Dynamic Islam

Liberal Muslim Perspectives in a Transnational Age

Jon Armajani

D1526047

University Press of America,® Inc.
Dallas · Lanham · Boulder · New York · Oxford

Copyright © 2004 by
University Press of America,® Inc.
4501 Forbes Boulevard
Suite 200
Lanham, Maryland 20706
UPA Acquisitions Department (301) 459-3366

PO Box 317
Oxford
OX2 9RU, UK

Library of Congress Control Number: 2004108502
ISBN 0-7618-2967-9 (paperback : alk. ppr.)

To Dr. Charles A. Ryerson III,
Professor, teacher, mentor, and friend

Contents

Acknowledgments   vii

1   Introduction   1

2   Fatima Mernissi   15

3   Leila Ahmed   41

4   Fazlur Rahman   77

5   Mohammed Arkoun   113

6   Conclusion   139

Notes   151

Bibliographies   193

Index   227

About the Author   237

Acknowledgments

There is no way I can thank everyone who made the completion of this book possible. The members of my dissertation committee, Juan Campo, Richard Hecht, Stephen Humphreys, and the late Ninian Smart were continually available for advice and support as I worked on my dissertation which formed the foundation of this study. I thank all of them for the time, effort, and attention they gave to my doctoral education and the completion of the dissertation. I am also eternally grateful to my parents, Robert B. and Mahvash Armajani, and to my brother, Cyrus, who have been unwavering in their love, generosity, empathy, and kindness. They have been and always will be the rock and cornerstone of my life and have given constant unconditional support to me and this project. I extend a deeply heartfelt thank you to my uncle and aunt, Siah and Barbara Armajani, who have offered their care, enthusiasm, inspiration as well as generous emotional and financial support which enabled me to pursue my doctoral studies and my professional aspirations. My uncle and aunt Michael (Manuch) and Jan Armajani have also from the time of my birth given their cheerfulness, generosity, and hospitality, graciously offering their home as a joyful sanctuary throughout my life, quite memorably during the strenuous period I was in Collegeville, Minnesota, working on the dissertation phase of this study. I am also very grateful to my aunt and uncle Pari and Ezat Bakshian for their love and support with respect to this and my other scholarly endeavors.

Without the wisdom and mentorship of Charles A. Ryerson III, Elmer K. and Ethel R. Timby Professor of the History of Religions Emeritus at Princeton Theological Seminary, I may have never embarked on the path of Ph.D. work in the History of Religions at all. I will always remember his attention to my development as a human being, student, and scholar. I am also profoundly grateful for his interest in this project and the guidance he provided in its various incarnations. I dedicate this book to him with respect and admiration.

A number of people at St. Mary's College of Maryland have also fostered my ideas and enabled the completion of this project. President Jane Margaret O'Brien, Trustee Terry Meyerhoff Rubenstein, Provost Larry E. Vote, Vice President for Development Salvatore M. Meringolo, Michael J.G. Cain, and Director of the Center for the Study of Democracy at St. Mary's College, Zach Messitte provided lively forums for me to explore and express many of the ideas in this book. Katharina von Kellenbach and Björn Krondorfer have consistently offered scholarly expertise and insight during the book's latter stages and I very much appreciate the encouragement and inspiration they have given me on this and other intellectual endeavors. I thank Melvin B. Endy Jr., Alan Paskow, Richard Platt, John Schroeder, Michael S. Taber, Thornton C. Kline III, Kathryn J. Norlock, and Celia E. Rabinowitz for all their help in obtaining the crucial library resources which enabled the completion of this book. I am also deeply grateful to Terell Lasane for his continued support of this project throughout its final phases. I extend my gratitude to Laraine Masters Glidden and David Finkelman who invited me to lead a College Faculty Seminar on Islamic revivalism in Spring 2002. This very engaging forum enabled me to further elucidate a number of my ideas about this aspect of Islam. My frequent and invigorating conversations with Asif Dowla about this book and other matters pertaining to Islam have sharpened my thinking about contemporary Islam and several crucial issues in this volume. Robin R. Bates, a continually supportive colleague and facilitator of the College's faculty writing group, together with Lois T. Stover, Anne Leblans, Garrey M. Dennie, and Holly Blumner offered numerous illuminating and penetrating comments on chapters of this manuscript from a variety of disciplinary perspectives. Louis Hicks offered a great deal of practical advice and enthusiasm during this book's final stages; he read the entire manuscript and provided numerous helpful comments. I am also very thankful to Pamela J. Hicks for her suggestions, scrupulous attention to detail, and tireless work in preparing this manuscript for publication. Emily Davis and Jesse Folks, my research assistants at St. Mary's College of Maryland, also did remarkable work as this manuscript came to completion.

I am grateful to Stephen Ryan and Beverly Baum at University Press of America/Rowman and Littlefield Publishing Group for their conscientious and focused efforts on this manuscript. I particularly appreciate the care which Stephen gave to the internal and external review processes as University Press of America/Rowman and Littlefield Publishing Group considered my proposal and initial manuscript and approved it for publication.

I wrote the bulk of this book as a Resident Scholar at the Institute for Ecumenical and Cultural Research on the campus of St. John's University in Collegeville, Minnesota. The formidable intellect and sound advice of the Institute's Executive Director, Patrick Henry, the sagacity and enthusiasm of Institute President, Kilian McDonnell, OSB, the compassionate help of Executive Associate, Dolores Schuh, CHM, and the perpetual good humor of Institute's Liaison Officer, Wilfred Theisen, OSB, went a long way towards making the writing of this book a joyous and exhilarating experience. It would have been impossible to conduct my research without the patient and understanding assistance of Sarah Blackburn-Renn, Interlibrary Loan Associate at the St. John's University Library, who ordered countless books and articles. Throughout the writing and research stages of this manuscript, the Revs. Greg Cootsona, Bob Hudnut, Al Jergenson, Dan McNerney, Steve Schibsted, and my good friend Katherine Komenda Poole offered the kind of grace I would have never found on my own. I also offer many thanks to my friend and colleague James E. Lindsay for reading the entire manuscript and providing invaluable comments.

I received generous financial support for this project from a Faculty Development Grant at St. Mary's College of Maryland, as well as the Islamic Studies Endowment Fund for Graduate Students, the Interdisciplinary Humanities Center Pre-Doctoral Fellowship, the J.F. Rowny Endowment Fund, and the General Affiliates Dissertation Grant, which were all provided through the University of California, Santa Barbara, and from the Presbyterian Church (USA)'s Racial-Ethnic Graduate Education Grant and the Chicago Presbytery's Higgins Scholarship Fund.

1

Introduction

The general problematic which this study explores is the way in which religious persons interpret and appropriate their own religious history to address current issues and difficulties that their religious tradition faces. One of the methodologies used here to examine questions related to the interpretation of religious history is comparison. Jonathan Z. Smith's reflection on the strength of a comparative method sets the tone for this study, "Comparison is, at base, never identity [rather], comparison requires the postulation of difference as the grounds of being interesting (rather than tautological) and a methodical manipulation of difference, a playing across the gap in the service of some useful end."[1] Here, the useful end of comparison is to gain a deeper understanding of how four modern Sunni Muslim diaspora thinkers — Fatima Mernissi, Leila Ahmed, Fazlur Rahman, and Mohammed Arkoun — have appropriated the sacred texts and religious history of their own religious tradition, Islam, as they construct their contrasting visions for Islam in the modern world.

In brief, Fatima Mernissi and Leila Ahmed combine various principles from modern feminism, including the equality of the sexes, with certain traditional Islamic principles, such as the unity of all believers before God, as they construct their distinctive feminist-oriented visions of Islam in the modern world. Fazlur Rahman and Mohammed Arkoun combine modern notions of human rights and democracy with Islamic principles related to social justice as they construct their contrasting visions of Islam which emphasize democracy, freedom, and liberty.

These four intellectuals are the focus of this study for several reasons. First, they are among the first generation of Muslims who have written the bulk of their works in western languages and intentionally direct their publications towards Muslims and non-Muslims in the West *and* the majority Muslim world. Second, these four intellectuals self-consciously identify themselves as Muslims and have interpreted, reflected on, and "theologized" about Islam and its place in the modern world using their religious tradition as a base. Third, each one is or was a scholar of significant stature who has written on a broad range of topics related to Islam and either holds or has held prominent scholarly positions. Fourth, all four have been influenced intellectually by lengthy or permanent residences outside of their majority-Muslim countries of origin. In this sense, each is a "Muslim diaspora intellectual" meaning each was born in a majority Muslim country, has either taken up permanent or extended residence in a non-majority Muslim country, and has intentionally interpreted the Islamic tradition as a Muslim with that context in mind. Fatima Mernissi is a liminal figure in this regard since although she received all her higher education in the West, she lives in Morocco and does most of her writing in Western languages. She can be considered a diaspora intellectual in that various Westerners comprise a significant audience for her.

Muslim Diaspora

My use of the term "Muslim diaspora" refers primarily (and at times exclusively) to the Muslim communities living *outside* of what has been classically referred to as the "Central Lands of Islam," an area which has been called the "narrow band of Islamic civilization" extending from Morocco in the west to Indonesia in the east.[2] This diaspora is neither uniform nor homogeneous. Rather, it consists of many diverse types of Muslims who have either emigrated from or trace their ancestries to a variety of predominantly Muslim countries.

Fatima Mernissi, Leila Ahmed, Fazlur Rahman, and Mohammed Arkoun have spent large segments of their lives either within or in some way related to the western Muslim diaspora. In examining the ways each one has interpreted and adapted the Sunna and Islamic history, this book's focus is on their *thought* and the ways in which they appropriate the pertinent primary source materials to their modern contexts.

Biographical Background

Moroccan-born Muslim feminist scholar, Fatima Mernissi (b. 1940) lives, works, writes, and teaches in Rabat, Morocco. She has, however, spent significant portions of her life in the West, studying and working in France from 1965 to 1969, where she earned her *license* in Sociology from the Sorbonne. She then studied at Brandeis University in Waltham, Massachusetts from 1970 to 1974 where she earned her Ph.D. in Sociology, writing her dissertation "The Effects of Modernization on the Male-Female Dynamics in a Muslim Society: Morocco" under the supervision of American sociologist Philip Slater.[3]

During her time in France, she was involved in the Moroccan Student Movement, which she says has had an enormous impact on the formation of her political and religious perspectives.[4] Since 1974, she has served as a faculty member and scholar-in-residence at Muhammad V University and the National Research Center in Rabat, has written extensively for the Moroccan women's magazines *8 Mars* and *Kalima* (which are distributed in Morocco and in France), has worked as an editor for the French scholarly journal *Peuples Méditerranéens*, and plays a leadership role in various women's organizations in Morocco and North Africa.[5] During the late twentieth and early twenty-first centuries, Mernissi has focused most of her attention on invigorating civil society and democracy in Morocco and the majority Muslim world through various technologies including the Internet. The organization she leads, Synergie Civique, and her website are two endeavors devoted to these objectives.[6]

Mernissi maintains strong links with Muslim communities in Europe and in the United States through her writings and speeches in those parts of the world. Indeed, like the three other intellectuals, Mernissi writes most frequently in western languages (in her case French and English), which has the effect of directing her writing to primarily Anglophone and Francophone audiences in the Muslim world and the West. The decision to write in English and French is quite conscious on Mernissi's part. She believes that she cannot freely express herself in Arabic and that when she does write in Arabic she has the feeling that a policeman is standing right next to her.[7] Since she does so little of her scholarly writing in Arabic, she says she belongs to the class of intellectuals who have intentionally exiled themselves from their mother tongue.[8]

Among her best-known works are *Beyond the Veil: Male-Female Dynamics in Modern Muslim Society; The Forgotten Queens of Islam; Islam and Democracy: Fear of the Modern World; Women and Islam: An Historical and Theological Enquiry;* and *Scheherazade Goes West: Different Cultures, Different Harems.*[9] These and other works by Mernissi have been published in English, German, Dutch, Japanese and other languages.[10] Mernissi writes regularly on women's issues in the popular press, participates in public debates promoting the cause of Muslim women internationally, and has supervised the publication of a series of books on the legal status of women in Morocco, Algeria, and Tunisia.[11] Mernissi's writings are directed toward several audiences: Muslims living in the Muslim world, Muslims and non-Muslims in the West, as well as Muslim and non-Muslim scholars in the West. For example, Mernissi's articles entitled "Fundamentalist Obsession with Women," "Sufis, Saints and Sanctuaries," and "Women in Muslim History"—all of which were published as pamphlets by Simorgh Women's Resource and Publication Center in Lahore, Pakistan—were also published as articles or chapters in books in western academic publications.[12] While these pamphlets and the scholarly articles have exactly the same content, the publishers of each one make these works available to different audiences, one primarily female and Muslim (in Pakistan), and the other primarily western and academic.

Egyptian-born Leila Ahmed is Professor of Women's Studies in Religion at Harvard Divinity School and is the first person appointed to that chair. She studied English at the University of Cambridge England, where she took her B.A. Hons. and earned her Ph.D. in 1970 and, under the supervision of British literary critic Gillian Beer, wrote her dissertation in the Faculty of English entitled "The Works of Edward William Lane and Ideas of the Near East in England 1800–1850: The Transformation of an Image."[13] She also worked closely with British Orientalists R.B. Serjeant and A.J. Arberry.[14]

Ahmed taught at the University of Ain Shams and Al-Azhar in Cairo and was Associate Professor and Chair of the Department of Foreign Languages at the University of the United Arab Emirates before joining the Women's Studies Program at the University of Massachusetts, Amherst in 1981, where she was director of the Near Eastern Studies Program from 1991 to 1992 and Director of the Women's Studies Program from 1992 to 1995.[15] She was a Distinguished Visiting Professor at the American University in Cairo in 1992 and was elected to a life membership at Clare Hall in the University of Cambridge in

1992. Her scholarly works include *Edward William Lane: A Study of His Life and Work and of British Ideas of the Middle East in the Nineteenth Century; Women and Gender in Islam: Historical Roots of a Modern Debate; A Border Passage: From Cairo to America—A Woman's Journey;* various journal articles on Islam and gender issues; as well as other works where feminist issues play a less substantial role.[16] Ahmed's articles are published in Western academic journals and her books are published by Western academic presses; her works are largely directed at western academics as well as academically-inclined Muslims.

Born in what is now Pakistan, Fazlur Rahman (1919–1988) held prominent faculty positions in that country and several North American and British universities. He wrote and translated a range of widely recognized scholarly works including *Avicenna's Psychology; Islamic Methodology in History; Islam; Islam and Modernity: Transformation of an Intellectual Tradition; Major Themes of the Quran;* and the posthumously published *Revival and Reform in Islam: A Study of Islamic Fundamentalism.*[17] In 1942, Rahman received a doctorate in Arabic from Punjab University in Lahore and, in 1949, a doctorate in Islamic Philosophy from Oxford University where under the supervision of the western Islamic Studies scholar H.A.R. Gibb he wrote a dissertation entitled "Avicenna's Psychology," which explored the metaphysical aspects of this medieval Muslim philosopher's work.[18]

The teaching career of Fazlur Rahman began at Durham University where he lectured in Persian Studies and Islamic Philosophy from 1950–1958.[19] In 1958, he accepted a teaching post at in the Institute for Islamic Studies at McGill University in Montreal, where he worked alongside Charles Adams who had become interested in the writings of Sayyid Abu'l-A'la Mawdudi, one of the most important leaders in the Pakistani Islamic revivalist group Jama'at-i Islami.[20] In 1962, Rahman was appointed director of the Central Institute of Islamic Research in Pakistan, which was given the task of interpreting "Islam in rational and scientific terms to meet the requirements of a modern progressive society."[21]

As a result of what Rahman calls "a cumulative effect" of various controversies between himself and Islamic revivalists in Pakistan, he felt compelled to leave his home country and accepted a Visiting Professorship at the University of California, Los Angeles in Spring 1969. He became Professor of Islamic Thought at the University of Chicago in the fall of 1969, a position he held until his death in July

1988.[22] Most of Rahman's writings have been published by Western academic presses. During much of the 1960's and 1970's Rahman was the founder and Editor-in-Chief of *Islamic Studies*, an academic journal which Rahman used to publish articles which were sympathetic to his point of view.[23] While Rahman published articles in Pakistani newspapers and magazines, he expressed his views largely through academic writings.[24]

Algerian-born Mohammed Arkoun (b. 1928) is Senior Research Fellow and member of the Board of Governors of the Institute of Ismaili Studies in London, Professor Emeritus of the History of Islamic Thought at the Sorbonne, former Director of the Institute of Arab and Islamic Studies there and editor-in-chief of the French scholarly journal *Arabica*. He has written such prominent works as *Lectures du Coran, La Pensée Arabe, Ouvertures sur l'Islam* and *The Unthought in Contemporary Islamic Thought*.[25] He has taught as a visiting professor at the University of California, Los Angeles, Princeton University, Temple University, the University of Louvain-la-Neuve, the Pontifical Institute of Arabic Studies in Rome, and the University of Amsterdam. He was a Gifford Lecturer at the University of Edinburgh in 2001–02 and received the Seventeenth Giorgio Levi Della Vida Award in 2002.[26] Arkoun was born into a Berber family in the hillside village of Taourirt-Mimoun in the Kabylia region of Algeria.[27] A native Berber-speaker, Arkoun learned French as a second language, then Arabic as a third.[28] He attended primary and secondary school in Algeria and earned his doctorate at the Sorbonne where his dissertation was a translation of the eleventh century Muslim philosopher Ibn Miskawayh's *Tahdhib al-akhlaq (Treatise on Ethics)*.[29]

Arkoun states that one reason he moved to France and does much of his writing in French is that he feels a greater sense of intellectual freedom there than in Algeria and that he is less fearful of recrimination in the West than in his home country. In addition to French, Arkoun's works have been published in Arabic, Dutch, Indonesian, English, German, Italian and Spanish.[30] The audience toward which Arkoun directs his writings is primarily academic. He believes that free expression and critical thinking, properly applied, can open new avenues for the renewal of Islam in the modern world.[31]

Interpreting Texts

The methods Mernissi, Ahmed, Rahman, and Arkoun utilize in interpreting and appropriating the Quran, Hadith, and Islamic history in order to construct their visions of Islam in the modern world play a central role in this study. This book examines the relationship between their historical methods and the conclusions they draw about Islamic history and early Islamic texts, on the one hand, and the role which they believe Islam should play in modernity, on the other. Each intellectual gives detailed attention to Islamic history, in general, and the Quran and Hadith, in particular, and their varying interpretations of these materials have a close relationship to their visions of Islam in the modern world.

The views of each thinker with respect to the role of Islam in the modern world are related to the interpretive or hermeneutical tasks in which each one engages. Hence, this study engages in a "hermeneutic of hermeneutics", that is, it analyzes how these thinkers engage in their hermeneutical endeavors and it compares and contrasts the varying methods and lines of argument which each author follows.

In attempting to understand how an interpretive or hermeneutical process can function in modern religio-political discourse, one can look to Martin Luther King's method of biblical interpretation in 1950s and 1960s America as one example. In many of King's speeches and writings, biblical passages related to justice together with constitutional themes such as liberty, equality, and freedom were vital hermeneutical presuppositions as he addressed the discrimination, injustice, and oppression which confronted African-Americans.[32]

King employed certain ideas from his contemporary situation in America (such as freedom, liberty, democracy, equality, and justice) and united these with comparable themes which he perceived in the sacred and historic texts of Christianity. He then used all these themes together as he addressed the circumstances in which he and other African-Americans found themselves. In his "I Have a Dream" speech, for example, King readily used specific language from the Bible, the Declaration of Independence, and the Constitution, as he articulated his vision for America's future.[33]

In my view, Fatima Mernissi, Leila Ahmed, Fazlur Rahman, and Mohammed Arkoun are involved in a similar hermeneutical process as they interpret their historical and sacred-textual traditions and appropriate them to the modern circumstances in which Muslims find themselves. Each intellectual unites certain principles gained from modern discourse such as human rights and democracy, for example, and unites these with comparable historic and sacred-textual themes which they believe to be present in the Quran and Hadith, such as the equality and unity of all believers in the eyes of God; they then utilize these and similar ideas as the primary presuppositions in "exegeting" sacred and historical texts and appropriating these texts for modern times in order to bring about change.

Fatima Mernissi's hermeneutical presuppositions primarily incorporate her idea of how all Muslims, particularly women and men, are deemed in the eyes of God as being full and equal partners in the Muslim community. Mernissi writes, "So, beyond its spiritual dimension, Islam was first and foremost a promise of power, unity, and triumph for a marginalized people, divided and occupied who wasted their energy in intertribal wars."[34]

These concepts of shared unity, equality, and triumph together with her notion that misogynist patriarchal Islamic elites had an overwhelming influence in shaping the content of Islamic texts and their interpretation are the hermeneutical presuppositions which shape Mernissi's discourse. Comparable interpretive principles are involved in the construction of Mernissi's vision for Islam's present and future. In her endeavor to establish and describe this vision Mernissi asks: "How is the principle of the equality of all believers (whatever their sex and ethnic or social origin) to be transformed into a practical political system which gives everyone the right to participate in the choice of the leader of the community?"[35] In answering this question, Mernissi envisions an Islamic world where women are freed from the isolation and hardship of the veil, male-imposed physical separation from many public spaces, and injustices in family life, career, economic opportunities, and education.

Much like Mernissi, Leila Ahmed believes that Islam's patriarchal misogynist structure played a significant role in determining the content and subsequent interpretations of most of Islam's texts and history. In terms of the hermeneutical presuppositions at work in Ahmed's writings, she unites concepts gained from modern western feminism with what she calls ideas of "Quranic Muslim egalitarianism." She writes:

> The egalitarian conception of gender inhering in the ethical vision of Islam existed in tension with the hierarchical relation between the sexes encoded into the marriage structure instituted by Islam. This egalitarianism is a consistent element of the ethical utterances of the Quran. Among

the remarkable features of the Quran, particularly in comparison with the scriptural texts of other monotheistic traditions, is that women are explicitly addressed: one passage in which this occurs declares by the very structure of the utterance, as well as in overt statement, the absolute moral and spiritual quality of men and women.[36]

This egalitarian ethical vision of Islam provides a vital basis for Ahmed's interpretation of the Quran, Hadith, and Islamic history, on the one hand, and the articulation of her vision for Islam in the modern world, on the other. Ahmed maintains, "The implications [of this passage] are far-reaching. Ethical qualities, including those invoked [in Sura 33:35]—charity, chastity, truthfulness, patience, piety—also have political and social dimensions."[37] These political and social dimensions involve an Islam that envisions and implements equality and justice for men and women in career, family life, education, and the various other social, personal, political, and economic spheres of human existence. Yet, Ahmed emphasizes that her vision is decidedly Islamic (and feminist) not western and feminist. That is, she does not advocate the Islamic world's comprehensive importation and adaptation of western feminist ideologies and lifestyles. Among the many aspects of traditional Islamic mores that she maintains is the option of the continued wearing of the veil (*hijab*) by Muslim women—even though the patriarchal environment where many Muslim women live has created the conditions which necessitate the wearing of it.[38]

While in his early works Fazlur Rahman takes a significantly different stance with respect to gender issues than Mernissi and Ahmed, he utilizes an interpretive framework based on social justice as he explains and appropriates the sacred texts and history of his tradition. Rahman writes:

Muhammad's monotheism was, from the very beginning, linked up with a humanism and a sense of social and economic justice whose intensity is no less than the intensity of the monotheistic idea, so that whoever carefully reads the early Revelations of the Prophet cannot escape the conclusion that the two must be regarded as expressions of the same experience.[39]

This "social-justice" view of Islam plays a significant role in determining the way in which Rahman interprets Islam's sacred texts and Islamic history.[40] He believes that much of Islamic history has been marked by the myopic, and tyrannical rule of religious and political leaders who influenced Islamic discourse and the method of Islamic education in such a way that critical thinking and the free-flow of ideas was discouraged. These weighty historic constraints on free thought in the Islamic world have had a negative impact on Islam in the modern world insofar as they have prevented many Muslim thinkers from exploring their history in ways that would enable them to develop meaningful and relevant solutions to the challenges confronting Muslims in the modern world.[41] Hence, in Rahman's view, the idea that the Quran envisions a just, equitable and free world and that the Islamic political and religious leadership have prevented Islam from achieving these ideals are important interpretive principles.

In structuring his vision for Islam's future, Rahman states,

> The heart of the problem which a Muslim must face and resolve if he wishes to re-construct an Islamic future on an Islamic past is: how shall this past guide him and which elements of his history may he modify, emphasize or deflate?[42]

Rahman is, in effect, asking what the proper hermeneutical presuppositions are (or should be) for interpreting Islam's past in such a way that will make the Islamic tradition relevant to the present and future. Rahman's vision of Islam's present and future involves, in large part, the implementation and construction of democracy, a renewed Islamic morality, and Islamic educational systems which foster and encourage free critical thought among Muslims.[43]

Mohammed Arkoun's interpretation of Islam's sacred texts and history is also guided by his belief that during the course of Islamic history many religious leaders' fear of chaos and mayhem, on the one hand, together with their desire for order and obedience, on the other, played a vital role in determining the content and trajectory of Islamic thought, jurisprudence, and theology. Arkoun's interpretive method involves his belief that Islam must free itself from these oppressive constraints and work in partnership with members of other religious traditions (primarily Christians and Jews whose histories, according to Arkoun, overlap significantly with that of Islam) in creating a world that is rooted in mutual understanding, equality, and harmony. Robert D. Lee describes Arkoun's dream:

> [Arkoun envisions a world where] there would be no margins and no center, no marginalized groups and no dominant ones. no inferior beliefs and no superior truth producing logic. [Arkoun] seeks a response to what may be the critical political question of our time: How can people be thoroughly themselves without isolating themselves by virtue of this identity from their neighbors and the rest of humanity? He poses it for Muslims in particular: Can the various Muslim identities be reconciled with each other and with non-Muslim identities, or does the contemporary reassertion of

cultural identities mean the world is necessarily divided between Shiites and Sunnis, mystics and traditionalists, Muslims and Christians, Berbers and Arabs, North Africans and Europeans?[44]

Arkoun's interpretive method is rooted in an examination of Islamic texts and history that adapts scholarly approaches from linguistics, semiotics, anthropology, and various social sciences. For Arkoun, the application of these methods must recognize the unique contribution which the ethics inherent in Islamic texts and history can make to Muslims in particular and humanity in general.

Differing Islamic Worldviews

These four intellectuals represent a strand of thought known as Islamic modernism or Islamic liberalism. Broadly speaking, three ideological groupings among Muslims include: Islamic revivalists (also known as "Islamists" or "Islamic Fundamentalists"), Islamic neotraditionalists, and Islamic modernists (or Islamic liberals).[45] These viewpoints function as ideal types, abstracted from a complex reality in which the values and attitudes of any one person are likely to contain a combination of all, tending towards one or the other viewpoint according to the issue or even time period involved.

Islamic revivalism is the reaffirmation, in a radically changed environment, of time-honored modes of understanding and behavior. In contrast to conservatism, which assumes that things can and should go on much as they have for generations past, Islamic revivalism recognizes and tries to speak to a changed cultural environment, an altered atmosphere of expectations. Islamic revivalists are not blind opponents of all social change, rather they insist that change must be governed by traditional values and modes of understanding. Islamic revivalists assert that the Quran's literal truth together with its legal and ritual injunctions based on Sharia must be applied to all Muslims and to religious minorities living in majority Muslim countries. These Muslims also believe that: (1) Islamic principles must dictate every aspect of life, both personal and societal; (2) Islam carries the exclusive truth and that other religions are either false or of limited validity; (3) traditional rules must govern sexual relations (i.e., sex may only take place within heterosexual marriage); and (4) western and secular cultures promote a range of consumerist and permissive lifestyles which are antithetical to Islam.

Islamic neotraditionalists live in diaspora settings as minorities, believing and practicing what they perceive to be the most classic (or even "conservative") aspects of Islam within those settings. They view themselves as interpreting "the true Islam" in a way that is appropriate to the circumstances of Muslims where they are a minority group.

Islamic neotraditionalists have much in common with Islamic revivalists. Among other similarities, they both: (1) exercise a strict or literalistic reading of the Quran;[46] (2) idealize the early Islamic community;[47] (3) stress the importance of Muslim women wearing the veil;[48] (4) reject Western-style critical and scholarly approaches to the Quran, Hadith and early Islamic history;[49] (5) agree on fastidiously adhering to the five pillars of Islam and five pillars of belief; (6) believe in abstinence before marriage; and (7) see themselves as being threatened by similar processes of westernization and secularization. There are a large number of Islamic neotraditionalist writers including Jamal Badawi, Abdur Rahman I. Doi, Suzanne Haneef, Hassan Hathout, Huda L. Khattab, and Sulaiman Mufassir.[50]

The publications of Muslim neotraditionalist intellectuals are widely available to Muslim diaspora audiences alongside books by Islamic revivalist writers such as Sayyid Qutb and Sayyid Abu)l-A(la Mawdudi in Muslim online and brick-and-mortar bookstores.[51] Also, neotraditionalist writers often quote revivalists in Muslim countries as one way of supporting their own claims.[52] There are, of course, differences between Islamic revivalist and neotraditionalist groups, the most salient pertaining to the role of religion and politics in the Islamic revivalist groups. Many of the revivalists in the Muslim world are confronting governments which are very hostile to their intentions and these groups often provide for various social, educational, and health needs which their Western Muslim counterparts do not. That is, the Islamic revivalist groups conjoin religious and political action in ways that the diaspora groups often do not, although Islamic neotraditionalists are frequently empathetic with the religio-political objectives of the revivalists in majority Muslim countries.

Islamic modernism (sometimes referred to as Islamic liberalism) constitutes an alternative interpretive stance to Islamic revivalism and neotraditionalism, yielding nothing to either orientation in its reverence for the traditional foundations of Islamic thought: the Quran, the life of the prophet, the example of the first Muslims, and the Sharia. However, Muslim modernists reaffirm and reevaluate the significance of all these principles for modern life; they view the Quran as

God's supreme revelation and believe that it calls for human progress. Modernists point to the Quran's restrictions on slavery, its enhancement of women's status, its limitations on the right of private vengeance, and its commands for beneficence, justice, equality, liberty, and social solidarity. For liberals, these ideals have propelled Muslims to make great leaps forward, beginning from Islam's origins in the seventh century through today. Muslim liberals do not want literal interpretations of the Quran to block Muslims from perceiving its true meanings as God's perfect revelation. They believe Muslims must seek the underlying moral purpose of the Quran and Hadith, and that of the lives of Muhammad and early Muslims — grounding their daily conduct on that ethical thrust.

As modernists, Mernissi, Ahmed, Rahman, and Arkoun affirm the authenticity of the Quran and Hadith, appropriate these texts to the modern milieu, give focused attention to issues such as justice, the status of women, ethical monotheism, democracy, social solidarity, and charity. These four intellectuals, like other modernists, believe that these are some of the most essential aspects of Islam's teachings and that they provide comprehensive models for Muslims and others in the modern world. One goal of this book is to elucidate further the at times converging and at other times diverging worldviews in the Islamic revivalist and modernist perspectives.

A Transnational Ethos

The ideas of these four thinkers and of many Islamic neotraditionalists and revivalists are conveyed within the cultural environment of transnationalism. While they express their ideas within their indigenous predominantly Muslim countries (such as Morocco, Egypt, Pakistan, and Algeria), they also direct their thought to Muslims across national boundaries.

Implicit in their perspectives is the notion that, even in its reinterpreted forms, the Sunna provides a universal message for all Muslims, no matter what their nationality or citizenship. These four intellectuals express this transnational character of their thought in many ways. First, they write in languages which can be understood by Muslims in different parts of the world. Fatima Mernissi, for example, while making some of her works available in Arabic, the primary language of her home country, writes in French and English in order to reach a broad transnational audience. Indeed, her works are available in many parts of the majority-Muslim world as well as in Europe and the United States. During the time Rahman was living in the United States, his scholarly work was directed at audiences in the West and in Pakistan. Arkoun's works are available to those who can read French (and to a lesser extent English) in many countries. Ahmed makes it explicit in her writings that Islam contains a universal message and suggests that her interpretations of the tradition transcend national boundaries. The fact that these speakers deliver lectures and engage in other forms of scholarly activities throughout much of the world testifies to the transnational character of their intentions and of their visions.

Yet, it is not only these writers who participate in a transnational ethos. Transnationality is one salient feature of much religious discourse and religious organization in much of the world today. One sees transnationalism at work in a number of religious and religio-political organizations including evangelical and fundamentalist Christians, as well as various Hindu nationalist and Jewish groups.[53]

With these concepts in view, the chapters which follow discuss significant features of the thought of Mernissi, Ahmed, Rahman, and Arkoun, focusing on matters of hermeneutics, the relationship of each thinker's worldviews with modernity and with Islamic revivalist and neotraditionalist perspectives, and the processes in which each thinker engages as she or he comes to terms with Islamic history. Chapter Two examines Mernissi's views on veiling, the appropriation of space in Muslim contexts, and her visions for Islam's future. Chapter Three analyzes Leila Ahmed's perspectives on veiling, the place of women in Muslim society, and the relationship between her views of Muslim history and her vision for Islam in the modern world. Chapter Four examines the egalitarian perspectives of Fazlur Rahman, his methodology for Quranic interpretation, and his views on Islamic education. Chapter Five presents Mohammed Arkoun's views on the Quran and his understanding of the relationship between the Sunni and other minority traditions (such as the Shiite, the Ismaili, and the Sufi) and the role this plays in terms of his understanding of interpreting the Quran and Islamic history. The book concludes with some observations on the interplay between modernism and neotraditionalism in cross-cultural perspective.

2

FATIMA MERNISSI

Mernissi asks, "Are we all going back to the veil, back to the secluded house, back to the walled city, back to the national, proudly sealed imaginary boundaries?"[1] This question sets the tone for much of Fatima Mernissi's thought. The wearing of the veil and the organization of private and public space in Muslim countries in such a way that they marginalize Muslim women and control their movements are key concerns in her major works. The hermeneutical presuppositions which shape Fatima Mernissi's inquiry are derived from modern Western feminism and modern Islamic thought, as well as Sura 33:35. Mernissi does not accept Western feminisms *in toto*; rather, she critiques certain aspects and adopts others. Although she makes passing reference to works by western feminists in the footnotes of her works, she does not specifically cite the strands within Western feminism which she adapts. Rather, she appropriates and critiques what she perceives to be general currents of thought within Western feminisms.[2]

Mernissi is more specific in her references to Muslim intellectuals who wrote about gender issues than in her references to western ones. She affirms Qasim Amin's and Salama Musa's position that "the liberation of the woman is a condition *sine qua non* for a total liberation of the Arabo-Muslim society from the humiliating hegemony of the West."[3] She maintains that when these two intellectuals speak of liberation of the woman they are referring "to a total equality with men in all spheres of social life."[4] With these writers, Mernissi affirms the "de-seclusion" of women and their being offered equal opportunities in such areas as employment and education. She joins Amin and Musa in their criticisms of Western colonialism and consumerism.[5]

Mernissi suggests the term "nisa'ism" (which is taken from the Arabic word for women), in contrast to "feminism," to define her unique theoretical and ideological position regarding the contemporary circumstances of Muslim women:

Nisa'i is for me an adjective which designates any idea, programme, project or hope which supports a woman's right to full-fledged participation and contribution in the remaking, changing and transforming of her society as well as the full realization of her own talents, needs, potentials, dreams and truths. And it is in this sense that I always live and define women's liberation regardless of the language that I use, whether it is feminism or nisa'ism, etc. I would like to add that this progressive, nisa'ist feminist current includes men as well as women. What is taken into account is the content of the historical work, and the ideological target of its conclusions and not the sex of the author.[6]

Mernissi first used the term *nisa'i* in her the 1986 pamphlet entitled *Women in Muslim History*, and while the word does not appear frequently in her writings, the definition which she gives guides much of her work. Mernissi believes she is espousing a position which adapts strands of western feminism, while critiquing it and using Islamic historic and textual positions as a basis for her viewpoint.

There are at least two distinctive ways in which Mernissi's nisa'ist perspective diverges from that of feminism: (1) in terms of the role which men play in the nisa'ist enterprise of working with women to gain equal rights; and (2) in terms of the nisa'ists pointed opposition to the aspects of traditional Islam which oppress women.

With respect to the first point, Mernissi observes that nisa'ists should reject any anti-male strands in Western feminism. She relates the following observations which she made in the early 1970s while she was a Ph.D. student at Brandeis University:

One of the big differences between Western and Muslim women's condition is that Western women have never really had a women's culture. You are more alienated here [in the West], alienated from each other by the men's world. . . . And American women are terrorized by men physically. I think. I felt that fear for the first time in this country [the USA], and I have never felt that in the Arab world. I think it is because American women are so physically terrorized that the American women's movement is so anti-male.[7]

Mernissi believes that the struggle for women's equality in the Muslim world should not involve demonizing Muslim men or perceiving them as the enemy; rather, women participating in the nisa᾽ist movement should work to co-opt men in the struggle and to proclaim the great benefits which women and men can gain from a Muslim society where all people are treated fairly and equally.[8] Participants in the nisa᾽ist movement should not naively believe that they share the same values as Western feminists nor should they believe that many Western feminists would be interested in acting as partners with the nisa᾽ists.

Mernissi relates a story about an experience she had with some American feminists in Boston in the early 1970's to highlight some of the differences in culture and values between nisa᾽ists and some western feminists. While she was studying in Massachusetts in the early 1970's, she visited a meeting of feminists in Boston where many of the women criticized her clothes, jewelry, and make-up. For these feminists, wearing jewelry and make-up (and even shaving one's legs) were *ipso facto* indications of a woman's submitting to patriarchal male-dominant preconceptions regarding women's appearance. Mernissi responded to these feminists by asserting that the cultural-historical circumstances of Muslim women differ radically from those of American women and the level to which women within each of these groups has been "emancipated" must be evaluated according to different criteria. For Mernissi, her clothing style and general appearance were emblematic of her rejection of the codes of dress (such as the veil) which were and are imposed upon many women in her culture. Thus the physical and cultural indications of feminist and nisa᾽ist emancipation differ substantially.[9]

Concomitantly, Western women and nisa᾽ists perceive and "lay claim" to their bodies in very different ways:

> It is interesting that while Western women's liberation movements had to repudiate the body in pornographic mass media, Muslim women are likely to claim the right to their bodies as part of their liberation movement. Previously, a Muslim woman's body belonged to the man who possessed her, father or husband. The mushrooming of beauty salons and ready-to-wear boutiques in Moroccan towns can be interpreted as a forerunner of women's urge to claim their own bodies, which will culminate in more radical claims, such as the claim to birth control and abortion.[10]

Thus, the hermeneutical presuppositions of nisa᾽ism at points converge with and at other points diverge from Western feminism. One point of convergence is in the priority they ascribe to equal rights for women. In Mernissi's view, some of the ways they diverge relate to the role of men in the respective movements and the priorities which the women in the two cultures must place on certain specific issues in terms of gaining equal rights.

The similarities and differences between the concerns of Western feminists and nisa'ists are evident in the emphasis Mernissi places on Muslim women reading and interpreting Muslim history for themselves, while applying their unique cultural and historical perspective to this task. This concern with women reading and interpreting history for themselves dovetails with the priorities of many Western feminists, but the challenges which many Muslim women face in their diverse circumstances may lead them to different conclusions than Western feminists:

> Muslim women in general and Arab women in particular cannot count on anyone, scholar or not, 'involved' or 'neutral' to read their history for them. Reading it entirely for themselves is entirely their responsibility and their duty. Our demand for the full and complete enjoyment of our universal human rights, here and now, requires us to take over our history to reread it and to reconstruct a wide open Muslim past. This duty, moreover, can turn out to be no drab, disagreeable task, but rather a journey filled with delight. And what is even more important, excursions into our past cannot only divert and instruct us, but also give us precious ideas about how to find happiness in life as a woman, a Muslim and an Arab, those three characterizations that they try to pin on us as a maleficent triad, an abyss of submission and abnegation in which our own wishes must inevitably be drowned.[11]

Mernissi suggests that the concrete historical circumstances of Arab Muslim women provide them with a unique orientation and a distinctive set of assumptions from which to interpret Islamic history. Muslim women's historical circumstances provide them with a set of hermeneutical presuppositions that positions them to understand Islamic history in a way that enables them to perceive women as active and important participants in that history.[12] The lessons learned from applying their natural hermeneutical presuppositions as Muslim women can have practical ramifications for them as well; one positive outcome of Muslim women reading and interpreting their history could involve them utilizing lessons and paradigms from their history in buttressing their demands for universal human rights in their own communities and nations.

Quranic Interpretation

In addition to the unique hermeneutical presuppositions which the nisaʾist perspective suggests, the Quran itself provides some hermeneutical presuppositions which offer Muslims a framework for interpreting that sacred text and other Islamic historic documents. For Mernissi, one of the most important passages which can guide Quranic as well as historical interpretation is Sura 33:35:

> Lo! Men who surrender unto Allah and women who surrender, and men who believe and women who believe, and men who obey and women who obey, and men who speak the truth and women who speak the truth, and men who persevere in righteousness and women who persevere, and men who are humble and women who are humble, and men who give alms and women who give alms, and men who fast and women who fast, and men who guard their modesty and women who guard (their modesty), and men who remember Allah and women who remember—Allah hath prepared for them forgiveness and a vast reward.[13]

According to Mernissi this passage is of pivotal significance in terms of understanding Islamic history. She explains its significance by saying that God spoke of the two genders in terms of complete equality as believers; that is, as members of one community. It is not sex that determines "who earns his grace; it is faith and the desire to serve him."[14]

For Mernissi, Sura 33:35 is the supreme Quranic hermeneutical concept which must be applied in interpreting the Quran, the Sunna, Islamic history and in constructing a vision for Islam's present and future. The nisaʾist perspective and Sura 33:35 are hermeneutical presuppositions which dynamically interact and reinforce one another as Mernissi interprets Islamic history.

The Veil and Veiling

One of the areas of Islamic history where Mernissi applies these hermeneutical principles is in her interpretation of Islamic historical texts as they apply to veiling. It would be helpful first to "unpack" the terms *veil* and *veiling* in different Islamic contexts, particularly as they apply to various types of dress and behavior. It is deceptive to think of the "veil" or "veiling" as one unitary and monolithic material or behavioral reality throughout Islam's history or even in the various regions of the contemporary Islamic world. Sherifa Zuhur in *Revealing Reveiling* discusses the wide varieties of modern and contemporary Islamic dress which fall under the category of the veil.[15] Zuhur observes that within the category of veiling in contemporary Egypt, in particular, as well as other predominantly Islamic countries, in general

> a variety of costume interpretations exist. Some women [wear] long skirts with sweaters or jackets. Some of the older women . . . [wear] stylish, conservative clothing along with a knit turban. However, they classif[y] themselves as *muhaggabat* (veiled) when asked. Many of the younger women and some of the older women [wear] plain, dark-colored, loosely fitting tunics and long skirts. Some of these garments are fitted at the waist, while others hang straight like a loose coat. One woman . . . [said] that although she had adopted the *higab* [veil], she still [wears] dresses with a waist, presenting herself as someone who had not completely transformed herself [into a veiled person].[16]

Zuhur interviewed veiled and unveiled women mostly in Cairo, Egypt. She found that some of the women who veiled themselves in their attempt to conform to their perceptions of Islamic injunctions about female dress also tried to adapt this style of dress to the latest fashions:

> There are ambiguities in the selection and categorization of the respondents. Certain women were described as partial *muhaggabat* [partially veiled], or fad followers, by other women. They wore the headcovering that covered their throat or went down to their shoulders. Below that they wore Western clothing. Quite a few wore rather daring styles — for example, tight pants, short skirts, or open necklines. There were women who also wore such combinations along with full make-up. They also wore brighter colors than other *muhaggabat*, patterned materials, and in some cases a brightly colored or metallic twisted scarf or cord to hold their headcloth in place, Bedouin style.[17]

Zuhur notes that some women have gone so far as to wear headcoverings and other types of Islamic dress which carry designer names such as Yves St. Laurent.[18]

One of the other significant distinctions pertaining to veiling relates to the wearing of the *niqab*, which refers to any of a wide variety of materials which cover the face. There are several types of *niqab*: some are in the shape of a plastic mask which cover the eyes, others are made of a semi-sheer cloth with no openings for the eyes which still allow the women to look out but prevent anyone from seeing her face, and others are made of a much thicker cloth with small openings for the eyes. The *niqab* is required by the Shafi'i and Hanbali schools of law (madhab) but not by the Maliki and Hanafi.[19] Jennifer Scarce, in *Women's Costume of the Near and Middle East* highlights many of the changes in Islamic women's dress throughout several centuries and in several different regions where Islam has historically predominated.[20]

From my own observations during trips to Turkey and pre-revolutionary Iran, I have seen variations in *practices* related to wearing the veil. For example, I have known Iranian Muslim women who made permanent residences in the West, and then upon their return to pre-revolutionary Iran veiled themselves in public in order to avoid harassment from certain Iranian men or in order to exhibit to their relatives living in pre-revolutionary Iran that they had not "strayed too far" from "traditional" Islamic mores. Alternatively, I met Iranian women living in Iran, some of whom remained veiled inside a house or apartment no matter who was present (whether family or not) and others who would put aside the veil upon entering any domestic space. Veiling is anything but a monolithic, cut-and-dry term; it can refer to wide varieties of dress and behavior, which not only may vary between regions but also between individuals.

Mernissi gives very little attention to the varieties of dress and behavior which surround veiling; she contends that the traditional Islamic imperatives regarding the wearing of the veil by Muslim women are not endemic to Islam's message of egalitarianism and are contradictory to the role of women (and their proper dress) as envisioned by the Prophet Muhammad in Islam's earliest years.[21] According to Mernissi, the requirement regarding the wearing of any type of veil arose not out of the original intentions of the Prophet and his egalitarian vision for his community.[22] Rather, these commands occurred as a result of the Prophet's and the early Muslim community's response to the hardships during their early years in Medina (roughly between 622 and 625) while the Meccans were attacking the Medinans during the Battles of Badr (624) and Uhud (625). For Mernissi, the verbal assaults of the *munafiqun* (hypocrites) against Muslim women increased the difficulties which the Muslim community faced.

Mernissi's opposition to the wearing of the veil is based at least in part on her interpretation of al-Tabari's narrative about the events surrounding the Prophet's wedding night with one of his wives, Zaynab Bint Jahsh, in Medina in 627.[23] Mernissi interprets al-Tabari's account of this story as suggesting that when Muhammad and his new wife wanted to engage in conjugal relations on their wedding night, several guests remained in Muhammad's house making noise, creating enough of a disturbance to distress the Prophet as he and his wife attempted to begin their conjugal activities.[24] As a result of this disruption, Muhammad asked his friend, Anas Ibn Malik, to place a curtain (*hijab*) between himself and Zaynab Bint Jahsh, on one side, and the male guests, on the other. Mernissi states it was during the early period of the Prophet's residence in Medina that this and related hardships occurred which gave rise to Sura 33:53–55, or "the descent of the *hijab*":

> If you ask [the Prophet's] wives for anything, speak to them from behind a curtain. This is more chaste for your hearts and their hearts. . . . Prophet, enjoin your wives, your daughters, and the wives of true believers to draw their veils close round them. That is more proper, so that they may be recognized and not be molested.[25]

This passage and Sura 24:31 have been traditionally interpreted as requiring Muslim women to wear the veil and, according to Mernissi, these passages and the context from which they emerged helped create a chain of events which led to the customs of veiling and the seclusion of many Muslim women.[26] Mernissi believes the Prophet's confrontation with his wedding guests and his irritation with them is a crucial event surrounding the revelation of Sura 33:53–55.[27]

For Mernissi, Muhammad's decision to place a curtain between himself and his male guests occurred during a period when the ordinarily calm and self-controlled Prophet was feeling a substantial amount of irritation toward his rude and "boorish" male guests who prevented him from spending some time in peace with his new wife.[28] Thus, Sura 33:53–55 was not revealed for the purpose of marginalizing or secluding women, but was intended to emphasize the importance of treating specifically the Prophet and his wives with courtesy, respect and tact.[29] In Mernissi's view, with these verses "Allah wanted to intimate to the Companions [of the Prophet] certain niceties that they seemed to lack, like not entering a dwelling without asking permission."[30]

The Prophet's frustration with his guests in Medina on his wedding night was not the only factor which gave rise to Sura 33:53–55 and subsequently to Sura 33:56–61; there were other significant historical circumstances which "precipitated a draconian decision like that of the *hijab* which split Muslim space in two."[31] Mernissi places Sura 33:53–62 in 627, which according to her was an enormously difficult and stressful time for the early Muslim community.[32] In addition to confronting the difficulties of relocating himself and his followers in Yathrib (Medina), Muhammad faced two fierce battles in 624 and 625:

The battle of Badr which Muhammad and his followers won and the defeat of the Prophet's armies at the Battle of Uhud, which Mernissi describes as "a disaster."[33]

In Mernissi's view during this period "Islam went through a time of severe military crisis, when the Prophet won a decisive victory over the Meccans, after which he conquered Mecca and then all of Arabia."[34] In the very tumultuous time leading up to late March 627, the Muslim community had to fight many battles such as the Battle of the Trench, which involved Muhammad's enemies mounting a ferocious attack against Medina.[35] Hence, Sura 33:53–55 and Sura 33:56–62 were intended to bring some peace to the difficult and troublesome circumstances which the early Muslim community faced:

> In addition to the incident about the lack of politeness of the guests at the wedding, it seems that the *hijab* came to give order to a very confused and complex situation. The *hijab* was to be the solution to a whole web of conflicts and tensions.[36]

Mernissi believes that her historical circumstance as a contemporary Muslim woman sensitizes her to the unique historical circumstance or the "occasion of revelation" in which Sura 33:53–62 was ostensibly revealed. Indeed, Mernissi makes the distinctive claim that the purpose of these verses was not the veiling and seclusion of women; rather, it was intended to instill in the Companions of the Prophet, and Muslims in general, habits of tact, courtesy, and politeness.

She asserts that it was particularly important to imbue many Medinese men with these attributes since, at the time, some of them (particularly the *munafiqun*) had a reputation for harassing and verbally abusing female slaves (who happened to be unveiled) as they walked the streets of the city.[37] In order to delineate female slaves, on the one hand, from free women, married women, and the wives of the Prophet, on the other, the Prophet instructed the latter to wear veils so that they would be protected.

For Mernissi, the division of space between men and women which the *hijab* created was not endemic to the Prophet's initial message and vision; rather the institution of the *hijab* was a specific response to the peculiar hardships which Medinese women in general and the Prophet's wives in particular faced during the early Muslim community's residence in Medina:

> In the struggle between Muhammad's dream of a society in which women could move freely around the city (because the social control would be the Muslim faith that disciplines desire) and the customs of the *munafiqun*

who only thought of a woman as an object of envy and violence, it was the latter vision that would carry the day. The veil represents the triumph of the *munafiqun*. Slaves would continue to be harassed and attacked in the streets. The female Muslim population would henceforth be divided by a *hijab* into two categories: free women, against whom violence is forbidden, and women slaves, toward whom *ta'arrud* (harassment) is permitted.[38]

Hence, Sura 33:53–62 were revealed during a difficult period at the beginning of Islam which was to introduce a troubling breach in space that had the effect of separating Muslim women from men and Muslim women from God.[39]

Mernissi validates the authority of classic Islamic texts, while offering fresh interpretations of them. Barbara Stowasser provides an analysis of Mernissi's hermeneutical method:

> At Mernissi's hands, the Quranic verses are related so closely to the historical events surrounding their revelation that a "causal" relationship between the two would logically follow; the *asbab al-nuzul*, "occasions of revelation" have (tacitly) become "occasions for revelation" and the verses themselves but a record of early umma history, while the question of their enduring relevance is (also tacitly) omitted. Nevertheless, the message is clear. In pitting the Prophet's early vision of gender egalitarianism against demands later imposed upon him by Medinan *Realpolitik*, this author stipulates that the Quranic dicta on Muhammad's wives and also women in general are of unequal "value." Even within the Quran, then, hierarchization of aspects of the message is here employed to yield that early, pristine, enduring ideal of an Islamic society in which men and women are truly equal.[40]

As Mernissi draws from her own tradition in articulating her views on veiling she applies two hermeneutical presuppositions which relate to the pre-eminence of egalitarianism: the first from Sura 33:35 which seems to suggest the equality of men and women and the second from her nisa'ist position. Her nisa'ist position and her selection of Sura 33:35 as being pre-eminent relate to the fact that she dwells in an era when the egalitarianism which these two ideas embody are valued and emphasized. She is defending her position in a principled way in the light of new knowledge, this knowledge being constituted at least in part by such "modern" ideas as freedom and gender equality. Much like other Muslim modernists such as Muhammad Iqbal, Ismail Faruqi, and the others in this study, she seeks the "underlying moral purpose" of the Quranic revelations (particularly in Sura 33:53–62 and 24:31) which to her do not pertain to veiling but to the moral purpose of encouraging men to treat women with courtesy, respect, and tact.[41]

Modernist thinking, either in Islam or in any other contemporary religious tradition, is not the only recurrent strand of thought; modernism dwells alongside and often in overt contradiction with neotraditionalism and Islamic revivalism. The modern neotraditionalist and Islamic revivalist positions on veiling, while grounding their viewpoint in many of the same sources as Mernissi, articulate a very different position on this issue. The Islamic revivalist position on veiling, which in every instance asserts that Muslim women should veil themselves, has had many proponents throughout modernity (and even throughout Muslim history) including such figures as Pakistani Islamic Revivalist Sayyid Abu'l-A'la Mawdudi, Ayatollah Ruhollah Khomeini, and the twentieth-century Egyptian Muslim activist Zeinab al-Ghazali. The discussion of the neotraditionalist and Islamic revivalist pro-veiling stance, is based on a collection of primary sources which are available to English-speaking Muslims throughout much of the Western and Islamic worlds. These works are distributed widely in these parts of the world through Muslim bookstores, mosques, various Muslim societies, such as the Muslim Students Association of North America and the Islamic Society of North America.[42] They are written by shaykhs and other Muslim leaders who feel that they know enough about their proposed subject to advise their fellow Muslims. These publications (which are usually in the form of paperback books, pamphlets, and brochures) are largely devoted to imparting knowledge regarding the "true" and "correct" Islamic way of life to all Muslims. Publications pertaining to women and gender issues carry titles such as *The Muslim Woman's Dress, The Muslim Woman's Handbook, The Position of Woman in Islam, Woman in Shariah,* and *What Everyone Should Know About Islam and Muslims.*[43]

Huda Khattab's *Muslim Woman's Handbook,* an example of a neotraditionalist work, calls itself "a practical guide to daily life [for any] Muslim woman in non-Muslim society" and is "aimed at Muslims and reverts [*sic*] alike." It devotes one of its eight chapters to practical matters related to the wearing of the *hijab,* which the writer believes is mandatory for all Muslim women.[44] Khattab is a British Muslim writer who received her BA (Hons) in Arabic from the School of Oriental and African studies in 1986, is the author of Muslim childrens' books and edits the monthly Muslim newsletter *Usra: The Muslim Family Magazine.* Khattab's work was chosen for consideration here because of its wide availability and because her viewpoint on veiling is similar to that of other neotraditionalist writers.[45]

In *The Muslim Woman's Handbook*, Khattab gives little attention to the passages in the Quran and Hadith which have been traditionally interpreted as requiring women to wear the *hijab*; she believes it is axiomatic for Muslim women to wear the veil; and she begins her discussion of this matter by addressing the specific issues of how female Islamic dress should be worn.[46] In setting out a dress code, she quotes contemporary sources which are within the same aggregate of publications for English-speaking Muslims as her book.[47] Khattab lists nine requirements for the proper wearing of the *hijab* in accordance with her perception of the Sunna. These include rules concerning the areas of the body which should be covered (the head and body), the appearance of the clothing itself (simple without any "adornments"), its thickness, its looseness, its aroma (it may not be perfumed), and its distinctiveness from male dress and the "costumes" of non-Muslims.[48]

In the scant reference which she gives to the Sunna in support of her stance on the *hijab*, Khattab writes, "The women at the time of the Prophet . . . used to have outer garments, the *jilbab* (cloak) and *khimar* (headcover), which they would don whenever they went out. . . ."[49] Khattab concludes from this reference that "[c]overing all the body, except the hands and face, is the *absolute minimum* extent of *hijab*."[50] Khattab takes the word *jilbab* from *Sura* 33:59 and *khimar* from Sura 24:31 and translates them as cloak and headcover respectively, yet scholars do not know for certain exactly what these garments looked like nor how they were worn during the time of the Prophet.[51] Khattab ignores whatever ambiguities there may be in translating or understanding these terms.

In addressing her mostly diaspora Muslim audience (although Khattab believes that the guidance she provides is applicable to all Muslims since Islam's teachings are universal), she takes for granted the notion that Muslim women are not to be secluded, nor should they necessarily be required to stay at home and care for children; rather, according to her, they may quite easily pursue careers while complying to what she believes are Islam's teachings concerning the veil:

> [Some] wonder if you can really be a lawyer/doctor/manager/journalist/ whatever [sic] in long flowing robes! . . . [Y]ou can look businesslike and professional in a *hijab*. . . . With a little effort, you can look businesslike enough to take on the world — without sacrificing your Islamic principles.[52]

While appealing to Islamic tradition to validate the wearing of the veil among Muslim women, she connects this validation of veiling with the affirmation of the very modern idea of women pursuing careers, perceiving no contradiction between these two principles. Khattab integrates her perception of her tradition (as marked by her affirmation of the veil) with the current of new practices (as marked by her support of women pursuing careers) and approves of both while believing that both are in conformity with Islamic tradition.[53]

Another neotraditionalist writer, ʿAbdur Rahman I. Doi (d. 1999), articulated the same stance on the veil as Khattab and supports his position by quoting Suras 24:30, 33:53 and seven Hadiths on the subject from the collections of al-Bukhari and Muslim.[54] Dr. Doi was a Professor and Director of the Centre for Islamic Legal Studies at Ahmadu Bello University in Zaria, Nigeria, serves on the editorial board of *The Search: Journal on Arabic Islamic Studies* based in Miami, Florida and his more than fifteen books and pamphlets are available through various outlets in much of the world.[55] His books are published through Muslim publishing houses in those countries and he traveled frequently to North America and Britain where he lectures to Muslim audiences.

Doi, Khattab and the other writers in this group quote the same Quranic passages and Hadith passages interpreting them as meaning that Muslim women are obliged to wear the veil.[56] Among other things, these writers view the veil as fully consistent with the practice of the wives of the Prophet; they believe it is a way of symbolically expressing a Muslim woman's chastity, her identity as a Muslim, and her desire to comply with every other aspect of Sharia.[57]

Thus, these neotraditionalists take a very different stance on the veil than Mernissi. They view what they perceive to be the injunctions requiring the veil in the Quran and the Hadith to be key aspects of the teachings of the Quran and Hadith, applicable to all Muslim women at all times. One can certainly infer from their writings that the difficulties which the Prophet and his early community experienced in Medina do not in any way contravene or alter what they believe to be the Prophet's clear intent: the wearing of the veil by all Muslim women who are beyond puberty.

Seclusion of Women

While the seclusion of women is not a significant issue for the neotra-ditionalists (since they take for granted the integration of women within various public spaces in the West), the seclusion of women and the division of public and private space within the predominantly Muslim world is a matter of great concern for Mernissi, who lives in Morocco and must either cope with, experience, or observe the hardships of these divisions of space on a daily basis. Mernissi asserts that the seclusion of women in Morocco and other predominantly Muslim countries contradicts the Prophet's original vision for the organization of space which, according to Mernissi, called for sexually integrated space that allowed men and women to interact with one another freely. Mernissi holds forth the egalitarian sexually integrated space of the first mosque which the Prophet built in Medina as the paradigm of equality for modern-day Muslims. (She notes that this type of sexually integrated space, which was emblematic of the Prophet's early years in Medina, stands in sharp contrast to the sexually segregated space which emerged during the Prophet's latter years in that city). This early structure which Muhammad is believed to have built had nine rooms, one of which he set aside as a prayer room, and the others of which he gave to his wives as their living quarters, "The *manazil* [bedrooms] of the Prophet's wives were on the left side [of the mosque], when [they rose] for prayer, facing the imam standing at the minbar [pulpit]."[58]

To emphasize the sexual integration of this sacred space Mernissi notes there was a door in the wall of the mosque (or prayer room) that faced Aisha's apartment into which the Prophet would often lean his head from the mosque before prayers so that she could wash his head for the purpose of ritual purification. Mernissi and other scholars familiar with the original texts maintain that the public sacred space of this first mosque was not limited to the Prophet and to his family but was open to the larger community who followed the Prophet: "When a new migrant arrived in Medina she or he tried first of all to find lodging in the vicinity of the mosque which was becoming not only a religious and political center but also the favored residential area for the community."[59] According to Mernissi's interpretation, the Prophet established his first mosque as a sexually integrated public sacred space where men and (quite possibly) unveiled women enjoyed equal access for the purpose of worshipping God.[60]

Mernissi draws some broad and pointed conclusions about the effects that the departure from this egalitarian paradigm had on virtually all later generations of Muslims:

> In conclusion, we can say that the Prophet's architecture created a space in which the distance between private life and public life was nullified, where physical thresholds did not constitute obstacles. It was an architec-

ture in which the living quarters opened easily onto the mosque and which thus played a decisive role in the lives of women and their relationship to politics. This spatial osmosis between living quarters and mosque had a consequence that official modern Islam did not see fit to retain or did not envisage. . . . [The institution of the *hijab*] is presented to us as emanating from the Prophet's will, [but] was insisted upon by Umar Ibn al-Khattab, the spokesman of male resistance to women's demands. Muhammad only yielded on this point when the community was in the middle of a military disaster and when economic and political crises were tearing Medina apart and delivering it [into a state of fierce political divisiveness].[61]

Clearly, for Mernissi the paradigm of Muslim women and men living as equal and free co-partners is the ideal circumstance for contemporary Muslims and the subsequent division of space between women and men was an adaptation which was contradictory to the Prophet's vision for Muslims. This democratic (or idealized) model of the early Muslim community demands that Muslim men and women share space as well as political, economic, employment and reproductive power. The veil and the attendant custom of secluding women (often in harems) from contact with men who are not their husbands (or close relatives) are concrete and symbolic obstacles to the gaining of equal rights for Muslim women in much of the Muslim world. Seclusion in particular has had, among other negative ramifications, the effect of barring many Muslim women from equal access to education, employment, and proper medical services.

Active Female Sexuality

While according to religious authorities and many other Muslims, the customs and requirements for the veiling of women are based in the decrees of the Quran and Sunna, Mernissi believes that there are more factors than simply the traditional interpretations of these texts that reinforce the custom of women's veiling. For Mernissi, one element which perpetuates the wearing of the veil is the Muslim concept of active female sexuality which suggests that women embody and exude an enormous amount of active sexual power.[62] This sexual power has the capacity of captivating men in such a way that they lose sight of their social and religious duties to the point that their lack of sexual control could actually cause a state of *fitna* (or chaos) to beset Muslim society:

In Islam, there is no . . . belief in female inferiority. On the contrary, the whole system is based on the assumption that women are powerful and dangerous beings. All sexual institutions (polygamy, repudiation, gender segregation, etc.) can be perceived as a strategy for containing their power.[63]

The elucidation of active female power and the potential it carries for causing fitna is succinctly stated in the philosophy of the medieval Muslim philosopher Abu Hamid Muhammad al-Ghazali who sees civilization as struggling to contain women's destructive, all-absorbing power. According to Mernissi's interpretation of al-Ghazali, women must be controlled to prevent men from being distracted from their social and religious duties. Women's power is the "most destructive element in the Muslim social order, in which the feminine is regarded as synonymous with the Satanic."[64] As a result of this perception of active female sexual power and its potentially destructive social consequences, institutional mechanisms, such as veiling and the seclusion of women, had to be established in order to contain women's power.[65] The late-nineteenth and early twentieth-century Muslim thinker Qasim Amin points to a similar sentiment among some Muslims regarding the relationship of sexual desire and fitna when he writes, "Preventing women from showing themselves unveiled expresses men's fear of losing control over their minds, falling prey to fitna whenever they are confronted with a non-veiled woman."[66]

Division of Public and Domestic Space

The Quranic injunctions which have been interpreted as demanding the veiling of women together with the traditional Muslim ideas regarding female sexuality have combined to create the concrete and oppressive division of public and domestic space in many Muslim countries. Public and domestic spaces are segregated along gender-specific lines with each area of space connected to its own set of institutionalized rituals and customs.

According to Mernissi, in the Muslim world virtually all public spaces (sidewalks, bazaars, parks, etc.) are believed to "belong" to men. Men perceive women (veiled or unveiled) as trespassing the appropriate spatial boundaries (*hudud*) whenever they go into public and women may occupy public space in a relative state of peace only if they are veiled. If women are not veiled in this "male-owned, male-dominated space," men come to the conclusion that women are sending them the message that they are sexually available:

> Women in male spaces are considered both provocative and offensive. . . . A woman is always trespassing in a male space. . . . A woman has no right to use male spaces. If she enters them, she is upsetting the male's order and his peace of mind. She is actually committing an act of aggression against him merely by being present where she should not be. A woman in a traditionally male space upsets Allah's order by inciting men to commit *zina* [fornication].[67]

There are certain severe ritualized penalties for women who enter public space in an unveiled state (*aryana*); they implicitly make themselves vulnerable to the crude and unrestrained behaviors of the men in these spaces. Mernissi maintains the segregation of the sexes in the Muslim world is so strict that that the very presence of an unveiled woman in public space carries the message that she is a sexual exhibitionist and would be willing to carry on sexual relations with any man in the street who would like to "woo" her.

While most Muslim women do not usually face the prospect of being verbally abused or harassed by strangers in the home, there are often rigid customs which regulate their behavior and the division of sexual space in the domestic sphere as well:

> The overlap between male and female areas [within domestic space] is limited and regulated by a host of rituals. When a man invites a [male] friend to share a meal at his house, he knocks on his own door and in a loud voice asks the woman "to make way" (*'amlu triq*). The women then run to hide in dark corners, leaving the courtyard free to be crossed by the stranger. The guest will remain with his host seated in the men's room. If he needs to go to the toilet, the ritual of *'amlu triq* is staged again, preventing the taboo interaction between strangers of different sexes.[68]

The segregation of men and women who are not close relatives is as tangible (albeit in different ways) in the household as it is in the street; in both contexts women are to remain invisible to strangers. They attempt to remain invisible in public by wearing the veil and they strive to be invisible in the home by staying out of the sight of male guests.[69]

Mernissi asserts that these divisions of space go far beyond the Quranic injunctions which have been interpreted as instituting veiling; these practices violate the egalitarian spirit of the Prophet's message by consolidating men's power through their self-serving and authoritarian appropriation of space. Space, the most fundamental domain within which human affairs are conducted, is not 'distributed freely' in many

Muslim societies. Rather, space is appropriated in a way that allows men to leverage and reinforce their power over women. The veil and the seclusion of women are two of the most salient examples of Muslim men's organization of space in order to serve their interests.[70]

Visions for Islam in the Modern World

The nisa'ist perspective and Sura 33:35 are the most significant aspects of Mernissi's hermeneutical presuppositions as she interprets early Islamic history to make normative statements about the ways in which Muslims should lead their lives and organize their societies today and in the future. These two hermeneutical presuppositions open up novel understandings of the early Muslim community. For example, the applications of these hermeneutical presuppositions lead Mernissi to the conclusion that the Prophet Muhammad's actions and decrees in their true and essential form embodied, and called upon Muslims to create, an egalitarian society where the rights and liberties of all Muslims, women and men, were affirmed and protected.

The external pressures which Muhammad's military enemies and the *munafiqun* placed on him and the early community caused that community to adapt the decrees and customs which demanded that women wear the veil. In Mernissi's view, one of the adaptations against these very difficult pressures is Sura 33:53–62, which has traditionally been interpreted as requiring Muslim women to wear the *hijab*.[71] She argues that these verses were not an essential part of the Prophet's message insofar as they were proclaimed during a period of serious and unexpected pressures on the community. In addition, the proclamations about the *hijab* created an unfair and unequal situation for women, a situation which contradicted the egalitarianism of the Prophet's earliest community and that of Sura 33:35. Consequently, these proclamations should not be accepted as normative or applicable to today's Muslims. Mernissi maintains that a proper interpretation of Sura 33:53–62, which considers the historical particularities surrounding that passage's revelation, could set into motion a chain of events where Muslim women could rid themselves of the veil, come out of seclusion, and eventually enjoy equal rights with men.

Two elements (which are related to Sura 33:35 and Mernissi's nisa'ist perspective) play an important role in the construction of Fatima Mernissi's vision for Islam's future: (1) Her view of the Prophet's early community as a model for democracy and free speech in the modern world; and (2) The United Nations Charter and the Universal Declaration of Human Rights as the basis for building a tradition of equal rights for people in the Muslim world and as a potential means for demanding that governments in the Muslim world remain accountable for ensuring these rights. For Mernissi, the oppressive and often tyrannical tactics of many governments in the Muslim world constitute a formidable barrier to liberty and the forms of political democracy which could reinvigorate Islam and the Muslim world.[72]

Even self-proclaimed secular governments in the Muslim world, such as those of Hafez al-Assad (d. 2000) of Syria and President Bourguiba (d. 2000) of Tunisia, while in large part secular in their ideology, ruled with reference to Islamic ideas and motifs. However, they did not embody the egalitarian and democratic spirit which Mernissi maintains was present in the Prophet's early community. The leaders of these and other states enforce policies which blatantly contradict the United Nations Charter and the Universal Declaration of Human rights to which all of these countries are signatories.[73]

In addition to providing a concrete paradigm for relations between men and women, the Prophet's early community also offers a model for the democratic political institutions which should be established in the Muslim world. The structure and political function of the mosque is the starting point of Mernissi's argument. She maintains that the mosque was the first and sole political space in which Muslims debated their problems in a group and that the Prophet never made any decision alone, taking care to debate every matter with those concerned.[74]

Mernissi presents the Prophet's early community as a type of democratic parliament where various members of that community gathered to debate freely and to express their opinions without the fear of negative repercussions from the Prophet or others in leadership. Mernissi's belief that the Prophet never made any decision alone, suggests that modern-day leaders in the Muslim world should heed the example of the Prophet and listen to the will of the people when making their decisions as well. Many contemporary Muslim political and religious leaders have misconstrued the role of the mosque in the time of the Prophet in order to serve their own despotic purposes:

> The idea that the mosque is a privileged place, the collective space where the leader debates with all the members of the community before making decisions is the key idea of that Islam which today is presented to us as the bastion of despotism.[75]

In this vein, Mernissi chooses an image from Islam's past to describe the current state of relations between the rulers and the ruled in many Muslim countries today. Much like the early caliphs of Islam, modern leaders in the Muslim world have lost contact with the people, have become less accountable to them, and formed barriers against them. For Mernissi, the first four caliphs slowly began to adopt practices which, in many ways, contradicted the principles of equality, freedom and democracy which the Prophet and his early community embodied. One way in which the early (and subsequent) caliphs contravened the ideals of Muhammad's early community was by separating themselves from the believers and avoiding contact with them.

As Islam spread, the caliphs became more tyrannical and less democratic.[76] This increased separation between the caliphs and the people whom they were supposed to lead functions, for Mernissi, as a metaphor for the separation between contemporary Muslim leaders and their people; contemporary leaders have lost sight of the democratic paradigm of Muhammad's early community, just as the caliphs did.

Mernissi argues that the people and the governments of Muslim countries should work together in making their laws and political institutions consistent with the "superlaws" of the United Nations. The United Nations Charter and the Universal Declaration of Human Rights offer a secular pattern of ideals for human rights which governments in the Muslim world could potentially utilize as models for reforming their laws in the interest of creating an environment where men and women receive equal rights and where all people are granted freedom of speech, religion, expression, and belief.[77]

Instead of building a future based on the ideals of the founding documents of the United Nations, the governments in most Muslim countries have acted in ways that are contradictory to the Charter which their predecessors signed. According to Mernissi, after the ratification of the United Nations Charter the governments of many Arab Muslim countries "monopolized the mass media and the schools to tell citizens that they must modernize and renounce tradition while refusing to grant them the essence of modernity: freedom of thought and participation in decision-making."[78] In addition to suppressing certain freedoms for their citizens, many Muslim states have violated the United Nations Charter by using violence to maintain their power.[79]

Sura 33:35 and Mernissi's nisa'ist perspective are the hermeneutical presuppositions which form the foundations for her Islamically-based critiques of the social customs and political systems which oppress

Muslim women in particular and Muslims in general. These hermeneutical presuppositions provide the ideals by which the spatial and
political organizations of the Muslim world are to be judged and they
also form a paradigm for the renewal and transformation of current
customs and political structures in the Muslim world.

Notions of Democracy in Mernissi's and Islamic Revivalists' Thought

Interestingly, many Muslim revivalist groups agree with Mernissi on
the point that oppressive governments exist in the modern Muslim
world and that instituting democratic structures should be the basis of
an Islamic state. John Esposito discusses the role which democracy
plays in the Muslim world today:

> In recent decades, many Muslims have accepted the notion of democracy
> but differed as to its precise meaning. The Islamization of democracy has
> been based upon a modern reinterpretation of traditional Islamic concepts
> of political deliberation or consultation (*shura*), community consensus
> (*ijma'*), and personal interpretation (*ijtihad*) or reinterpretation to support
> notions of parliamentary democracy, representative elections, and reli-
> gious reform. . . . [M]any Islamic activists have "Islamized" parliamentary
> democracy, asserting an Islamic rationale for it, and appealed to democracy
> in their opposition to incumbent regimes. Islamic organizations such as the
> Muslim Brotherhoods in Egypt, the Sudan and Jordan, the Jama'at-i-Islami
> in Pakistan, Kashmir, India and Bangladesh, and Algeria's Islamic Salva-
> tion Front, Tunisia's Renaissance Party, Kuwait's Jama'at al-Islah (Reform
> Society) . . . among others have participated in parliamentary elections.[80]

The Muslim Brotherhood in Syria also emphasizes the importance of
instituting an "Islamically-based" democratic form of government in
Syria; they maintain that democracy is inherent in the Prophet's original
message.[81] The Proclamation of Syria's Muslim Brotherhood states the
belief that freedom and democracy are as essential to Muslims as the
need for "air, water and food."[82] Among other demands, this Proclamation calls for equality between citizens, the abolition of political
prisons, freedom to form political parties and trade unions, free and
direct elections, and the protection of the rights of ethnic and religious
minorities.[83]

Indeed, those who wrote the Proclamation view democracy as being
inherent to Muhammad's vision for the early Muslim community:

> The messenger of Allah (peace be unto him) used to consult his companions in both major and minor affairs; he used to consult both men and women in peace and war alike. . . . But the Prophet (peace be upon him) wanted to teach his people the principles of mutual consultation [*shura*] and to train them to abide by them. He used to emphasize the necessity of mutual consultation even in the most critical circumstances; he used to say to his companion 'If you agreed on one matter, I would not oppose you on it.'[84]

For the members of Syria's Muslim Brotherhood, shura and *ijma(* are concepts that are inherently tied to an Islamic form of democracy and are the bases of "good government."[85] These principles are like "a lifeboat in storms, a protection against political and military dictatorship, and a safeguard against personal ambitions and party or sectarian domination."[86]

In terms of the Brotherhood's stance on women, they assert an "Islamic conception" of the equality of men's and women's rights.[87] The Proclamation states, "The woman has the right of ownership, work, and participation in the progress of the society provided that this remains within the boundaries of Islam and does not transgress over the duty of the woman toward her home, husband, and children."[88]

It is precisely this qualification on the part of Islamic revivalists which causes concern on the part of Fatima Mernissi. In her work *The Fundamentalist Obsession With Women*, Mernissi states that Islam provides women the right to choose their destinies, and that the Islamic revivalists' prescription regarding women staying in the home violates the egalitarian principles of the Prophet's message which permitted women choice and the opportunity to consult (engage in shura) with the Prophet.[89] For Mernissi, shura and *ijma(* are just as applicable in the domestic sphere as they are in the public. Thus, while Islamic revivalists and modernists such as Mernissi understand democracy as being inherent in Islam they differ regarding the roles which they believe that women should play within a democratic system.

In *Islam and Human Rights*, Ann E. Mayer analyzes the contemporary discussion among Muslims about women's rights and human rights by setting the various Muslim viewpoints on this subject into historical context.[90] She also examines the ways in which Muslim intellectuals and governments in the Muslim world have approached the issue of human rights. While "there is much in the sources of Islamic law that bespeaks a fundamentally egalitarian philosophy," these sources do distinguish "in a number of areas between the rights of Muslims and non-Muslims, men and women, and free persons and slaves."[91] Although Muslims generally agree that slavery is a retrograde institution that is now unacceptable, "Muslims today disagree about whether a legal system in which women . . . are given equal rights with Muslim men would be compatible with the requirements of Islam."[92]

Mayer asserts that members of the ulema and Islamic revivalist groups believe that the Sharia demands equality and, at the very same time, they maintain that the differing ways in which men and women are treated in these societies are *in full accord* with the Sharia's requirement for equality.[93] How can the ulema and Muslim revivalists maintain this apparently contradictory stance? Mayer maintains that social conditioning plays a crucial role in how people think about the principle of equality, as is clear, for instance, from the history of the United States.[94] Although egalitarianism was a fundamental tenet of the political and legal order envisaged by the Declaration of Independence and the Constitution, almost no white men in the era of the American Revolution thought that the principle of equality extended to women and black slaves, who were assumed to be different and unequal.

Mayer parallels the circumstance of late eighteenth-century white men in America to that of many modern Muslim men:

Because of the cultural conditioning that prevails in the Middle East, it is easy for conservative Muslims to think that the distinctions made between different groups of persons in Islamic law are part of the natural order of things and to believe that that the retention of premodern Islamic rules does not in any way contravene the principle of equality. Thus, one finds Muslims who argue that Islam recognizes the principle of equality even while they maintain that women and non-Muslims must be accorded an inferior status.[95]

Hence, Islamic revivalists, such as those in Syria's Muslim Brotherhood, may perceive no inconsistency between what they believe to be their Islamically-based egalitarian stance, on the one hand, and their belief that Muslim women must perform their duty toward their "home, husband, and children," on the other.[96] According to Mayer, this stance is fully consistent with the cultural conditioning which is prevalent in the Middle East. Although the Muslim revivalists' position on women may seem consistent to the revivalists themselves, according to Mayer "those Muslims have a problem when they try to deal with international human rights standards, which clearly say that the principle of equality is not compatible with a regime of discrimination against women. . . ."[97]

It is precisely this apparent contradiction between the Revivalists' stance regarding women, on the one hand, and the Universal Declaration of Human Rights' explicit stipulations regarding gender equality, on the other, which makes this document a very attractive platform for Mernissi. She quotes this document extensively in *Islam and Democracy* as she criticizes government policies toward women in various Muslim countries and as she condemns Islamic revivalist groups' stance on this issue.[98] Her interpretation of the Quran, Hadith, and early Islamic history combined with her support of the Universal Declaration of Human Rights provide her with a textual foundation for her attacks against these institutions.

Even though Mernissi is in many respects opposed to Islamic revivalism (in part for what she believes to be its misogynist stance), she believes members of the Muslim women's movement can learn at least two things from the Islamic revivalists. First, she believes their organizational strategy is strong and worth emulating:

> Women can learn something from the effective way in which fundamentalists use the media to disseminate information throughout Islam. This is because the fundamentalists have a comprehensive regional and international strategy involving translation into the main Islamic (Turkish, Persian, Arabic, Urdu) and Western (English and French) languages, as well as well-organized distribution systems; [they are able] to disseminate printed material around the world at affordable prices.[99]

Secondly, Mernissi believes that Islamic revivalists are adept at using their interpretations of the Quran and Hadith in constructing their visions for Islam, and that nisa'ists need to gain this skill:

> What makes fundamentalist Islam so strong is that it uses religious texts, traditional Muslim heritages as a launching ground for its vision of a different Arab world. Women have to do the same. They have to investigate the past, the traditional literature and the sacred texts to identify in them features, profiles, events where sexual equality is stated.[100]

Thus, Mernissi admits that she has some admiration for some of the strategies of Islamic revivalists, while she disagrees with many aspects of their message.

Ursula Günther sums up Mernissi's overall worldview and method in the following way:

> Mernissi's intent is to utilize the positive impulses within Islam as a motive and as a means for appropriating Islam's history . . . in constructing a vision which she believes to be the very center of Islam's message; a message which focuses on *the complete and total equality of all human*

beings. While pursuing this endeavor in a culture which has adopted many Western technological and intellectual "achievements," she sees no alternative other than cautiously and critically adapting certain positive features of these western strands into her own framework.[101]

In conclusion, while Mernissi criticizes many characteristics of Western culture such as aspects of Western feminism, many Western countries' propensity to use violence in geo-political affairs, and their colonialist past, she carefully appropriates certain aspects of western thought, such as democracy and equality, perceives these as being inherent to Islam and adapts them as part of her vision for Islam. She views certain hoped-for changes, such as the setting aside of the veil and the institution of a democratic system where women are equal partners, as absolutely necessary for instituting some of the ideals which are most important to Islam's initial message, a message of equality which she believes must form the foundation for the lives of all Muslims.

3

LEILA AHMED

The hermeneutical presuppositions which shape Leila Ahmed's perspectives are similar to those of Mernissi's, but with respect to some crucial issues, particularly those related to the role of minority movements such as Sufism and Qarmatianism, Ahmed expresses viewpoints which differ from Mernissi's. The two hermeneutical presuppositions which are important to Ahmed's viewpoints are Sura 33:35, which she interprets as declaring the equality of men and women, and some of the perspectives inherent to various forms of western feminism. For Ahmed, two of the central messages of the Quran relate to justice and egalitarianism. She believes that these two ideals are inextricably tied to the meanings of the revelations which were transmitted to Muhammad; they were the ideals which are supposed to set the standard for the Muslim community.[1]

Ahmed maintains that Sura 33:35 forthrightly proclaims the equality of men and women under God; by balancing virtues and ethical rewards as well as "concomitant rewards, in one sex with precisely identical virtues and qualities in the other, the passage makes a clear statement about the absolute identity of the human moral condition and the common and identical spiritual and moral obligations placed on all individuals regardless of sex."[2] Yet, according to Ahmed, as Islam spread and became institutionalized after the time of the Prophet, many of the dimensions of this egalitarian ethic were either forgotten or intentionally ignored by those participating in the patriarchal structures of "establishment Islam."[3] Ahmed maintains that historically there have been at least two distinct voices within Islam and two competing understandings of gender, one expressed in the pragmatic regulations for society and the other in the articulation of an ethical vision.[4]

Ahmed maintains that while the voice of Islam which relates to the pragmatic regulations of society has been "extensively elaborated into a body of political and legal thought, which constitutes the technical understanding of Islam," the second voice which proclaims Islam's egalitarian ethical vision "has left little trace on the political and legal heritage of Islam."[5]

While the voice related to pragmatic regulations was the one which more or less "won" and constitutes some of the central features of majoritarian Sunni perspectives, there have been those within Muslim history, namely for Ahmed the Sufis and Qarmatians, who have based their communities and their ideals primarily on the egalitarian ethical vision. Ahmed maintains that the Sufis and Qarmatians have believed that the "regulations which Muhammad put into effect, even his own practices, were merely the ephemeral aspects of the religion, relating only to that particular society at that particular moment."[6] According to Ahmed, the Sufis and Qarmatians contended that these regulations were never intended to be normative or permanently binding for the Muslim community.

These groups' perspectives on women and their rules and practices pertaining to them differed in important ways from those perpetuated by the Islamic establishment.[7] Implicit in the worldviews of such groups was the idea that the laws applicable to the first Muslim society were not necessarily applicable to or binding upon later ones. In substantiating this position, Ahmed points to the notion that the Kharijites and Qarmatians both rejected concubinage and the marriage of nine-year old girls (which came to be permitted by the Sunni majority). In addition, the Qarmatians banned polygamy and the veil, while the Sufis "implicitly challenged the way establishment Islam conceptualized gender" by permitting women to put their spiritual pursuits and priorities at the center of their lives.[8]

However, according to Ahmed, the ones who have held power through much of Islamic history have not been groups such as these. Rather, the groups which did hold power were the ones whose androcentric perspectives came to shape the majoritarian legal viewpoints in Islam. Ahmed believes that "those in power" during the Abbasid period (750–1258) had an enormous impact in creating the legal structures which contributed to the inequalities inhering in much of subsequent establishment Islam.[9] Ahmed does not specify what she means by "those in power" during the Abbasid period, but she seems to be referring to the ulema, other influential Muslim intellectuals, and the caliphs who wanted to interpret Islam's textual tradition in ways that would benefit them.

Ahmed recognizes that her stance regarding the importance of the ethical vision contrasts with the views which have been historically accepted by the majority of Sunni Muslims. The hermeneutical presuppositions which are tied to Ahmed's interpretation of Sura 33:35 converge with her feminist stance as she presents her understanding of Islamic history and the role of women within that history. She expresses one aspect of her feminist stance in terms of what she calls "cultural betrayal." That is, as she criticizes certain patriarchal and misogynist tendencies within Islam, she does not want to be perceived as contributing to Western anti-Muslim polemics.

She begins describing the predicament she faces by characterizing some of the features of Islam's relationship with the West:

> The Islamic civilization has a very special, even unique, relation with the West so that the issue of cultural loyalty and betrayal perhaps at issue in any culture in this new age of the simultaneity and accessibility of a range of cultures is experienced with unique force and intensity in that civilization.[10]

The current socio-cultural environment in which many Muslims live, which is characterized by Western hegemony and anti-Muslim bigotry on the part of many westerners, has a significant impact on the way Muslims perceive themselves and their history; these factors help account for many Muslims' defensive posture with respect to Islam:

> For centuries [Islam] and the West [have been] in a confrontational stance [during which] in the first centuries Islam was in the ascendant; and then for centuries, as the balance began to shift in favour of the West, in mutual fear and hostility, each was afraid that the Infidel power would triumph and [that] the Infidel [would] take over. In our [i.e., the Muslim] case, the Infidel has taken over: first gallingly as colonizers and now in the flood of ideas and general appurtenances of Western civilization abstract and material it is pervasively everywhere. So that the Islamic civilization is not only a civilization unambiguously on the defensive, emphasizing and reaffirming old values, but also a civilization that finds itself reaffirming them the more intransigently and dogmatically and clinging to them perhaps the more obstinately because it is reaffirming them against, and safeguarding them from, an old enemy.[11]

Ahmed believes that she and some other Muslim feminists (who she does not specify) face a similar predicament; that is, in critiquing aspects of the Islamic tradition, they could be perceived as contributing to the continuing Western discourse against Islam and, by doing so, betraying their own cultural and religious tradition.

> It is only when one considers that one's sexual identity alone (and some would not accept even this) is more inextricably oneself than one's cultural identity, that one can perhaps appreciate how excruciating is the plight of the Middle Eastern feminist caught between those two opposing loyalties, forced almost to choose between betrayal and betrayal.[12]

Yet, Ahmed suggests that this notion of the "betrayal of one's culture" may well be rooted in a very traditional (and possibly outdated) notion of culture. Ahmed maintains that in this current age in which we live, many people (particularly those living in the West) do not necessarily have to belong to a given culture by virtue of their birth:

> As members of this new world of cultural simultaneity with a range of cultural systems before us, we have now the onus and the privilege of not belonging to (and therefore also of not being morally owned by) any culture simply by birthright, and our culture can now, must now, be a matter of positive personal choice and commitment, and to (it may be) understandings, ways of perception, and systems of analysis drawn from different cultures.[13]

Ahmed observes that Muslim feminists, on the one hand, and Western feminists, on the other, find themselves in very different circumstances as they critique their respective cultures. Although Western feminists face criticisms and pressures toward conformity and acceptance, Muslim feminists feel these pressures much more acutely because in engaging in their critiques, they must be careful not to appear to be betraying their cultures and their religion. Because of the danger of appearing to betray one's religion and culture, the Muslim feminist is often confronted with forces which "bear down on her urging her to silence her criticism, remain loyal, reconcile herself to, even find virtue in the central formulations of her culture that normally she would rebel against. . . ."[14]

Sources of Ahmed's Thought

Ahmed draws from the strands of feminism which emphasize the priority that scholars must give to gender as they write about history. In critiquing Ira Lapidus' inattention to the role of gender in the *History of Islamic Societies*, Ahmed cites the work of Joan W. Scott.[15] Scott indicates the inaccuracies which have arisen from the disregard for women in historical scholarship and she outlines the implications which considering gender can have for historical analysis. In her work, Ahmed emphasizes the distinctive experiences of Arab Muslim women in history and she discusses the ways in which class, ethnicity, and local culture have an impact on scholarly discourse. The works of Nancy F. Cott and Judith Butler, whom Ahmed cites, consider these issues as they critique Western feminist scholars who universalize their own ideas and apply these concepts to non-Western cultures in ways that do not adequately take into account cultural differences.[16] Ahmed aligns herself with these ideas as she examines the distinctive role of gender in Arab Muslim societies.

Ahmed adopts themes from the writings of Egyptian feminists as well. Huda Sha'rawi (1879–1947), Malak Hifni Nassef (1886–1918), Zeynab al-Ghazali (b. 1918), and Doria Shafik (1914–1976) are four women who Ahmed maintains have had a tremendous impact on Muslim feminism and the discourse about women in Arab societies during the late nineteenth and twentieth centuries.[17] Sha'rawi who, among other things, is famous for publicly removing her veil in Cairo after returning from an International Women's Conference in Rome in 1923, affiliated herself with the westernizing, secularizing tendencies of society and promoted a feminism that assumed the desirability of progress toward Western-type societies.[18] She was a leader of the Egyptian Feminist Union and believed in raising Egyptian women's intellectual and moral level while enabling them to attain political, social, and legal equality.[19] The Union's specific goals were obtaining access to education at all levels for women, reforming marriage law, in particular laws relating to polygamy and divorce, and setting a minimum marriage age of sixteen for girls.[20]

Malek Hifni Nassef agreed with Sha'rawi regarding the political, social, and legal equality of women. However, in contrast to Sha'rawi she took a strong stand for the veiling of women and believed that the Quran, Hadith, and Islamic history should be taught in Egyptian schools.[21] Yet, Nassef did not articulate Muslim women's roles in society as thoroughly as someone Ahmed believes is a second generation Egyptian feminist, Zeynab al-Ghazali, who was a student of Sha'rawi's and broke with her at the age of eighteen.[22]

Al-Ghazali founded the Muslim Women's Association in Egypt in 1938 which helped women study Islam, maintained an orphanage, assisted poor families, and assisted unemployed men and women in finding useful employment.[23] She believed that Islam provided women with "everything: freedom, economic rights, political rights, social rights, public and private rights," although these rights were unfortunately not manifest in Islamic societies.[24] The way to bring about a society in which women had freedom and human rights was also the way to revive the Islamic nation, which had to be governed by the unerring dictates of the Quran and Sunna.[25]

Ahmed calls mid-twentieth-century Doria Shafik, "who underscored the superiority of the West" and adopted western concepts of liberty, freedom, and justice in her thought the "exact opposite" of al-Ghazali. Shafik founded three women's magazines one of which was *Bint al-Nil* (Daughter of the Nile). This magazine formed the nucleus of Shafik's political organization which went by the same name.[26] During her life, Shafik was actively involved in several political struggles. In 1951, she led a thousand women in a demonstration at the Egyptian parliament demanding that women be given the right to vote and equal job and educational opportunities as men.[27] In 1952, Shafik's *Bint al-Nil* organization, which had its own paramilitary unit of two hundred women, surrounded the building of Britain's Barclay Bank in Cairo as a protest against British colonial domination in Egypt. Her final significant political action took place in 1957 when she went on a hunger strike to protest Israel's delay in pulling out of the Sinai after the "Tripartite Aggression" and the "dictatorship" of Nasser which she believed was leading Egypt "into bankruptcy and chaos."[28] As a result of these actions, which Ahmed says "seem overdramatic and disproportionate," the members of Bint al-Nil forced her to resign. In subsequent years, she devoted herself to writing and finally committed suicide in 1976. Although Ahmed critiques the actions which Shafik took late in her political career, she states Egyptian "society would doubtless have been healthier and state abuses perhaps somewhat curbed had there been many more Doria Shafiks."[29]

Ahmed incorporates aspects of secular feminism from Egyptian feminists (Sha'rawi and Shafik), strands of Western secular feminism (Scott, Cott, and Butler), together with approaches from Islamically-oriented feminism (Nassef and al-Ghazali). Her presupposition that the Quran calls for justice and that Muslim's must heed this call is certainly one adaptation of certain forms of Muslim feminism. While Ahmed maintains that the Quran contains the ethical basis for the transformation of Muslim societies and the establishment of political structures which give equal rights to women, she would disagree with al-Ghazali's and Naseef's specific ways of articulating the Quran's pronouncements.

Ahmed would probably find too simplistic al-Ghazali's belief that Muslims must "purify the world of unbelief, atheism, and oppression."

Ahmed's claims are a bit more reserved. While she believes in the validity of Islam's teachings regarding justice and equality, she takes great care in examining the context within which these ideas were originally proclaimed and the ways they can be applied to Muslim communities today. She affirms the value of the contributions of Middle Eastern secular feminists such as Sha'rawi and Shafik, but believes that they too readily accepted Western biases regarding veiling and Western ideas which asserted that Western societies offered women more freedom and justice than Islamic societies.[30]

Ahmed agrees with Western feminists' ideas regarding the importance of reading history with gender-issues in mind and she employs feminist conceptions of patriarchy and misogyny. Although she recognizes the contributions of Western feminism to scholarly discourse, she criticizes some Western feminists (whom she does not name) for their prejudices against Muslim women:

> Although Western feminists have succeeded in rejecting their culture's myths about Western women and their innate inferiority and irrationality, they continue to subscribe to and perpetuate those myths about Muslims . . . as well as to assume superiority towards the women with them. To conceive of us [Muslim women] as existing mindlessly passive, indifferent, perhaps unaware of our oppression. tolerating a situation no Western woman would tolerate . . . is to assume, and imply, our inferiority. Such docility toward the received ideas of their culture on the part of Western feminists creates barriers between us that sometimes seem insuperable.[31]

Thus, Ahmed carefully adapts secular western, secular Middle Eastern, and Islamic forms of feminism in her thought, while remaining critical of what she perceives to be the disadvantages of each.

Western and Muslim feminism are certainly not the only influences on Ahmed's thought. Gillian Beer, literary historian and Ahmed's dissertation adviser at Cambridge University, and British Orientalists A.J. Arberry and R.B. Serjeant had a substantial impact on Ahmed's work as well.[32] Beer had a role in guiding Ahmed in her close reading and interpretation of modern historical narrative, which is manifested in Ahmed's analyses of the writings of nineteenth-century British Orientalist Edward Lane. Arberry and Serjeant contributed to Ahmed's knowledge of Middle Eastern and Islamic history, which is evident in *Women and Gender in Islam* and in the articles she published in the 1980s and 1990s pertaining to Islamic history.[33] Ahmed's intellectual movement from her work on Edward Lane to her emphasis on feminism and gender issues is an intriguing one. Her work on Lane carries the antecedents for this movement. In her book on Lane, Ahmed praises him for his ability to live and work comfortably in Arab and Western cultures,

> [Lane] is . . . remarkable in that the experience of living between, or within, two cultures seems to have been for him unperplexing and even enriching, rather than the splintering, disintegrative experience it was to be for a later generation of Englishman. . . .[34]

Ahmed may have taken an interest in Lane because she also found herself living and working in both the Arab and Western worlds. She also states that while writing about Lane's life and work, she found that his love for Egypt, after her own alienating experiences there, brought the country back into her life in "a positive, restorative way."[35] Lane also taught Ahmed the renewing quality of disciplined work and his deeply religious habits—which interwove Islam and Christianity—were valuable to her when she experienced "a tremendous inner crisis."[36] While Edward Lane combined Arab and Western influences in his works as an Englishman, Ahmed does so as a person whose land of birth and parentage is Egypt. Lane's ability to live comfortably within two cultures and be enriched by them seems to be one model to which Ahmed herself aspires.[37]

Ahmed was born in Egypt, studied at Cambridge from 1966 until 1971, taught at Ain Shams University and al-Azhar University in Cairo and at the University of the United Arab Emirates, was Professor in the Women's Studies Program at the University of Massachusetts in Amherst, and is currently Professor of Women's Studies in Religion at Harvard Divinity School.[38] While she has lived in the Arab and Western worlds, Ahmed has directed her works primarily to a Western academic audience, publishing mostly through Western presses and scholarly journals.[39]

Women in Early Islamic History

Conscious of what she perceives to be Islam's inherent egalitarian message together with an understanding of what her position as a Muslim feminist entails, Ahmed analyzes the historic development of what she believes to be misogynist tendencies in the legal and cultural structures of Sunni Islam. In her work *Women and Gender in Islam*, Ahmed sets forth a three-part thesis regarding the development of misogynist interpretations and practices within Islam. First, she believes that the practices sanctioned by Muhammad within the first Muslim society were "enunciated in the context of far more positive attitudes toward women than the later Abbasid society was to have, a context that consequently tempered the androcentric tendencies of Islamic practices. . . ."[40] Secondly, she argues that "the decision to regard androcentric positions on marriage as intended to be binding for all time was itself an interpretive decision, reflecting the interests and perspectives of those in power during the age that transposed and interpreted the Islamic message into the textual edifice of Islam."[41] Thirdly, she argues that the "social context in which this textual edifice was created was far more negative for women than that in Arabia, so the spiritually egalitarian voice of the religion would have been exceedingly difficult to hear."[42] For Ahmed, the practices and living arrangements of the Abbasid era "were such that at an implicit and often an explicit level, the words *woman*, and *slave*, and *object for sexual use* came close to being indistinguishably fused. Such practices, and the conceptions they gave rise to, informed the dominant ideology and affected how Islam was heard and interpreted in this period and how its ideas were rendered into law."[43]

She indicates that the three areas of life where she believes women played an active role during the early Islamic and even *jahiliyya* times were warfare, marriage, and religion. Ahmed claims that women played a far less active role in these areas during and after the Abbasid period. In terms of warfare, Ahmed writes that it seems that the Prophet permitted the participation of women in these activities insofar as early accounts, such as those of the Battle of Uhud, portray women, including Muhammad's wives, actively and freely participating in the ostensibly male domain of warfare.[44] She points to an account by al-Bukhari in his Hadith collection where he includes a description of one man during the Battle of Uhud

> seeing 'A'isha and another wife of Muhammad's, their garments tucked up and their anklets showing, carrying water to men on the battlefield. Other women on the Muslim side are mentioned as caring for the injured and removing the dead and wounded from the field.[45]

In addition, Ahmed asserts that Umm 'Umara continued to fight in Muslim battles during Muhammad's lifetime and afterward, until she lost her hand in the battle of 'Uqraba in 634.[46] In support of her position,

Ahmed points to several other instances of women's involvement in warfare during the early Islamic period.[47] According to Ahmed, this type of free participation in community affairs would soon be curtailed by the formal introduction of seclusion and by the continuation of the barring of women from the mainstream of public affairs during the Umayyad period and increasingly so during the Abbasid period.[48]

Regarding the issue of marriage, Ahmed suggests that as Islam became more formalized over time, practices related to marriage became quite restrictive for Muslim women living after the early Islamic period. She maintains that during the transition from the first Muslim community to Abbasid society attitudes toward women and marriage changed extensively. Everything from the acceptability of marrying nonvirgins, such as widows and divorcées, to women's legitimate expectations in marriage, was revised.[49]

This relative freedom which women may have enjoyed during *jahiliyya* and early Islamic times is indicated by some evidence which suggests that women during those periods frequently remarried after divorce or widowhood without a great deal of stigma, a state of affairs which changed dramatically during the Abbasid era. Umm Khulthum and ʿAtika bint Zaid are examples of women who could remarry without stigma. After Umm Kulthum married Muhammad's adopted son, Zaid, and he died in battle in 629, she married another Muslim, Zubair ibn al-ʿAwwam, whom she divorced after he treated her harshly; this was a divorce which the Prophet condoned. Afterwards, she had two more husbands in succession: ʿAbd al-Rahman and ʿAmr Ibn al-ʿAs, conqueror of Egypt. In this early Islamic period, she was able to marry four different men without great difficulty or opposition from the Prophet or his companions.[50] ʿAtika bint Zaid also had four husbands. Of all of Muhammad's wives, the only one who had not been previously married was ʿAʾisha, indicating that there was little restriction regarding women being married more than once in pre-Islamic times.[51] Besides illustrating that no stigma was attached to men marrying nonvirgins during this early period, the information on ʿAtika bin Zaid and ʿAʾisha also indicates that neither age nor previous marriage barred women from making socially prestigious matches.[52] Other aspects of the stories of these two women indicate that the Islamic type of marriage which was introduced by Muhammad retained a degree of flexibility insofar as there was some room for women to negotiate marriage terms acceptable to them.[53] According to Ahmed, the practice of women being able to remarry and to stipulate the conditions of marriage continued on a less frequent basis into the Umayyad (661–750) and the early Abbasid periods.[54]

In sharp contrast to certain majoritarian Muslim perspectives which maintain that the status of women improved with the establishment of Islam, Ahmed suggests there is historical evidence which indicates that in certain respects some freedoms which women in *jahili* times enjoyed were severely inhibited or banned by Islam.[55] She indicates that evidence regarding marriage practices in pre-Islamic Arabia is fairly scant and its implications are not always certain. In light of these difficulties, she points to the works of W. Robertson Smith and Montgomery Watt which have suggested that women may have enjoyed substantial freedoms during the *jahiliyya*. W. Robertson Smith wrote that evidence of matriliny from pre-Islamic Arabia is distinctive enough to suggest that certain pre-Islamic Arabian societies were matriarchal and that Islam replaced a matriarchal order with a patriarchal one.[56] More recently, Montgomery Watt contends that evidence of the practices of uxorilocal marriage and polyandry in some parts of Arabia indicates that pre-Islamic Arabia was not matriarchal, but that it was predominantly matrilineal. It was a society in which paternity was of little or no importance. Ahmed interprets these studies as indicating that Arabian society around the time of Muhammad's birth was in the process of changing into a patrilineal one. She maintains that this was a change which Islam was to consolidate.[57]

For Ahmed, the customs surrounding the lives and marriages of Khadija and ʿAʾisha represent some of the shifts from *jahili* to Islamic practice. Khadija owned her own business, and she was the one who proposed to Muhammad — a man several years younger than herself. Ahmed believes that Khadija's economic independence, her marriage overture — apparently without a male guardian to act as an intermediary — her marriage to a man many years younger than herself, and their monogamous marriage all reflect *jahili* rather than Islamic practice.[58]

These customs were to undergo some significant changes as Islam began to establish itself during Muhammad's life. The type of autonomy which seemed to characterize much of Khadija's life became increasingly absent as Islam grew. Unlike the monogamous life which Muhammad had led with Khadija, after her death, as Muhammad became the established prophet and leader of Islam, "the control of women by male guardians and the male prerogative of polygyny were . . . to become formal features of Islamic marriage."[59] The customs and social circumstances which surround ⟨A⟩isha were to prefigure the limitations that would thenceforth restrict Muslim women's lives: "she was born to Muslim parents, married Muhammad when she was nine or ten, and soon thereafter, along with her co-wives, began to observe the new customs of veiling and seclusion."[60] Ahmed believes that the differences between Khadija's and ⟨A⟩isha's lives, especially with regard to their varying autonomy, were to foreshadow the changes which Islam was to effect for subsequent Muslim women as the acceptance of women as participants in and authorities on the central affairs of the community steadily declined in the ensuing periods under Islam.[61] She concludes her analysis of marriage practices within Islam and her argument that the changes in these practices increasingly served male interests by claiming that Islam selectively reinforced certain existing pre-Islamic practices which benefited men.[62]

Clearly, Ahmed maintains that the social circumstances and practices surrounding ⟨A⟩isha's life (such as the fact that she married Muhammad when she was nine or ten, had co-wives, and was veiled and secluded) were emblematic of the patriarchal and misogynist tendencies which became heightened during her lifetime. In contrast to ⟨A⟩isha, she cites Khadija's life as representative of the higher level of freedom and independence which some women during *jahiliyya* times enjoyed. By elevating the position of Khadija over that of ⟨A⟩isha, Ahmed's work deviates with the vast majority of Muslim biographies of ⟨A⟩isha which, in spite of her flaws, have often glorified her and what the biographers believe to be her patient and humble support of the Prophet, the favored status which he accorded her, and her care in transmitting thousands of very important Hadith traditions.[63]

In addition, Ahmed's approach to the source material about ⟨A⟩isha's life may be somewhat problematic. The two sources which Ahmed uses most extensively in her historical depictions of ⟨A⟩isha are ninth century Muslim historian Ibn Sa⟨d⟩'s *Kitab al-Tabaqat al-Kabir* and Nadia Abbott's *Aishah, The Beloved of Muhammad*, which was the first biography of ⟨A⟩isha to be written by a Western scholar.[64] Denise Spellberg notes some of the difficulties in these two sources. Ibn Sa⟨d⟩ began writing his biography of ⟨A⟩isha one hundred and fifty years after she had died and his work was based on oral reports transmitted over three to four generations. Spellberg argues:

> even the earliest Arabic written sources on ⟨A⟩isha's life already capture that life as a legacy, an interpretation, not simply because of the issue of chronology or mode of transmission, but because of the distinctly different

historical contexts in which the later written preservation of her recorded life took place. . . . ʿAʾisha's legacy demonstrates the power of interpretation in the formation of historical meaning. Her life, as retold in an increasingly elaborate series of reflections and contexts, refracts the emergence of a complex Islamic communal identity in the medieval period. In writing about ʿAʾisha, Muslims honed their own vision of themselves. They used her example to define their past in new ways for a community that sought always to follow the precedent of the Prophet Muhammad and his first followers, male and female.[65]

Thus, accounts such as Ibn Saʿd's exhibit the "medieval process of selectively retelling and emphasizing parts of her life and its meaning."[66]

In her critique of twentieth century scholarship on ʿAʾisha, Spellberg maintains that although Nabia Abbott's biography of her is a "thorough Western study of ʿAʾisha's life," it suffers from two flaws.[67] First, in Abbott's attempt to present "a linear chronology in which the subject is traced from birth to death," she does not give adequate consideration to the divergences and apparent contradictions about ʿAʾisha's life which appear in the medieval sources.[68] Second, Abbott's portrayal of ʿAʾisha is colored by her own presupposition that the Prophet's wife was a "sage and a saint"; Spellberg calls this designation both "inaccurate and misleading."[69]

Thus, one of the difficulties in Ahmed's presentation of ʿAʾisha's life is that it does not provide enough attention to the possible weaknesses in the source materials. Ahmed's presentation does not, for instance, qualify her depiction of ʿAʾisha by stating that Ibn Saʿd's *al-Tabaqat* represents one of several interpretations of ʿAʾisha's life.[70] Ahmed's work also does not adequately consider the problems which may arise from the fact that Ibn Saʿd was writing one hundred and fifty years after ʿAʾisha's death and that his account was based on oral traditions, each of which carried its own biases. Also, Ahmed's treatment is not critical of Abbott's biography and may underestimate the potential weaknesses in Abbott's biases and her inattention to divergent interpretations of ʿAʾisha's life.[71]

Misogyny and Medieval Islamic History

According to Ahmed, women's active role in the religious sphere also became increasingly restricted after early Islamic times. She writes that the evidence on women in early Muslim societies suggests that they characteristically participated in and were expected to participate in the activities that preoccupied their community, and that these activities included matters pertaining to religion.[72] Ahmed maintains that women were not passive, docile followers but were active participants "in the domain of faith" as well as other areas.[73]

For Ahmed, the Hadith narratives show that early Muslim women acted and spoke out with the understanding that they were entitled to participate in religious life; they were permitted "to comment forthrightly on any topic, even the Quran, and to do so in the expectation of having their views heard."[74] Concomitant with women's active participation in the religious life of the community, Muhammad welcomed their viewpoints and seemed to engage them in conversation.[75]

Women's involvement in the religious life of the early Muslim community also provided an occasion for the revelation of Sura 33:35 which Ahmed, Mernissi, and others interpret as decreeing the equality of men and women before God. Ahmed believes that this revelation was occasioned when women asked why many of the revelations up until that time were addressed almost exclusively to men, when women too had accepted God and his Prophet.[76] According to Ahmed, after these events, Sura 33:35 and subsequent revelations addressed women explicitly a number of times.

The habit of listening and giving weight to women's expressed opinions and ideas which seemed to be evident in Muhammad's attitude during his lifetime continued to be a feature of the Muslim community in the years immediately after Muhammad's death, and is vividly manifested by the acceptance of women's contributions to the Hadith.[77] ʿAʾisha in particular (with "Umm Salama and Zeinab as distant seconds") was consulted by many in the Muslim community after Muhammad's death for guidance regarding his actions and sayings. According to Ahmed, ʿAʾisha's accounts served to settle points of conduct and sometimes points of law.[78] In the six widely accepted Hadith collections there are a total of 2,210 Hadiths attributed to ʿAʾisha while al-Bukhari and Muslim in particular, whose Hadith collections are often understood to be the most authoritative, included some three hundred Hadith which were transmitted by ʿAʾisha in their works.[79]

In addition to their role in passing down the traditions of the Prophet, women played an active role in other areas of religious and political life as well. For example, according to Ahmed, during his last illness Abu Bakr, the first caliph, gave ʿAʾisha the responsibility of disposing certain public funds and properties and of distributing his own property among his other sons and daughters.[80] A woman was even entrusted with safeguarding the first written version of the Quran. This was Hafsah, one of the wives of the Prophet and a daughter of ʿUmar, who, according to some accounts, kept this written version during ʿUthman's caliphate.[81]

For Ahmed, the relative freedom of women and their involvement in some of the central affairs of the early Muslim community were to become severely restricted during the Abbasid period.[82] Ahmed notes that during the Abbasid period women were conspicuous for their absence from all areas of the Muslim community's most important activities.[83] Ahmed asserts that in the records relating to this period there is a marked decrease in accounts pertaining to the activity of women in warfare and religious life; there are also scant descriptions of them as participants in or key contributors to the cultural life and productions of their society.[84] According to Ahmed, beginning with the Abbasid period, women of the elite and bourgeois classes lived out their lives in seclusion, guarded by eunuchs if wealthy.[85] The institutions which were to play influential roles in containing women during this and subsequent periods were polygamy, concubinage, and seclusion.[86]

The texts which were produced during the Abbasid period reflect the marginalized role which women played at that time; women are virtually absent from these texts. In their textual productions, the Abbasid writers inscribed "an implicit and explicit ideology of gender."[87] Ahmed argues that the patriarchal and misogynist nature of these texts relates to the fact that the writers of these texts

> grew up experiencing and internalizing the society's assumptions about gender and about women and the structures of power governing the relations between the sexes, assumptions and structures that were encoded into and manifested in the ordinary daily transactions of life.[88]

These practices then became inscribed in the texts which the men wrote; they took the form of normative injunctions about the nature and meaning of gender or at other times "silently informed their texts as assumptions about the significance of women and gender."[89] These patriarchally-based texts are regarded as the core prescriptive texts of Islam and have been used by many Muslims throughout history to oppress and marginalize women, most often barring them from the central decision-making and interpretive processes within the tradition. Ahmed believes that Muslim supporters of patriarchy gave endorsement and license to the various pre-Islamic mores and prejudices directed against women. Particularly during the Abbasid period Islam lent itself to interpretations that endorsed "a deeply negative and debased conception of women." As a result, a number of "abusive uses of women" became legally and religiously sanctioned Muslim practices.[90]

While the texts which the Sunni majority produced during the Abbasid period came to be the "orthodox texts" of Islam, there were concurrent movements within Islam such as Sufism and Qarmatianism, which for Ahmed more truly embodied the Prophet's vision of a just Islamic society. Implicit in Ahmed's position is the idea that many of the laws and practices which were either perpetuated or created during the Abbasid period contradicted some of the essential aspects of Muhammad's teachings pertaining to justice and equality of the sexes. For Ahmed, what she calls "orthodox Islam" (a reference to the majority Sunni position) gave a paramount status to androcentrism while paying little heed to women. In doing so, those who elaborated the laws ignored Islam's ethical teachings, particularly its emphasis on the equality of women and men and its injunctions to treat women fairly.[91] Ahmed's critical stance regarding the Sharia and its development is one that in many respects contradicts the majoritarian Sunni perspective that Islamic law represents the ultimate jurisprudential standard toward which Islamic society is to strive; this is one aspect of her thought which is distinctly modernist.

Quran and Sharia

In another viewpoint which contrasts sharply with that of many majoritarian Sunni perspectives, Ahmed questions the extent to which the Quran can be a valid basis for formulating specific legal prescriptions. For her, Quranic precepts consist mainly of "broad general propositions chiefly of an ethical nature" rather than "specific legalistic formulations."[92] To illustrate what she believes to be the intrinsic complexity and ambiguity of the Quranic text and the crucial role played by interpretation, Ahmed points to Sura 4:3, which pertains to the appropriate number and proper treatment of wives. She states that the Quran permits a man to have up to four wives, but at the same time, husbands are enjoined to treat co-wives equally and not to marry more than one wife if they feel they will not be able to treat them equally well. These teachings regarding the number of wives have given rise to varying interpretations in Islamic history: some interpreters have stated that Muslim men should limit themselves to one wife since it is very difficult to treat all of one's wives equally, while others have stated it is possible for Muslim men to treat multiple wives equally and that men should be permitted to marry that number, if they are can afford it financially.[93] Thus, for Ahmed the ambiguity of this and other verses related to other matters calls into question the Quran's reliability as a coherent basis for the formulation of Islamic law.

How does Ahmed's position on the Quran and Sharia compare with those of other modern Muslims whose ideas are representative of classic majoritarian Sunni perspectives regarding these issues? The Sunni majoritarian view is that the Quran and Hadith form the basis for the formulation of Sharia law (in its various historical manifestations) and that the purpose of the Sharia is to guide the life of the entire umma or Muslim community. In *An Introduction to Islamic Law*, Joseph Schacht summarizes the central role of Islamic law to Muslims and to many Islamic societies:

> Islamic law is the epitome of Islamic thought, the most typical manifesta-
> tion of the Islamic way of life, the core and kernel of Islam itself. The very
> term *fiqh* 'knowledge,' shows that early Islam regarded knowledge of the
> sacred Law as the knowledge *par excellence*. . . . The whole of life of the
> Muslims, Arabic literature, and the Arabic and Islamic disciplines of learn-
> ing are deeply imbued with the ideas of Islamic law: it is impossible to
> understand Islam without understanding Islamic law.[94]

Schacht's observation reinforces the immense degree to which Ahmed's near-total rejection of Islamic law, in favor of Sufism's and Qarmatianism's egalitarianism, varies from majoritarian Sunni Muslim perspectives on this issue.[95] In turning aside from Sharia as a basis for guiding the Muslim community, Ahmed is opposing what Schacht calls the very "core and kernel" of Islam itself. Yet, Ahmed's deep-rooted belief in the pre-eminence of Islam's inherent egalitarianism seems to leave her with little choice. For her, Islamic law and "orthodox Islamic history" (as she calls it) have been so thoroughly imbued with patriarchy and misogyny that they leave little precedent on which to base a future of egalitarianism and liberty, which for her are the core principles undergirding the Quran's teachings.

Ismail Faruqi, a modernist Islamic thinker and Professor of Islamic Studies at Temple University in Philadelphia until his untimely death in 1986, expressed viewpoints on Sharia which are relatively consistent with majoritarian Sunni positions on Islamic law. Faruqi is quite adamant in his belief regarding the centrality of Islamic law to Muslims and to Muslim societies as well as the unique contribution Sharia has made and can continue to make in the history of religions. For Faruqi, the principles of the Sharia embody

> the quintessence of Islam [and] of Islamic culture and civilization . . . The Sharia . . . is the greatest contribution of Islam to humanity. It is the outpouring of Muslim genius and the real forte of Islam itself. It is the response to the perennial questions. 'What ought man to do?' 'What can man accomplish?' and 'What may he hope for?'[96]

Faruqi continues by stating that the hundreds of millions of people during the fourteen centuries of Islam who have become Muslims were transformed by the Sharia while being "lifted out from the nethermost depths of primitiveness, ignorance or debauchery to the uppermost heights of discipline, refinement and civilization."[97] Faruqi also maintains that the Sharia "integrated and unified" the disparate millions of Muslims whose lives it touched into a "homogenous world umma or universal community."[98]

For Leila Ahmed the creation and continued formulation the Sharia and *fiqh* through the Umayyad, Abbasid and subsequent periods had effects that were, in her view, very negative for women. While Islamic law may have had the effect of helping to unite very diverse groups of people under its sway, for Ahmed this reality does not justify giving Sharia a prominent place in the life of the umma today. Its power and history in the oppression and marginalization of women is more than enough reason to reject it as a legal or moral basis for Muslim communities. Additionally, Ahmed maintains that the Sharia does not embody the egalitarianism which she believes is central to and inherent in the Quranic revelations and the Prophet's teachings.

The question of how the Sharia is to be appropriated and understood in Western diaspora settings where (at least in the public sphere) secular law is the norm poses a dilemma for some diaspora Muslims.[99] One question which diaspora Muslims face with respect to Sharia is: How are Muslims to live in accordance with Sharia law when the societies in which they reside are ruled by secular law?[100]

Scholars have noted that the hijra, or the emigration of Muhammad and the newly formed Muslim community in the seventh century from Mecca to Yathrib (later to be renamed Medina), forms one significant paradigm for many Muslims living in the United States and Europe.[101] Many members of emigrant Muslim communities perceive themselves as having left their familiar home countries and settled in nations where as Muslims they constitute a minority — similar to the way in which Muhammad and his early community constituted a minority group during their early years in Medina. Many diaspora Muslims even draw parallels between the hostilities they encounter in their newly adopted homelands and the hostilities which Muhammad and the early Muslim community experienced in Medina.[102] Following what they believe to be Muhammad's model, these diaspora Muslims believe that they are to follow the Sharia law to the extent possible in countries where the "laws of the land" are not based on Sharia.[103] That is, they believe that much like Muhammad enforced Sharia law among his followers in Medina, a city which according to their view did not come under Sharia until several years later, they are to follow Sharia within their own communities today. As these diaspora Muslims strive to live in accordance with Sharia, they do so with the hope that through *da'wa* (the process of converting people to Islam) the wider societies within which they live will eventually become Muslim and, concomitant with that occurrence, Sharia will become the law of their adopted homelands.[104]

Consistent with this viewpoint, Ismail Faruqi maintained that God had placed Muslims in the West for the purpose of spreading Islam's message and converting westerners to Islam. He stated his belief in God's purpose to Muslims by saying, "If you look upon [your emigration to the West] as an event in world history, you will see that Allah, *subhanahu wa ta'ala*, has prepared the course of history to welcome you in the West. . . . By bringing you here . . . Allah, *subhanahu wa ta'ala*, has carved out a vocation for you, a new mission, and this mission is to save the West."[105]

Some Muslims living in the West have adapted their understandings of the two types of dictates of Sharia — *'ibadat* (religious observances) and *mu'amalat* (social transactions) — to their diaspora settings.[106] That is, some Muslims continue to follow the dictates of *'ibadat* (such as praying five times per day, fasting during Ramadan, making the pilgrimage to Mecca, almsgiving, eating foods in accordance with the Sunna, etc.) until the time when Sharia will become the law of the land and everyone can live every aspect of their lives in accordance with the *'ibadat* and *mu'amalat*. The *mu'amalat* (Islamic laws covering areas such as family law, marriage, divorce, criminal law, inheritance, trade and commerce, distribution of wealth, and international law) cannot come into full force in Western countries until Muslims have succeeded in converting the vast majority of people in Western countries to Islam, thus opening the way for the full establishment of Sharia in these nations.[107] These broad characterizations are not meant to suggest that all diaspora Muslims living in the West hold to any or all of these ideas.

Rather, these are some general trends which emerge among from books and other publications produced by such organizations as the Islamic Society of North America, the Muslim Students Association, American Trust Publications, and Jama'at al-Tabligh.[108] These represent one type of neotraditionalist approach to Sharia and hijra in diaspora settings. These views stand in sharp contrast to those of Leila Ahmed who does not mention da'wa in her writings and maintains that the Quran largely provides broad and general guidance on ethical issues.[109]

While there are a variety of attitudes regarding Sharia and hijra in contemporary Muslim diaspora circles, these particular diaspora Muslims are not the first to reinterpret the symbolism of the hijra in order address their changed circumstances. The hijra, which marks the beginning of the Islamic calendar, has been rearticulated by Muslims during various times in history as they have adapted to diverse situations. For instance, the symbolism of the hijra was used by Shehu Usuman dan Fodio (1754–1817) as a way of justifying his jihad and opposing the religious syncretism, injustice, and corruption of the Hebe Muslim rulers in West Africa,[110] and by Islamic revivalist groups in Egypt in the twentieth century to oppose secular rule there.[111] Ideas pertaining the hijra were also appropriated by the Muslim emigrés from Russia (1783–1914) as a way of reshaping their Muslim identity in the face of their forced migration from Russia and the Balkan states[112] and by the twentieth century Khilafat movement to legitimize its call to Indian Muslims to migrate from British India to Afghanistan and Pakistan.[113] In articulating the idea of hijra to address their new socio-cultural environment, contemporary diaspora Muslims are reformulating a pivotal symbol which has helped Muslims understand their changing historical circumstances in meaningful ways during much of Islamic history.[114]

Ahmed's stance that the Quran is an ambiguous and relatively incoherent basis for the formulation and exposition of Islamic law is a significant departure from classic majoritarian Sunni perspectives on the relevance of the Quran's teachings to all aspects of life and its role as one important foundation for Sharia. Suzanne Haneef, a North American Muslim and author of *What Everyone Should Know About Islam and Muslims*, offers a viewpoint which contrasts sharply from that of Leila Ahmed and is consistent with majoritarian Sunni perspectives on the clarity of the Quran and its applicability to all spheres of life. Haneef writes:

The Quran is complete and perfect, and its principles and teachings are as valid and binding today as at the time when they were revealed; for although the style and mode of human life have changed, the Ultimate Realities, the nature of good and evil, and man's own nature are unalterable and permanent verities which are in no way affected by the passing of time or changes in the human condition.[115]

For neotraditionalist diaspora Muslims such as Suzanne Haneef and Abdur Rahman Doi, the Quran and Hadith form the definitive and absolute bases for Sharia which is to guide the lives of Muslims in the personal and social spheres. For these Muslims, the teachings of the Quran and Hadith provide a clear, specific and absolute basis for Sharia. In the chapter entitled "Holy Quran: The First Primary Source of Shariah" in his book *Shariah: The Islamic Law*, Abdur Rahman Doi writes that, as the basis for Sharia, the Quran

contains the knowledge (*al-ʿilm*) imparted by Allah and the guidance (*al-huda*) for men who are righteous for all time to come. It is a declaration (*bayan*) of the truth and light (*nur*) to show the right path. It is the wise (*al-hakim*) the complete exhortation (*mawzat*) and the clear message (*al-balagh*) . . . The Quran provides a code of conduct for every believer and is the commandment (*amr*) and a warrant (*tadhkira*) for him.[116]

Ahmed, on the one hand, and neotraditionalists such as Haneef and Doi, on the other, come to terms with religious tradition and modernity in contrasting ways. Ahmed uses the relative freedom which her circumstance as a Muslim living in the West permits her to dramatically re-interpret Islam, all the while maintaining that her viewpoints regarding the tradition express what really was essential to the Prophet's teachings all along: justice and liberty for all Muslims. Neotraditionalist thinkers such as Haneef, while believing in the importance of justice and liberty, respond to the rapid changes and skepticism of modernity by making absolute claims regarding the Quran, Hadith, and the pre-eminence of the Sharia. This neotraditionalist vision of Islam suggests that Muslims must be completely sure-footed in their interpretations of these traditions and that Muslims must appreciate the fact that they live their lives in ways that differ substantially from the non-Muslims around them. In contrast to Ahmed, who maintains that the Quran primarily provides broad ethical commands and is ambiguous regarding the particular ways Muslims are to lead their lives, Haneef maintains that the Quran is direct and detailed regarding the ways in which Muslims are to live.

This difference suggests one possible difficulty in Ahmed's thought: if a Muslim or a community of Muslims is to accept her understandings of the Quran and Sharia how are they supposed to lead their lives? What would a Muslim community which would "live out" Ahmed's perspectives look like? It is very difficult to answer these questions in terms of Ahmed's thought insofar as she seems primarily concerned with illuminating the hardships which majority Sunni cultures have caused for women throughout Muslim history. Ahmed suggests that these matters pertaining to women must be resolved before Muslim communities can live their lives in accordance with her understanding of Islam.[117]

Sufis and Qarmatians

While Ahmed maintains that Islamic law in various historical forms has not fully represented the essential ethical teachings of Muhammad, she contends there have been particular movements in Islamic history — which Sunni authorities have denounced as *kafir* (or heretical) — which embody the most important ethical teachings of Islam better than Islamic law. Two of the movements which she discusses in this regard are Sufism and Qarmatianism. She explains that both of these movements diverged from what she calls "orthodox Islam" in that they

> emphasized the ethical, spiritual and social teachings of Islam as its essential message and viewed the practices of Muhammad and the regulations which he put into effect as ephemeral aspects of Islam relevant primarily to a particular society at a certain stage in history.[118]

For Ahmed, the differences between groups such as the Qarmatians and the Sufis, on the one hand, and the "orthodox" Sunni majority, on the other, are more significant than the fact that members of these groups interpret particular words or passages differently. Rather, the Sufis and the Qarmatians differ with respect to the majoritarian position "in a more radical, pretextual, or supratextual sense of how to 'read' Muhammad's acts and words and how to construe their relation to history."[119] In this vein, Ahmed poses a question, the answer to which forms the basis of her understanding of Islam's most important feature: "Was the import of the Islamic movement a specific set of ordinances or that it initiated an impulse toward a juster and more charitable society?"[120] For Ahmed, the answer lies in affirming the latter.

Ahmed argues that in many respects Sufism is one example of a movement within Islam which represents Islam's egalitarian voice. For Ahmed, Sufism was a movement in which pietism, asceticism, and mysticism were dominant elements; it broadly opposed the politics, religion, and culture of the dominant society as well as its view of women. Ahmed also maintains that Sufi pietism had political dimensions, being a form of dissent and passive opposition both to the government and to established religion.[121] Sufism's oppositional relation to the dominant society is most clearly evident in the values it enunciated as "fundamental to its vision."[122] Sufi asceticism and its emphasis on the inner spiritual meaning of the Quran are two key features of Sufism which contrasted with what Ahmed believes were the relatively unegalitarian customs and laws of much of Abbasid society. She asserts that Sufi asceticism's emphasis on celibacy and its renunciation of money and material goods stood in direct contrast with the "materialism, exploitation of the labor of others, and unbridled sexuality for men" that were characteristic of the customs of elite Abbasid society.[123] Sufi Quranic interpretation, which emphasized the inner and spiritual meaning of the text, countered the "letter-bound approach of orthodoxy."[124]

For Ahmed, several elements in Sufism suggest that its perspectives and practices with respect to women also stood in contradistinction to those of the majority culture. She maintains that from

> early on, [Sufism's] proponents counted women among the important contributors to their tradition and among [their] elect spiritual leaders. . . . Moreover, Sufi tales and legends incorporate elements that also suggest that they engaged with and rejected the values of the dominant society with regard to women.[125]

Ahmed points to the many Sufi stories and poems about the eighth century figure Rabia al-ʿAdawiyya as exemplifying Sufism's distinctly countercultural elements with respect to ideas about gender.[126] The notion underlying all male-female interaction in the dominant society "that biology and sexuality governed relations between the sexes" is repudiated by several narratives which involve some of the legendary interactions between Rabia and Hasan al-Basri. Many of these stories depict Rabia as being smarter and "more spiritual" than her protagonist, Hasan al-Basri.[127] Other stories within the Sufi tradition emphasize the idea that women have spiritual powers, wisdom, patience, and insight which equal or exceed those of men.[128]

While little is known about the Qarmatians, Ahmed maintains that certain of their beliefs and practices seem to have embodied many of the important aspects of Islam's ethical voice. She asserts that the apparent Qarmatian practice of sharing all things in common (which implies a radical egalitarianism and communalism on their part) is emblematic of one way in which the Qarmatians manifested Islam's ethical voice in opposition to what Ahmed calls the material "corruptions practiced by the dominant society."[129] Ahmed also says that there is evidence that suggests that Qarmatian women were not veiled, that both sexes practiced monogamy, and that men and women socialized together.[130] These and similar practices apparently led Abbasid writers to assert that the Qarmatians were debauched and obscene. Ahmed maintains that the Sufi and Qarmatian movements show that

> there were ways of reading the Islamic moment and text that differed from those of the dominant culture and that such readings had important implications for the conceptualization of women and the social arrangements concerning gender.[131]

These ethical voices of Islam were to be marginalized and oftentimes considered heretical by the Abbasids and others who subsequently held sway over interpreting Islamic history.[132]

When Ahmed's representation of Sufism is compared to those of other scholars of Sufism, some potential questions arise. Ahmed presents Sufi orders as having an egalitarian ethos, which supported the equality of men and women. There may be two difficulties in this viewpoint. First, her work does not adequately account for the hierarchization within Sufi *tariqas* (or Sufi orders) which characterized these orders beginning in the eleventh century. Second, it seems to downplay the predominant role that men and male saints played in much of Sufi history.

Regarding the history and hierarchization of Sufi orders, Spencer Trimingham divides the development of these orders into three stages.[133] During the first stage, which began in the eleventh century, small circles of students gathered around a single master and these Sufi groups had "minimum regulations for living a common life."[134] Around the middle of the twelfth century, "undifferentiated and unspecialized" lodges began to grow and guidance under a single master became a generally accepted principle.[135] In the second stage, which lasted from approximately the thirteenth to fourteenth century, the orders became hierarchized with the shaykhs or murshids (Sufi masters) taking on greater authority and power. Sufi doctrines took on a more codified form than previously, and there were written rules to regulate life within them and prescribed methods for such Sufi rituals as prayer (*dhikr*) and dance (*raqs*) came into being.[136] During the third stage, which began in the fifteenth century and lasted until the beginning of the nineteenth century, members of many Sufi orders' "individual creative freedom ... was fettered [and] they were subjected to conformity...." while the adherents were subjected to the "arbitrary will of the sheikh," and who turned them into "spiritual slaves."[137]

One potential difficulty in Ahmed's presentation of Sufism is that it seems to idealize the "classical period" of Sufi poetry from the eighth to thirteenth century without providing discussion of the subsequent hierarchization of the Sufi orders. It is difficult to discern whether the Sufi orders were as democratic or egalitarian as Ahmed suggests. Even during the first stage of Sufism, adherents were compelled to follow the instructions of their shaykhs. In the stages which followed, according to Trimingham's presentation, the authority of the shaykhs became greater while the codes which governed the orders became increasingly rigid. Ahmed's treatment tends to idealize what may be some of the egalitarian strands of Sufism without fully taking into account the hierarchy and rule-oriented structure which increasingly characterized the orders.

Ahmed's work espouses a representation of a Sufi "golden age" without giving full attention to the complex character of Sufism in much of Islamic history. Carl Ernst critiques some Muslims' and western scholars' attempts to reconstruct a Sufi "golden age,"

> Reformist and fundamentalist thinkers have not hesitated to appropriate the Orientalist tendency to venerate past 'golden ages'; this strategy permits them to pay respectful homage to selected early Sufis who can be described as pious Muslims, and at the same time to complain bitterly of the decline of modern Sufism [or Islam] into corruption.[138]

Ahmed's work seems to utilize an idealized vision of Sufism as a basis for constructing a modernist- and feminist-oriented vision for Islam.[139]

There also may be little evidence to indicate that the prevailing attitudes of Sufi men toward Sufi women were as egalitarian as Ahmed's work indicates. There were certainly female Sufi orders in Aleppo, Baghdad, Cairo, and elsewhere during the twelfth and thirteenth centuries.[140] Women may also have had more of an impact within Sufism than they did on the rest of Islamic society.[141] This, however, seems to be only part of the story. During Sufi history, the shaykhs of most Sufi orders were men, males comprised the vast majority of adherents, many Sufi orders prohibited the admission of women, the initiation rituals for women varied from those of men, and most Sufi saints and poets were men.[142] In addition, women's veneration of Sufi saints, which Mernissi argues plays a significant role in the psychological and physical well-being of Moroccan women, is usually centered on male saints.[143] Ahmed's treatment does not adequately consider these relatively male-dominated aspects of Sufism.

Ahmed's presentation of Qarmatianism may be a bit idealized and downplays certain key characteristics of Qarmatian society. While her analysis does not specify to which period in Qarmatian history she refers, her discussion of Qarmatian communalism seems to be drawn from aspects of this religious movement's history in Bahrayn from 899 to 1078, when Qarmatianism was the "official religion" of this Persian Gulf island.[144] According to Daftary, historical evidence indicates that "communal and egalitarian principles seem to have played an important role in the organization of the Qarmatian state of Bahrayn, especially in terms of the ownership of property, cultivation of agricultural land, collection of taxes, distribution of public expenditures, and various types of state assistance to the underprivileged."[145] This evidence certainly supports Ahmed's assertions.

However, as in Ahmed's discussion of Sufism, her analysis of Qarmatianism omits the dominant role which men played in Bahrayni Qarmatian society. For example, even though the leaders of the Qarmatian state conferred in major decisions with a council known as *al-ʿIqdaniyya*, which was comprised of "some high-ranking officials and the representatives of influential families," all the leaders of the Qarmatian state as well as the members of the ʿIqdaniyya were men.[146] Although the revenues from the customs received from ships passing near Bahrayn went to the male and female descendants of Abu Saʿid, the founder of the Qarmatian state in Bahrayn in 899, the vast majority of all other revenues (from taxes, fees, war booty, etc.) went to males.[147] The ʿIqdaniyya's ownership of at least thirty thousand slaves in the eleventh century is another unegalitarian practice which Ahmed omits from her discussion.[148] Ahmed's work also does not give adequate attention to the more violent strands of Qarmatian history such as the Qarmatians' attack on Basra in 923, their sacking and pillaging of Kufa in 925 and 927, their assaults on and imprisonment of pilgrims to Mecca between 923 and 930, as well as their desecration of the Great Mosque and their carrying away of the Black Stone in 930.[149] In setting forth the Qarmatians as a model of Islam's ethical voice, Ahmed's interpretation does not give adequate consideration to the events in their history that stand in contradistinction to their egalitarianism. In sum, her work stresses the aspects of Sufi and Qarmatian history which buttress her thesis, while giving little attention to the events and practices which contrast with that line of argument.

Qarmatianism, Sufism, and Sunni "Orthodoxy"

Ahmed's emphasis on Qarmatianism and Sufism as models of Islam's ethical voice and as examples for the Muslim community to follow constitutes another area where her viewpoints contrast sharply from majoritarian Sunni perspectives. The Qarmatian movement probably had its origins in the late ninth and early tenth centuries in southern Iraq and the northern Arabian peninsula. It was an offshoot of the Ismaili movement and, at least in its early stages, was comprised of poor peasants, other economically underprivileged persons and people who felt marginalized by Abbasid society. While the Qarmatians practiced a communal egalitarian ethic, their worldview and basic doctrines differed substantially from those of most Sunnis. For example, the Qarmatians believed in the idea of the Imamate in ways that were similar to Twelver Shiites (although the Qarmatians believe that only seven of the Imams were authoritative); they held to the notion of the exoteric (*zahir*) and esoteric (*batin*) meanings of the Quran and they believed there would be seven major historical cycles which would be repeated until all souls were emancipated and return to the Universal Soul. Finally, they believed that those who understood the inner meaning (*batin*) of the Quran would comprehend the ephemeral nature of Sunni law and ritual and would abstain from practicing them.[150] In all these ways, the Qarmatians differ substantially from traditional Sunni belief and practice which rejects the idea of the Imamate, usually holds rather exclusively to the notion of the exoteric meaning of the Quran, and emphasizes the central role of proper ritual and law. [151]

As for Sufism, during various times in Islamic history members of the Sunni majority have claimed that certain Sufi groups or individuals strayed from the "true" Sunni path.[152] From the persecution of the Sufi poet Husayn ibn Mansur al-Hallaj to the Wahhabis' polemical attacks against various Sufi groups in the modern era, there have been many periods in Islamic history when some Sunni authorities have denounced Sufis as *kafir* or heretical.[153] Sufi concepts such as *fana'* (which means the annihilation of the body and its desires), *baqa'* (which connotes becoming united with God and remaining with him), Sufi veneration of saints and the graves of saints, as well as the respect that they often show to their master (*murshid* or *shaykh*) are believed by some strict Sunnis to contradict the "essentials" of Sunni belief and practice.[154]

This characterization of Sufism is not intended to disregard recent scholarship which indicates that many Sunni ulema (such as medieval Muslim scholars Ibn al-Jawzi and Ibn Taymiyya) were members of Sufi orders and that the Sufi emphasis on devotion to God was important to "mainstream" Sunnis as well. Undoubtedly, the relationship between Sufism and Sunni Islam has been complex. Rather, the above characterization of Sufism and majoritarian Islam is meant to indicate the tense relationship which sometimes existed between those who emphasized inner mystical experiences, and others, who were more exclusively Sharia-minded.[155]

While there are a diversity of viewpoints among diaspora Muslims about Sufism, there is quite a preponderance of "anti-Sufi" literature available in Muslim diaspora circles within the United States, particularly in publishing companies which are affiliated with ISNA and MSA.[156] These are diaspora perspectives which contrast sharply from Ahmed's. In contrast to these organizations, there are many Sufi organizations and publications in North America, such as the Sufi magazine *al-Muslimun*, the American Sufi Institute, the Sufi Psychology Association, the Threshold Society, and the International Association of Sufism which foster mystical ideas and practices.[157] Although Ahmed espouses her own Sufi ideals, she does not specify whether any of these contemporary organizations embody her vision for Islam; she does not mention them in her writings.

Since an adapted form of feminism and an egalitarian interpretation of Sura 33:35 function as her primary hermeneutical presuppositions, Ahmed applies these principles to whichever groups in Islamic history which she believes have encouraged the equality of men and women, such as the Qarmatians and Sufis. She does not feel bound by traditional Sunni presuppositions or worldviews because she believes that many in the Sunni majority throughout Islamic history have contradicted the most essential teachings of the Quran which decree that women must have roles equal to those of men in Islamic society. In criticizing and dissenting from majoritarian Sunni views on such issues as the role of women, the place of Sharia in the Muslim umma, and the affirmation of certain Qarmatian and Sufi beliefs and practices, Ahmed is directly attacking what Bernard Lewis would call the "remembered history" of the Sunni tradition.[158]

For Lewis, remembered history is put forward by those in positions of political or religious power so that the mythic and symbolic nature of that history may help justify their position while providing a sense of a common past for the "commonfolk".[159] Ahmed is using a scholarly method of reviewing the primary and secondary sources on women in Islamic history in order to highlight what she believes to be a pattern of Islamically-based androcentric oppression which has been directed against them. Yet, her examination of Islamic history is not done for the exclusive purpose of looking at issues that other scholars have ignored. Her own scholarly investigations are related to a *moral purpose*; that is, she believes that Islam's essential teachings carry a set of *objective ethical proclamations* which demand that Muslims treat women and men equally. She contends that through much of Islamic history those who have held power have strayed from these ethical proclamations and instituted policies and belief structures which have undercut Islam's foundational teachings regarding the equality of the sexes. That is, her rejection of Sharia law, her criticism of Abbasid policies, and her embracing of certain forms of Sufism and Qarmatianism do not undercut Islam's most important teachings, they reinforce them.

The Veil and Veiling

Ahmed's discussion on veiling is complex and intriguing. On the one hand, her interpretation of the historical context of the Quranic verses regarding veiling resembles that of Mernissi. While Ahmed rejects the notion that Muslim women are required to veil themselves (she is an "unveiled" Muslim herself), she explains to her primarily Western audience the phenomenon of "reveiling" among many Muslim women today, and describes why many of them understand the veil in terms of "liberation" as opposed to oppression.[160]

In terms of the historical background which may have set the stage for the origins of veiling and the seclusion of women in early Islam, Ahmed points to evidence which suggests that veiling and seclusion were practiced among Persians, Assyrians, and Byzantines. These customs were, in all likelihood, in place before the rise of Islam in the seventh century.[161] In Assyria, for example "respectable" women who were of the upper class and/or who were married were required to veil as a symbol of the fact that they were sexually unavailable to men, whereas female slaves and prostitutes were to remain unveiled.[162] As Muslims began to formulate their religious law, they adapted preexisting practices of veiling and seclusion, codified them, gave them religious sanction, and applied them to Muslim women.

Ahmed points to three sets of events which may have occasioned the practices of veiling and seclusion during the life of the Prophet and subsequently: (1) the events surrounding the Prophet's marriage to Zeinab bint Jahsh (which — like Mernissi and many other Quranic interpreters — Ahmed accepts as the occasion of revelation, for Sura 33:53); (2) the attacks on the Prophet's wives by the *munafiqun* in Medina (which — like Mernissi and many other Quranic interpreters — Ahmed accepts as the occasion of revelation for Sura 24:31); and (3) ʿUmar ibn al-Khattab's advice to Muhammad that he should enjoin the veiling and seclusion of his wives in order to assure their protection and fidelity in view of the fact that the many visitors who were traveling to Mecca may pose a threat to the security and faithfulness of the Prophet's wives.[163]

Ahmed and Mernissi are in virtual agreement regarding the occasions of revelation for Suras 33:53 and 24:31; their interpretations of these Suras are also very similar. Ahmed suggests that the term *hijab* in 33:53 should be translated as "curtain" and believes that the wearing of the veil is "nowhere explicitly prescribed in the Quran."[164] She maintains that the only verses dealing with women's clothing instruct them "to guard their private parts and throw a scarf over their bosoms (Sura 24:31–32)."[165] She also states that during the Prophet's life and soon after his death veiling and seclusion were still considered peculiar to Muhammad's wives and she writes that "it is not known how the custom spread to the rest of the community."[166]

While Ahmed rejects the notion that the Sunna requires women to wear the veil, she describes the issue of veiling with respect to colonialist and Islamic discourse and she provides some explanations as to why increasing numbers of contemporary Muslim women are deciding to veil themselves, a phenomenon which some scholars have termed "reveiling."[167]

Regarding the contextualizing of aspects of modern Western and colonialist discourse about the veil, on the one hand, and certain types of Islamic discourse about it, on the other, Ahmed asserts that as Western colonizers occupied various Muslim countries they pointed to the veil as "backward." For the colonizers the veil functioned as an example of the way in which Muslim men oppressed "their" women and many of the colonizers believed that veiling was a "problem" which needed to be "eradicated."[168]

According to the colonialist discourse, since the veil was one indication of the "backwardness" of Islamic societies (in comparison with Western societies) and Muslim men's "oppression of Muslim women," one way to "solve" the "problem" of the veil, was for the colonizers to encourage Muslim women to put the veil aside so that they could make "progress." In this vein, Lord Evelyn Baring Cromer, the British Colonial Governor of Egypt in the late nineteenth and early twentieth centuries, wrote that veiling was the "fatal obstacle" to the Egyptians' "attainment of that elevation of thought and character which should accompany the introduction of Western civilization" and only by abandoning practices such as veiling might the Egyptians attain "the mental and moral development which [Cromer] desired for them."[169]

Ahmed continues by illuminating some of the underlying hypocrisies in the viewpoints of Cromer (and of other colonizers like him). Even as Cromer announced these "anti-veiling" points of view that, as he claimed, were to serve the long-term interests of Egyptian women and eventually Islamic societies as a whole, he pursued policies that were, taken together, quite detrimental to Egyptian women. For example, he placed restrictions on Egyptian government schools which severely curtailed girls' education and he discouraged the training of female doctors because he believed that "throughout the civilized world, attendance by medical *men* is still the rule."[170] Yet while Cromer implicitly claimed that his "anti-veil" stance was meant to assist Muslim women, it was through his activities in his own country that Cromer's "paternalistic convictions and his belief in the proper subordination of women most clearly declared themselves:" Cromer was a member of the British Men's League for Opposing Women's Suffrage.[171]

These attitudes about the veil and attendant hypocrisies were not limited to Western colonizers in the political realm. They were often present among many Western missionaries in the Islamic world and other people who Ahmed calls "well-meaning European feminists" living in the Middle East such as Eugénie Le Brun, a French aristocrat who encouraged Muslim women to cast off the veil as the essential first step in their struggle for female liberation.[172] Ahmed wryly summarizes the apparent self-contradictory nature of these Western claims:

> Feminism on the home front and feminism directed against the white men was to be resisted and suppressed; but taken abroad and directed against the cultures of colonized peoples, it could be promoted in ways that admirably served and furthered the project of the dominance of the white man.[173]

Thus, in the periods following World War II, as various anti-colonialist independence movements (which often contained pro-Islamic themes as features of their ideologies) took shape, the veil became a rallying point for many Muslim women. Women who may never have been veiled previously began to veil themselves to symbolize the authenticity of their Islamic faith and practice as well as the sincerity of their anti-Western/anti-colonialist convictions. One context where the veil had this pro-Islamic/anti-colonialist function was among Muslim women during the Algerian independence movement in the late 1950s and early 1960s. In such movements, the veil came to symbolize

> not the inferiority of the [Islamic] culture and the need to cast aside its customs in favor of the West, but, on the contrary, the dignity and validity of all native customs, and in particular those customs coming under the fiercest colonial attack — the customs relating to women — and the need to tenaciously affirm them as a means of resistance to Western domination.[174]

In the Algerians' struggle for independence, many Algerians affirmed the wearing of the veil because in the words of some of the independence-minded Algerians "tradition demanded the rigid separation of the sexes" and "because the occupier was bent on unveiling Algeria." Thus, many of the Muslim Algerian women who veiled themselves during and after the Algerian independence struggle were turning the colonialist discourse on its head — the very article of clothing which many Westerners viewed as a sign of backwardness and the "oppression" of Muslim women became a symbol of what the Muslim women believed to be authentically Islamic and genuinely good.[175]

This description of the role of the veil in the Islamic revivalists' anti-colonialist discourse is just one part of Ahmed's explanation (to a primarily Western audience) of the significance of veiling to some Muslims. Besides analyzing the veil's relationship to the Islamic revivalists' resistance narratives, Ahmed describes some of the practical reasons which many Muslim women, particularly veiled Muslim women in Egypt, have for wearing the veil. First and foremost, the vast majority of women who veil themselves believe that injunctions in the Quran and Hadith require them to do so.[176]

In addition, Ahmed indicates that many Muslim women living in Egypt find it much easier to walk around and conduct their daily activities in public space without harassment from men when they are veiled.[177] Since the veil functions as an affirmation of traditional religious and social customs (such as strict adherence to the Sunna, chastity, and humility) it allows women to talk and interact with men in a relatively relaxed manner. The veil sends males the message that the veiled woman would be available for sexual contact exclusively to her husband only after marriage.

Furthermore, in an age when "arranged marriages are disappearing and women need to find their own marriage partners, clothes that enable women to socialize with men to some degree and at the same time indicate their adherence to a strict moral code (which makes them attractive as wives) are advantageous in very tangible ways."[178] Finally, Ahmed notes that veiling carries at least one other practical advantage — in most cases, women who veil do not need to spend any extra money staying current with the latest fashions since a veiled woman can wear a limited number of veils over a relatively long period of time. This is a feature of veiling that is particularly beneficial for the economically disadvantaged.[179]

In her discussion about veiling Ahmed is not attempting to justify its use among Muslim women; rather, she intends to explain to a Western audience the reasons why many Muslim women choose to veil. She pointedly criticizes the largely patriarchal nature of Muslim societies that causes some women to feel that they must veil themselves in order to protect themselves against undesired male advances. Ahmed believes that male aggressiveness in many of these public spaces lends the spaces a "coercive" quality; it is this negative character of the public spaces in some Middle Eastern contexts that leads many Muslim women to the personal decision of veiling.[180]

She quotes one veiled Egyptian women who expressed her decision to veil in rather cynical terms, "If I carry a gun, . . . I will also be protecting myself. Wearing the veil is like having to carry a gun."[181] Ahmed goes on to assert:

[I]ndeed it should not be necessary for women — any more than for men — to have to either wear a veil or carry a gun to protect themselves or guarantee that their fellow citizens respect their dignity.[182]

As mentioned earlier, one of the most noticeable differences between Ahmed's and Mernissi's treatment of the issue of veiling is that while Ahmed provides a sociological and even phenomenological description of the reasons for the increase in veiling among Muslim women, Mernissi (even though she is a sociologist by training) spends very little time in her works explaining this trend. What accounts for this difference? Mernissi states in several of her works that, as a woman living in the majority Muslim culture of Morocco, she is confronted with familial and societal pressures to veil herself virtually everyday.[183] Given this situation, she believes that commands that Muslim women must veil are based on faulty patriarchal interpretations of the Quran and Hadith and that the practices of veiling have served to subjugate Muslim women both today and throughout Islamic history.[184] If Mernissi were to provide a set of sociological and/or phenomenological descriptions for the practice of veiling among contemporary women she would risk undercutting her own anti-veil stance. Because Mernissi lives, works, teaches and writes in a country where there are enormous social pressures to veil, she must maintain a direct and consistent approach on this issue.

For her part, Ahmed recognizes that she can oppose the practice of veiling, on the one hand, while explaining why many Muslim women have chosen to veil, on the other, because she lives in a society (the United States) where there are very few pressures being put upon her to veil. She writes, "It is obviously easier for those of us currently based in societies where such a choice [of veiling] is not exacted of us to discern and analyze the perilous ambiguities of adopting the veil."[185] The fact that Ahmed lives in a society where veiling is not widely practiced (and is often frowned upon) compels her to explain to some of the members of this society (i.e., most of her Western readers) the reasons why many Muslim women choose to veil. Even though Ahmed has chosen not to veil, one way that she exhibits her sense of what she calls "cultural loyalty" to her Muslim counterparts who have chosen to veil is to explain to Westerners why they have chosen to do so. Ahmed praises Mernissi directly for working and articulating her feminist position in a society where some of its members adamantly criticize her for her Islamically-based feminism:

> . . . [O]nly one woman, I believe, to date — Fatima Mernissi in, for instance, her book *Beyond the Veil* — has succeeded (while based in the Middle East and so in that sense making that total commitment) in extricating herself from the issue of cultural loyalty and betrayal, and the entrammelling arguments into which it precipitates one, and moved to surveying, considering, analyzing and debating the implications of a feminist perspective from a position that is cool and culturally assured, undistracted and unworried by issues of cultural rivalry.[186]

Ahmed herself seems to be unencumbered by traditional Sunni perspectives as she rejects Sharia, majoritarian Sunni perspectives of history, and embraces "sectarian" movements such as Qarmatianism and Sufism as central models for the expression and formulation of Islamic ethics. She rejects the remembered history which has marked much of Sunni history, replaces it with a recovered history which takes seriously the role of women throughout the Islamic past, while using aspects of the sacred textual tradition to define and justify her egalitarian ethic: an ethic she believes the patriarchal cultures of Islam have suppressed and which embodies the true and ultimate foundation for the Islamic community.

4

FAZLUR RAHMAN

The idea of socio-economic justice is the central hermeneutical presupposition which shapes Fazlur Rahman's perspectives regarding the Quran's message to humanity. According to Rahman, Muhammad manifested this sense of justice in his actions and teachings, while admonishing the members of the early Muslim community to do the same.[1] Before turning to a consideration of Rahman's views on the Quran, its pronouncements on justice, and the ways in which these ideas shaped his scholarly writings and worldview, it is important to consider the context within which Rahman wrote and worked.

Throughout much of his life, Fazlur Rahman debated and disagreed with respect to the Quran and other issues with Sayyid Abu'l-A'la Mawdudi (1903–1979), another twentieth-century Pakistani intellectual who was the leader of Pakistan's Jama'at-i Islami, which continues to be one of Pakistan's most popular Islamic revivalist organizations.[2] In his untitled autobiographical essay, Rahman points to the most significant influences on his intellectual life: his home environment, his father's six years of study at the Deoband madrasa in north India, and Rahman's own graduate studies in Islamic and Western Philosophy and Western Orientalism at Oxford University, where British Orientalist H.A.R. Gibb was his dissertation adviser.[3]

Rahman writes that he was born into "a Muslim family that was deeply religious" and that they "practiced [the] Islamic rites of prayer, fasting, etc. with meticulous regularity;" he notes that by his tenth birthday, he was able to recite the entire Quran from memory.[4] From his mother, Rahman was taught the "virtues of truthfulness, mercy, steadfastness, and, above all, love."[5] Rahman writes that the influence of the Deobandi School on his thought came to him most directly from his father who, while Rahman was growing up in north India during the 1920s and 1930s, provided him "with the traditional course of Islamic study he had undergone at the Deoband Seminary. . . ."[6] One of the most significant impressions which the Deobandi school had had upon Rahman's father and, subsequently upon Rahman himself, was the relatively open-minded attitude of those scholars in integrating Islam with modern ideas:

> Unlike most traditional Islamic scholars of that time, who regarded education as a poison both for faith and morality, my father was convinced that Islam had to face modernity both as a challenge and as an opportunity. I have shared this belief with my father to this very day.[7]

In her work on the Deobandi school, Barbara Metcalf notes that the scholars of Deoband discouraged a "rigidity of views" and open-mindedness while encouraging students to "express their opinions."[8] This attitude and the fostering of critical thinking is most evident in Rahman's vision for the future of Islamic education.[9] The early training he received in the Quran was an aspect of Rahman's childhood that influenced his later scholarship as well; he gives an enormous amount of attention to the Quran in his works and his interpretation of the Quran undergirds his worldview.[10]

Rahman writes that his doctoral studies in Islam and philosophy during the 1940s at Oxford University engendered "a conflict between his modern and traditional educations" and from the late 1940s to early 1950s he experienced "an acute skepticism" which "shattered [his] traditional beliefs."[11] While the study of philosophy influenced his thought in many ways, it caused him to focus deeply on ethical issues in some of his writings during the 1970s and 1980s.[12] H.A.R. Gibb and S. Van Den Bergh, among the other Orientalists with whom Rahman studied at Oxford University, grounded Rahman in a Western scholarly critical approach to Islamic history and the sacred texts of Islam, a method which was foundational to virtually all of Rahman's scholarship.[13] Gibb was to have an influence on his student in at least one other way: Rahman adopted an attitude toward Sufism very close to that of Gibb's.[14]

After completing his Ph.D. in 1949, Rahman taught at Durham University in England from 1950 to 1958 and McGill University in Canada from 1958 to 1961. He returned to Pakistan in 1962, where he served as Director of Pakistan's Central Institute of Islamic Research and as a member of Pakistan's Advisory Council of Islamic Ideology until he felt compelled to leave the country in 1968. These positions provided him with two platforms from which to attempt the implementation of his modernist vision of Islam through public policy.[15] He was appointed to these posts by Pakistani President Muhammad Ayyub Khan whose government gave Rahman, the Institute of Islamic Research, and the Advisory Council the task of "interpreting Islam in rational and scientific terms to meet the requirements of a modern progressive society"; this was a very important undertaking since during this period Pakistan was continuing to develop its religio-political identity and its educational and governmental structures in the wake of its independence from India in 1948.[16] In addition to his books, one channel through which Rahman disseminated his ideas was the scholarly journal *Islamic Studies*, which he founded in Pakistan in the early 1960s and edited through much of that decade and into the early 1970s.[17] While the professional positions in Pakistan's Islamic advisory council and the Institute of Islamic Research gave Rahman opportunities to attempt to implement his modernist stance on various issues such as education, biomedical and family planning issues, financial interest, and the mechanical slaughter of animals, he was unable to influence the Pakistani parliament to enact any of his policy initiatives, largely because of the opposition of the Jama'at-i Islami and various influential members of this group, including Mawdudi.[18] After leaving Pakistan in 1968 (as a result of pressure from Islamic revivalists), he continued to articulate his modernist perspectives as a professor at the University of California, Los Angeles and the University of Chicago.[19] The vast majority of Rahman's writings have been published by Western presses in English and seem more accessible to Western audiences than audiences in the Islamic world.

Sayyid Abu'l-A'la Mawdudi, a contemporary of Rahman's who was also born in north India, was a populist writer, speaker, and leader of the Pakistani Revivalist group, Jama'at-i Islami. Mawdudi and Rahman disagreed on many points, including Quranic interpretation, and the roles of education, government, and Islamic law in Pakistan. Much like Rahman, Mawdudi's home life was characterized by his parents emphasis on teaching him the Quran.[20] Unlike Rahman, however, Mawdudi was descended from one of the most prominent branches of the Chisti Sufi order, a lineage that was an important aspect of Mawdudi's claim to authority and which gave him a tolerant attitude toward Sufism in many respects.[21] Mawdudi's father attended the madrasa at Aligarh (founded by nineteenth century Indian modernist Seyyed Ahmed Khan), but was pulled out by his parents because they believed the school had adopted too many British ideas and customs.[22] The resulting anti-colonialist attitude of his father was one that Mawdudi himself adopted.[23]

In 1921, Mawdudi studied the classic areas within Islam (including Quranic interpretation, Hadith, law, logic, theology, and literature) in Delhi under the shaykh Mawlana ʿAbd al-Salam Niyazi. Niyazi promulgated his own strict interpretive stance, leaving little room for alternate opinions.[24] This lack of openness to alternative viewpoints came to characterize Mawdudi's own approach to the Quran, Hadith, and Islamic history. During the 1920s and 1930s, Mawdudi expressed his revivalist view of Islam and his opposition to British rule through magazines, pamphlets, books and lectures.[25] In 1941, he founded the Jamaʿat-i Islami, Pakistan's most powerful Islamic revivalist organization, and played a major role in the movement's leadership until his death in 1979.[26] Unlike Rahman, who spent portions of his life in India and Pakistan and the West, Mawdudi spent his entire life in his homeland. In addition, Mawdudi's writings, many of which took the form of inexpensive pamphlets and were published in Pakistan, were not directed to an academic audience; their direct style and content were aimed at a broad cross-section of Indian and Pakistani Muslims.[27] Rahman and Mawdudi were well-aware of each other's viewpoints and of the impact that they were having on the formation of their homeland's emerging religious, political, and cultural milieu at the time of the Partition in 1948 and thereafter.

Rahman's Views on Quranic Interpretation

Rahman's process of Quranic interpretation consists of a "double movement, from the present situation to Quranic times, then back to the present."[28] In engaging in the first part of this double movement (i.e., analyzing the socio-historical context within which the Quran was revealed), Rahman contends that the acute problems in seventh century Arabia consisted of "polytheism (idol worship), exploitation of the poor, malpractices in trade, and general irresponsibility toward society."[29] As Rahman moves from the historical context within which he believes the Quran was revealed to the contemporary situation which Muslims face, he states that the general message of the Quran is the same for people living in both contexts: "The Quran put[s] forward the idea of a unique God to whom all humans are responsible and the goal of eradication of gross socioeconomic inequity."[30]

Rahman states that one of the first steps which Muslim individuals and communities must take as they attempt to establish a just socio-economic order is adopting the attitude of *taqwa*. *Taqwa* is a Quranic word which Rahman defines "as that attitude or rather quality of mind, whereby a person becomes capable of discerning between right and wrong and makes the necessary effort to do so"; *taqwa* can be translated as "conscience".[31] Rahman believes that taqwa embodies the spirit with which the umma must approach Quranic interpretation and it is also the attitude which must pervade the individual and communal life of all Muslims. While *taqwa* involves the attitude of being able to discern right from wrong, there are rewards for those who do right and punishments for those who do wrong; Rahman believes that God rewards the good and punishes the evil in this world or the next.[32] Consistent with this idea, Rahman writes that the Muslim community, both individually and corporately, must make every effort to live its life in accordance with the moral teachings of the Quran and Hadith and that Muslim political and religious leaders have a particular responsibility to express and manifest the Quran's virtuous moral teachings in their lives and works.[33]

In addition to engaging in the "double movement" (from present to past and back to the present) and approaching the Quran and the whole of life with *taqwa*, interpreters of the Quran must attempt to explain the Quranic text, paying attention to the idea that the Quran is a unity and that it is primarily a "book of religious and moral principles and exhortations and is not a legal document."[34] One of the most significant errors which Muslims legists (i.e., the ulema) made throughout history in interpreting the Quran was that they approached it "atomistically" as primarily a legal text in their attempts to utilize the Quran as a basis for rendering religio-legal decisions.

Rahman maintains that this approach was wrong on at least three counts. First, these legists did not render their decisions (in the form of the establishment of Sharia and the issuance of fatwas, for example) in light of the Quran's unity and cohesive meaning (of which obedience to God and the establishment of a just socio-economic order play a large part). Secondly, during much of Muslim history most of the legists gave little or no consideration to the concrete historical context within which the Quran was revealed. By ignoring the various social, political, and historical circumstances within which the Quran was revealed the Muslim legists often misinterpreted and misappropriated various Quranic passages. For example, the ulema often attempted to apply

Quranic passages, which were meant for the specific circumstances of seventh century Arabia, to their own settings. Thirdly, the ulema frequently "misunderstood" the underlying purpose of the Quran; they approached it primarily as a legal document with specific legal prescriptions (which Fazlur Rahman believes it decidedly is not) instead of as a revealed book which contains general moral guidance.

The history of Muslim legal pronouncements surrounding the interpretation of Sura 2:282 is emblematic of the ways in which ignoring the socio-historical context of various revelations can lead to inappropriate (and in Rahman"s view, incorrect) interpretations. This verse indicates that when a loan is made and a record of debt is written for this transaction, two male witnesses are to be called. It goes on to state "if two men be not at hand then a man and two women, of such as you approve as witnesses, so that if one errs (through forgetfulness) the other will remember." Traditionally, Muslim legists have interpreted this passage as meaning that in virtually all legal cases the testimony of two female witnesses is equal to that of one man.[35] Rahman believes that interpretations such as this one are exemplary of the misappropriations of Quranic passages throughout much of history.

He asserts that the specifics of Sura 2:282 pertain to certain unique features of society in seventh-century Arabia. According to him, the reason "for having two female witnesses instead of one male is that women would be more 'forgetful' than men, since women in those days were normally not used to dealing with credit."[36] The traditionalist understanding states that the law that two female witnesses equal one male is "eternal and a social change that enabled a woman to get used to financial transactions would be 'un-Islamic.'"[37]

In contrast to this position, Rahman attempts to interpret this passage in terms of what he believes to be its own context and in terms of the modern socio-historical circumstances within which Muslims find themselves (i.e., he is exercising his interpretive "double movement" process). In doing so, he says that the testimony of a woman being considered of less value than that of a man was contingent upon her weaker power of memory concerning financial matters *around the time the passage was revealed* since many women at that time were unaccustomed to dealing with financial issues. When women became conversant with such matters (as is the case today), "their evidence can equal that of a man" and this state of affairs would be "for the betterment of society."[38] Thus, while the Quran for Rahman is God's revelation for humanity through Muhammad, it must be interpreted within the full scope of its own historical context as well as that of the modern-day situation.

Rahman notes that throughout much of Islamic history, legal pronouncements were accompanied by a *ratio legis* (i.e., a legal rationale) which explained why a law was being enunciated. The *ratio legis* is the "essence of the matter" and the actual legislation is supposed to be its embodiment "so long as [this legislation] faithfully and correctly realizes the ratio; if it does not, the law has to be changed."[39] Rahman criticizes traditional Islamic legists in this regard insofar as they generally stuck to the letter of the law and enunciated the principle that "Although a law is occasioned by a specific situation, its application nevertheless becomes universal."[40] In the long-run, this relatively rigid custom of interpretation has been counterproductive within Islam since it has not permitted Muslim legists the flexibility to adapt their Quranic interpretations and legal decisions to changing situations.[41]

Mawdudi's Views on the Quran

The interpretation of the Quran was one of several areas where Rahman's and Mawdudi's perspectives differed substantially. While Rahman believed in interpreting it with very careful consideration of its historical context in seventh century Arabia, Mawdudi emphasized that he could read the Quran and decipher its "plain meaning" with minimal effort.[42] Mawdudi indicates that in all his writings he tries to express "as faithfully as possible" in his own words the meaning conveyed to him by the Quranic passages and the impressions they have made upon his mind.[43] Mawdudi believed that the Quran contained the complete and perfect revelation for all human beings at all times and that its single true and clear meaning would become obvious to those who sincerely sought to understand this message.

Mawdudi maintained that the Quran emphasized four interrelated concepts, *ila* (divinity), *rabb* (lord), *'ibada* (worship) and *din* (religion).[44] Mawdudi argued that these four terms would lead one to understanding the essential meaning of the Quran. The terms *ila* and *rabb* are supposed to be understood in terms of God's characteristics, while *'ibada* and *din* are to be understood in terms of the duties which faithful Muslims must perform.[45] *Ila,* among other things, refers to God's holiness, sacredness, purity and "separateness" from human beings, while *rabb* refers to God's oneness (*tawhid*) and his complete sovereignty over the entire universe.[46] Linked to these two terms are *'ibada,* which relates to the proper rituals (such as *salat,* making the hajj, eating halal, etc.) performed in obedience to God, and *din,* which Mawdudi defines as the *totality* of the entire Muslim community's obligations, including, but not limited to, the establishment of an Islamic state under Sharia law.[47]

Thus, for Mawdudi the Quran was to be the guide for Muslims' personal and communal devotion to God; it also provided clear injunctions for the establishment of Sharia and the proper structure of an Islamic state, since for him Islam made no distinction between the religious and political realms.[48] Unlike Rahman, who believed that in order to properly understand the Quran one had to be well-educated and take into consideration various types of scholarly literature which were written about it, Mawdudi maintained that Quranic interpretation was a simple and straightforward task and that those who truly sought to understand it would agree with each other regarding its meaning.[49] Mawdudi believed that the Quran was comprised of a direct dialogue between God and humankind; each *aya* or verse expressed a separate conversation and all the verses were interrelated and could be fully understood in terms of the four underlying concepts.[50] The Quran, Mawdudi argued, was not only supposed to be recited, and reflected upon, but Muslims were to read and understand it at face value and implement its teachings. Since the Quran explained the "ultimate causes of man's successes [and] failures," if Muslims properly implemented its teachings, they would be able to solve their social, political, and cultural maladies.[51]

While Rahman and Mawdudi both affirm the authority and authenticity of the Quran for the Muslim community, they differ markedly in terms of the way they believed the Quran should be interpreted. They disagreed on three significant points. First, Rahman believes that the Quran contains general ethical teachings and purposefully lacks relevant specifics regarding the concrete formulation of Sharia law.[52] He maintains that the Islamic community has relative freedom in terms of appropriating Quranic teaching for the establishment of Sharia so long as its stipulations are consistent with the Quran's general moral guidelines.[53] In contrast, Mawdudi maintains that the Quran (often together with the Hadith) provides self-evident injunctions regarding every aspect of private and communal life, including the proper observance of rituals, appropriate personal and public morality, and the proper structure of the Islamic state.[54]

Second, Rahman and Mawdudi differ regarding the importance of the contexts within which the Quran was revealed to modern Quranic interpretation. Rahman places an enormous amount of emphasis on examining and analyzing the various sources which bear on the Quran's historical milieu when interpreting various passages. An interpreter can make the "double movement" (from present to past and back to present) effectively only after she or he becomes familiar with the historical circumstances within which a passage was revealed.[55] Mawdudi, in contrast, believes that because the Quran contains the universal and immutable message of God to humanity for all times and places; the particular historical context within which it was revealed is far less important than its *application* to the modern historical situation. Since the Quran is universally applicable, implementing its teachings properly is more important than comprehending the milieu within which it was revealed.[56]

Third, Rahman and Mawdudi differ regarding the role of the individual believer in Quranic interpretation. Rahman maintains that in order for the Islamic community to be reinvigorated, Islamic educational systems must be established which, among other things, would teach the proper methods of Quranic interpretation and even create an environment where differences of opinion could emerge.[57] Mawdudi contends that the Quran's teachings are unitary and monolithic, and that the purpose of Islamic education should not be to encourage the learning of proper methods or critical thinking but to convey these unitary ideas to the students so that they may understand and implement them.[58]

These specific differences are indicative of the more overarching contrasts between Mawdudi's and Rahman's approaches towards Quranic interpretation and Islamic history. One of the main areas of contrast between their approaches is that Rahman favors a more "open-ended" methodology where the answers to every question are not known in advance and where individuals and communities apply rigorous methods of analysis to reach conclusions.[59] Mawdudi's approach, in contrast, is one where the individual can come to rapid conclusions regarding Islam's teachings about various issues, and then move on to implement these universal injunctions in the modern world.[60]

Rahman and Mawdudi on Sharia

Rahman believes that rigid practices surrounding Quranic interpretation and legal decision-making represent a set of problems which became a significant part of Islamic jurisprudence after the middle of the eighth century. He maintains that the Sharia itself, and concepts surrounding it, developed in two phases. The first phase began in the seventh century after the Quran began to be revealed and lasted until approximately the middle of the eighth century. The second phase began in the middle of the eighth century and continued for some time afterwards.[61]

Rahman states that during the first phase, Muslims enjoyed considerable freedom in terms of formulating their understandings of the Quran and Muhammad's teachings. The principle concept which guided the early Muslims during this first phase was *din* (or "duty to God" as Rahman defines it). Because during this period "the impulse of the Quran was fresh and lively the Muslim was more likely to stress his effort to submit to and follow God's guidance [i.e., act in accordance to *din*]."[62] Under this attitude, "whatever the Muslim 'understood' of God's Sharia, he would naturally regard as his attempt at *Din* [sic] rather than claim it as Sharia from God."[63] During this period, the idea predominated that it was "up to God to know" whether a person's or the community's actions were really in accordance with Sharia or not.[64]

Secondly, during this initial period *fiqh* (which Rahman defines as the interpretive *process* involved in establishing or understanding Islamic law as opposed to the law itself, which is Sharia) was "personal, free and somewhat subjective rather than an objective discipline."[65] Given what Rahman believed to be this prevailing attitude in the first phase, it would have been "impossible for any single person to claim that the result of *his* thought was the unique content of the Sharia."[66]

One of the salient features of the second phase of the development of the structures surrounding Quranic and legal interpretation was the rise of the ulema and their efforts to formalize the hermeneutical processes.[67] In this period, members of the emerging ulema utilized four principles (the Quran, the Sunna, *ijtihad,* and *ijmaʿ*) which began the concretizing of Islamic legal methodologies. With the establishment of these methods in the madhabs, a "radical change took place in the nature of *fiqh* which passed from being a personal activity to mean a structured discipline and its resultant body of knowledge."[68] This emerging body of knowledge became standardized and members of the ulema established it as an objective system. Whereas in the first phase, "one used to say 'one should exercise *fiqh* ('understanding'),'" the proper thing to say [during the second phase] was 'one should *learn* or *study fiqh.*'"[69] In Rahman's view, Quranic interpretation and Islamic jurisprudence became increasingly "routinized" throughout the Umayyad (661–750) and Abbasid (749–1258) periods. While there were positive developments during these periods (such as the establishment of the four Sunni madhabs or schools of legal thought and the emergence of certain forms of Islamic philosophy and theology), various types of interpretive, legal, and governmental structures came into existence which contradicted what Rahman believes was the Quran's basic message of egalitarianism, justice and devotion to God.[70]

Concomitant with these changes, Islamic society became increasingly stratified. This increased stratification took several forms. For example, during the Umayyad and Abbasid periods the caliphs viewed themselves and desired others to view them as kingly leaders. They resided in opulent palaces with all the accoutrements of royal power and they became increasingly separated from the masses of people who comprised the majority of the umma. For these caliphs, maintaining their power and order in society seemed to be far more important than acting as God's representatives on earth and as successors of Muhammad. Over time, members of the ulema engaged in interpretive practices and perpetuated modes of thought which maintained their positions of power (as interpreters of the law) and the overarching religio-political power of the caliphs. Rahman believes that a deterioration and calcification of interpretive, intellectual and educational structures characterized developments during much of the Umayyad and Abbasid periods. Particularly in the field of Islamic jurisprudence, the ulema's lack of attention to the relationship of law, on the one hand, with ethics and theology, on the other, put them in a position where they made decisions which contradicted (what Rahman believes are) the basic teachings of the Quran, and which were detrimental to the overall well-being of the umma.[71]

Four factors which contributed to the deterioration of Islamic jurisprudence, education, and government during the Umayyad and Abbasid periods were: (1) a lack of attention to the relationship between law and theology; (2) a weak relationship between law and ethics; (3) the closing of the doors of *ijtihad*; and (4) a movement away from shura (which in Rahman's view was Muhammad's exemplary practice of consulting several people in his decision-making). Each one of these issues will be examined in turn.

According to Rahman, as theology and law began to develop during the beginning of the ninth century, some Muslim legists expressed hostility at times toward what they considered the "overly speculative" nature of much of Islamic theology.[72] Yet, Rahman believes that many Muslim theologians and philosophers (such as Abu Hamid Muhammad al-Ghazali, Sadr al-Din Shirazi, and Ibn Sina to name a few) constructed perspectives which attempted to relate Quranic themes to human circumstances and which could have been of enormous help to legal decision-making within Islam. From various points of view, theologians and philosophers such as those mentioned above discussed topics including the nature of God, human beings as individuals and as members of society, prophethood, and revelation in ways which could have been enormously helpful to legists, but which legists often attacked or ignored. For Rahman, considering these broader Quranically-based themes may have prevented various members of the ulema from being overly "atomistic" in their approach to law and may have allowed them to create legal structures which were more consistent with what Rahman believes are the Quran's views on justice and egalitarianism. Lack of attention to theology contributed to the ulema rendering much of Sharia into "an empty, rigid, and lifeless shell."[73]

Rahman believes that difficulties also arose in Islamic history as a result of a bifurcation between law and ethics (or what Rahman calls "Quranic ethics").[74] Before formulating a system of Quranically-based Islamic ethics, however, "a proper Quranic theology is necessary in order to define the God-man relationship."[75] After Muslims create a proper set of theological perspectives, they can move on to constructing ethics since Quranic "ethics presupposes a satisfactory theology."[76] Islamic theology and ethics when properly constructed take into account "the demands of the Quran as a unitary teaching."[77] A lack of attention to the Quran's "underlying unity" (particularly its theological and ethical coherence) caused the Sharia to become "rigid, its rigidity being softened only by casuistries which, however, further tended to make it ineffective."[78]

The third difficulty which contributed to the straying of the umma from the "main tenets" of the Quran was the "closing of the door of *ijtihad*" at the end of the ninth and the beginning of the tenth centuries. Rahman writes that during this period when Islamic law and doctrines had taken a definite shape the *ijma* or consensus regarding these issues was declared final "and the door of *ijtihad* was closed."[79] *Ijtihad* is a legal principle in Islamic jurisprudence which often allows a legist considerable freedom in interpreting and appropriating the Quran and Sunna in making legal decisions. Rahman believes that this closing of the door of *ijtihad* has had long-lasting and deleterious effects on the history of Islamic legal interpretation.[80]

Why did this closing of the door take place? Rahman provides several answers to this question. In one set of analyses regarding this issue, Rahman writes that Islam had passed — during the time leading up to the closing of the door of *ijtihad* — through "a period of great conflict of opinions and doctrines."[81] As this period came to a conclusion, certain interpretive rules began to attain stability "through the emergence of an orthodoxy . . . towards the beginning of the tenth century."[82] The Quran and Sunna, now "dislodged from fresh thought or *ijtihad*, could not continue [their] function for the organism needed [all these elements] for its growth."[83] Rahman comments on the negative ramifications of this new state of affairs by stating, "A stabilizing principle without a principle of expansion necessarily becomes a static tool of oppression."[84] Thus, the Sharia, instead of functioning as the "path or the road leading to water [or] to the very source of life," served as an instrument of power, reinforcing the authority of the caliphs and the ulema at the expense of the people's right devotion to God and the justice which Rahman believes that the Quran teaches.

Wael Hallaq forcefully disputes the idea that the door of *ijtihad* was ever closed.[85] One of the arguments Hallaq makes is based on his reading of Muhammad Ibn Idris al-Shafi'i's (d. 820) *Risala*, which many Muslim and western scholars have considered to be the work which marked the concretization of the rules for interpreting Islamic law (*usul al-fiqh*) and which brought about the closing of the doors of *ijtihad*.[86] Hallaq contends that far from providing any specifics in terms of *usul al-fiqh*, the *Risala*, among other general prescriptions, affirmed that (1) law must be derived from revealed scripture; (2) the Sunna of the Prophet constitutes a revelation binding in legal matters; (3) there is no contradiction between the Sunna and the Quran; and (4) the procedures of *qiyas* and *ijtihad* and the sanctioning instrument of consensus are prescribed by the revealed texts.[87] Hallaq asserts that Shafi'i's exposition of these propositions is "rudimentary and erratic" and that the *Risala* "has little to offer in the way of systematic methodology."[88]

Hallaq also maintains that from the ninth through twelfth centuries, *ijtihad* was "deemed a perennial duty and the actual practice of Muslim jurists."[89] Further, "all groups and individuals who opposed *ijtihad* were finally excluded from Sunnism" and that up until the twelfth century there was "no mention whatsoever of the phrase *insidad bab al-ijtihad* (closing of the door of *ijtihad*) or of any expression that may have alluded to the notion of the closure."[90] To support these views, Hallaq quotes the works of such medieval scholars as Mawardi (d. 1058) who explains that *ijtihad* must be one of the imam's skills, because knowledge of the law and of the means by which new problems (*nawazil*) must be solved are an essential part of his duties.[91] He cites the exclusion of the anti-*ijtihad*-oriented Dawud al-Zahiri (d. 883) and his school, the Hashwis, who "found no place in the pale of Sunnism," as an example of the exclusion of individuals and groups who stood against *ijtihad*.[92] He also states that the works of the eleventh century Hanbali jurist and theologian Ibn ʿAqil were the first place where the term *insidad bab al-ijtihad* appeared.[93]

Although Hallaq's article criticizing the closing of the doors of *ijtihad* appeared in the *International Journal of Middle East Studies* in 1984 (which was four years before Rahman's death), Rahman did not respond to Hallaq's arguments in his writings which appeared after that time. If one were to accept Hallaq's viewpoint, this would certainly call into question Rahman's argument that the closing of the door of *ijtihad* were one element that contributed to the stagnation of Islamic legal interpretation. Yet, even if one were to agree with Hallaq's position, Rahman's two other arguments about the deterioration of legal methods in the medieval period (i.e., the bifurcation of law and theology, on the one hand, and law and ethics, on the other) could remain intact. Accepting Hallaq's viewpoint would also not threaten Rahman's argument that the authority of shaykhs in madrasas compelled their students to accept their opinions, without encouraging the students to think critically.[94] That is, Rahman could continue to claim that these developments during the medieval period were significant and long-lasting enough to have a negative effect on Islamic legal thought and education well into the modern period.

While Rahman criticizes many of the patterns in legal thinking and education during medieval Islamic history, Mawdudi's understanding of Islam's history is much more dualistic. In the words of Seyyed Vali Reza Nasr, "[t]he lines of demarcation that defined Islam [for Mawdudi] were perforce steadfast: there was either Islam, as it was understood and defined by Mawdudi, or there was un-Islam."[95] For Mawdudi, there has been one period in Islamic history which has embodied "true Islam" and that was during the period of the Prophet and the Rightly

Guided caliphs in the seventh century.[96] After that initial golden period, "three-quarters" of Islam became defective and incorrect (Mawdudi does not specify which three-quarters that was).[97] This very long phase within Islamic history (which has lasted, with a few exceptions, until the present time) was comprised of several characteristics: ignorance (or *jahiliyya*), atheism, polytheism, and monasticism. The ignorance which pervaded much of Islamic history took many forms and in one of its manifestations it "professed belief in the Unity of God and Prophethood, performed pious acts of fasting and praying and feigned eagerness to refer disputes to the Quran and Sunna."[98] The combining of Islam and un-Islam in the same body politic, as a result of this ignorance, gave rise to great complications. Atheism took the form of people submitting to the authority of "kings" (probably a reference to the Abbasid and Umayyad caliphs) and the emergence of various forms of philosophy and theology which resulted in hair-splitting and "the creation of a number of new sects."[99] Polytheism primarily took the form of people worshipping saints' tombs and confusing these saints for gods. Monasticism, for its part, "attacked the religious scholars and guides, righteous and good-natured people and infused into them" all the evils which flowed from polytheism.[100]

Although for Mawdudi much of Islamic history was marked by corrupt and disdainful un-Islamic beliefs and practices there were certain individuals whose ideas represented true Islam. These *mujaddids* or "renewers" of the religion included the founders of the four schools of Sunni law, the medieval Muslim philosophers and legists al-Ghazzali (1058–1111) and Ibn Taymiyya (1263–1328) as well as the modern Muslim reformers Shaykh Ahmad Sirhindi (1564–1624) and Shah Waliullah (1703–1762). All of these great *mujaddids* were distinguished for their insight into problems which Muslims faced, for their reform of religious practices, for initiating an intellectual revolution and defending Islam in the political sphere, for establishing the primacy of the Sharia, and for their opposition to the self-proclaimed orthodoxy of the ulema.[101]

The most significant difference between Rahman's and Mawdudi's views of Islamic history is that while Rahman gives meticulous attention to the nuances and changes within that history, Mawdudi sweepingly separates the good from the evil, the pure from the corrupt, and the Islamic from the un-Islamic. Seyyed Vali Reza Nasr describes Mawdudi's dualistic perspective:

By putting everything in black and white, [Mawdudi] brought moral pressure to bear on his audience, manipulating the psychological impulse that is inherent in a consequential choice between such diametric opposites as truth and falsehood, salvation and perdition. By dramatizing the conflict between good and evil, Mawdudi decided how social or theological issues were interpreted, what issues were of relevance and how and in what manner they would be discussed.[102]

While both Rahman and Mawdudi are critical of Islamic history, they are critical of it in different ways. Rahman's primary criticisms regarding Islamic history have to do with at least two developments: (1) the rigid socio-economic stratification of Islamic society which began after the beginning of the Umayyad period and lasted for some time afterwards[103] and (2) the absence of an emphasis on original and critical thought within the Islamic educational system, which was one of the factors that weakened Islamic societies and made them vulnerable to colonialist penetrations.[104]

Although Mawdudi condemns the rigid social stratification which emerged after the beginning of the Umayyad period, he maintains that the primary cause of the decline of Islamic societies was their lack of attention to the four primary Quranic concepts (*ila, rabb, ʿibada,* and *din*) — the most important of these being *din*, which involved the complete obedience of the individual and Muslim community to God and Sharia.[105] While Mawdudi and Rahman are in agreement that one of the weaknesses of Islamic education during the medieval period and afterward was its emphasis on the rote memorization of various texts, they disagree with respect to the importance of fostering critical thought within the educational process. For Mawdudi, the most salient weakness within the medieval Islamic education was not its lack of attention to promoting critical thought; rather, the educational systems suffered from inattention to the Quran's most important teachings and from not inculcating students with a proper sense of *din*.[106]

Both Mawdudi and Rahman are critical of the purported "closing of the door of *ijtihad*" and advocate its reinvigoration, but differ as to what form *ijtihad* in the modern world should take. Rahman maintains that one of the characteristics of a genuine and constructive Islamic educational system is that it promotes a variety of interpretive stances and viewpoints.[107] That is, Rahman believes that *ijtihad* should be a fluid and dynamic process whose results may vary somewhat from one time to another and even from one social context to another.[108] Even when well-educated people within the same socio-historical context differ with respect to their interpretations, he holds out that these differences can often be allayed by appealing to philosophical principles of logic and rationality.[109]

For Mawdudi, *ijtihad* consists of understanding the unitary and monolithic meanings which the Quran contains for the whole of humanity and implementing them.[110] He believed that one of the primary tasks of the *mujtahidun* (the interpreters who engage in *ijtihad*) was to lay the interpretive and ideological groundwork for the Islamic revolution.[111] Mawdudi perceived himself as a very important *mujtahid* who had the obligation to interpret the Quran in such a way as to promote an Islamic revolution and bring a truly Islamic state and society into existence.[112] For Mawdudi, *ijtihad* had the very practical objective of bringing to the fore the true meanings of the Quran. Mawdudi wanted to utilize these meanings as a vehicle for rejecting un-Islam in the modern period (which included various corruptions and immoralities introduced by the West) and ushering in a truly Islamic state.[113] Mawdudi perceived the Jamaʻat-i Islami as being one very important vehicle in implementing the true teachings yielded by *ijtihad* and spearheading the Islamic revolution.

Rahman's Critique of Medieval Political Structures and Education

For Rahman, shura was another concept that embodies justice and egalitarianism which Muslim leaders during the Umayyad and Abbasid periods and other subsequent leaders ignored through most of Islamic history. According to him, Muhammad often practiced shura when he was faced with an important decision.[114] Rahman believes that after the Prophet's death there was only one other time that shura was properly exercised. That was when Abu Bakr was elected to the caliphate by "consensus" (excluding, according to the Shiite view of history, the opinions of the partisans of Ali).[115]

In addition to several instances in the Quran where the term shura is used, Rahman points to the Hadith tradition which states "My community shall not agree on an error" as part of the Prophetic emphasis on the importance of Muslim leaders consulting with and reflecting the will of the community.[116] Unfortunately, over time the "orthodoxy" (a term Rahman seems to use in reference to many of the caliphs and members of the ulema during the Umayyad and Abbasid periods) developed and clung "to the one-sided doctrine of inculcating absolute obedience to the ruler."[117] He points to two Hadiths that he believes may have been written sometime in the early Umayyad period which helped buttress caliphal power and stood in contradistinction to the Quran's (and other Hadiths') emphasis on shura. These pro-caliphal/ anti-shura Hadiths state: (1) "The Sultan is the shadow of God on earth" and (2) "Even an unjust ruler must be obeyed."[118] During the Abbasid period, the saying "one day of political chaos and lawlessness is worse than thirty years of a tyrannical ruler" became popular as well.[119] While absolute obedience to the ruler became the prevailing mode of thought during the Umayyad and Abbasid periods, the ulema "devised nothing to control the absoluteness of the ruler himself."[120] This state of affairs related directly to the demise of the notion of shura as a viable *modus operandi.*[121]

Thus, for Rahman, a movement away from shura, the lack of attention to the relationship between law and theology, and law and ethics, the closing of the doors of *ijtihad*, and a shift away from shura were some of the problems associated with the deterioration of Islamic government and jurisprudence during the Umayyad and Abbasid periods. These trends resulted in the umma living its life in contrast to the ethical teachings of the Quran, which emphasize justice and devotion to God. These shifts away from what Rahman believes forms the essence of the Quran's teaching created a host of problems throughout Muslim history and for today's umma.

Rahman believes that historically, while it has made certain substantial contributions, Islamic education has also suffered from some significant flaws. He analyzes the historical problems with Islamic education by outlining the history of various modes of Islamic education. During the first and second centuries of Islam, "scattered centers of learning grew up around persons of eminence."[122] In this early stage, students gained their Islamic education, which usually consisted of memorizing the Quran, copying down traditions from the Prophet and his Companions, and deducing legal points from them, through individual teachers as opposed to fully institutionalized schools or colleges.[123] Beginning in the eleventh century, Sunni Muslims established freestanding madrasas (Islamic schools), where students studied the Quran, Hadith, *fiqh*, Islamic philosophy and theology and, in some cases, disciplines related to the sciences. The "graduates" of these madrasas who had studied religious sciences received a certificate or a permit (*'ijaza*) in order to become a teacher in one or more of these subjects and/or to become a member of the ulema, while others who studied the sciences went on to become physicians.[124]

Rahman maintains that the "most fateful distinction that came to be made in the course of time" was between the religious or traditional sciences (*ʿulum sharʿiya* or *ʿulum naqliya*), which included Quran and Hadith study, on the one hand, and what Rahman calls the "rational or secular sciences" (*ʿulum ʿaqliya* or *ghayr sharʿiya*) which included disciplines related to what would be termed today as the "hard sciences," on the other.[125] As this bifurcation within the educational system developed, one area of the religious sciences, the science of rhetoric and eloquence (which Rahman calls "peculiarly Arab"), established itself "besides theology, [as] the major intellectual field among orthodox scholars."[126]

As a result of this shift to an emphasis on rhetoric and eloquence, "it came to pass that a vibrant and revolutionary document like the Quran was buried under the debris of grammar and rhetoric."[127] One of the characteristics of medieval madrasa education was that "the Quran was never taught by itself, most probably through the fear that a meaningful study of the Quran by itself might upset the status quo, not only educational and theological, but social as well."[128] Madrasa teachers came to believe that they needed more interesting "extrinsic props" to understand the Quran, and the one prop which they found to be the "most delicious" and "intoxicating" was the science of rhetoric and eloquence.[129]

Alongside the development of rhetoric, another development which Rahman believes

adversely affected the quality of learning in the later medieval centuries of Islam was the replacement of the original texts of theology, philosophy, jurisprudence, and such, as materials for higher instruction with commentaries and supercommentaries.[130]

One unfortunate consequence of this pedagogical mode was "the preoccupation with hair-splitting detail to the exclusion of the basic problems of a subject."[131] Additionally, philosophical and rhetorical disputation (*jadal*)

became the most fashionable procedure of 'winning a point' and almost a substitute for a genuine intellectual effort at raising and grappling with real issues in a field.[132]

The emphasis on rhetoric and disputation coupled with the rote memorization of texts led to a situation where teachers discouraged analysis and creative thought and students found themselves learning about very arcane subject matter such as the content of commentaries and supercommentaries.[133]

With these pedagogic practices came "the steady dwindling of original thought," and, consequently, the Muslim world witnessed the "rise of a type of scholar who was truly encyclopedic in the scope of his learning but had little new to say on anything."[134] One important and implicit assumption of this type of pedagogical system is that education and scholarship are not regarded

> as an active pursuit, a creative 'reaching out' of the mind to the unknown— as is the case today—but rather as the more or less passive acquisition of already established knowledge.[135]

Rahman believes that this rather static form of pedagogy which was primarily devoted to the absorption of facts was an additional short-coming of Islamic society in the medieval period. The flaws of the Islamic educational system together with the rigid systems of *fiqh* and tyrannical leadership during these times contributed to the weakening of Islamic civilization which made the Islamic lands vulnerable to the onslaughts of Western colonialism.

Sufism

Rahman points to the rise and popularity of Sufism from the late ninth century onwards as another trend which had a deleterious effect on the religious life of masses of Muslims throughout much of Islamic history. Rahman uses antagonistic language in his criticisms of Sufism. He calls Sufism "morally harmful"; he asserts that Sufism's "incalculable harm to Muslim society is . . . a glaring fact of history," and that its effects have been "various, deep, and paralyzing."[136] Why does Rahman use such strong language in his criticism of Sufism? Most importantly, Rahman believes that historically Sufism has deluded large numbers of Muslims and blocked them from the "true Islamic path" which is proclaimed in the Quran.

According to Rahman, Sufism has several characteristics which led to its negative impact on many Muslims and Islamic societies. First, as Sufism developed, it created "a dichotomy between inner, spiritual development, on the one hand, and what it termed the Sharia on the other."[137] He argues that Sufism's emphasis on inner piety (through its stress on such concepts as *fana'*, the complete annihilation of the individual within God, and *baqa'*, the idea that a person can eternally remain with God in this world and the next) gave much of Sufism an "anti-Sharia" quality. That is, many Sufis believed that the Sharia did not provide the true and ultimate path toward devotion to God, but that inner piety and seeking to unite themselves with him spiritually did. However, Rahman qualifies this assertion by noting that there were individuals in Islamic history who combined their own understandings of Sufism with a focus on Sharia. He cites thirteenth century Muslim jurist Ibn Taymiyya, who was a strident defender of Islamic law and engaged in certain Sufi practices, and seventeenth century Sufi Ahmad Sirhindi, who, among other things, asserted that Sufi meditation gave a person a deeper understanding of Sharia, as positive examples of individuals who properly combined mystical and legal teachings in their writings.[138]

A second aspect of Sufism's "spiritual delinquency" has been beliefs it has promoted in the second coming of Jesus, in the Mahdi, and in the miracles of the saints.[139] Rahman believes that Sufism and Shiism are both responsible for the spread of such "questionable" ideas.[140] In these criticisms of Sufism, Rahman does not provide specific citations. He seems to characterize Sufism in accordance with his own observations and he articulates this condemnatory stance in broad generalities which make it difficult for the reader to understand to which specific Sufi groups he is referring. In his attempt to provide some context for his characterizations, Rahman writes:

> The Muslim masses, from the shores of the Atlantic to Indonesia, are . . . in the grip of that Sufistic spirituality which, as a whole, is no better than a form of spiritual delinquency often exploited by the clever Sufi leaders for their own ends.[141]

For Rahman, one positive aspect of Sufism in history is the role which certain strands within it played in Islamic reform movements in the sixteenth century and thereafter. He cites the seventeenth century Muslim reformer Ahmad Sirhindi's reform movement in India and the nineteenth and twentieth century Sanusi organization in North Africa as examples of what he calls "neo-Sufi" reform movements, which stripped Sufism "of its ecstatic and metaphysical character and content" replacing it "with a content which was nothing less than the postulates of the orthodox."[142] Rahman notes that one of Ahmad Sirhindi's reforms pertained to the idea of the Unity of Being, which was first articulated by thirteenth century Sufi mystic Ibn 'Arabi, who stated that one goal of the believer was to unite himself with God.[143] According to Rahman,

Sirhindi affirmed that the unity of being was a real experience, but that for Sirhindi this unity does not necessarily entail unity with God; rather, it involves the sense of peace the believer feels when obeying Sharia.[144] This is one tendency in Sufism which Rahman believes is valuable.

Another significant example of a Sufi reform movement which Rahman affirms is the north African Sanusi organization which he presents as playing a substantial role in Muslim resistance to Italian colonial rule in Libya and British rule in Egypt in the early twentieth century.[145] Rahman presents Ahmad Sirhindi's thought as well as the Sanusi movement as two positive examples of neo-Sufism in that they appropriately combined mystical understandings with an emphasis on Islamic law or political action.

In recent academic scholarship, the concept of "neo-Sufism" has come under sharp attack, most notably by R.S. O'Fahey and Bernd Radtke, who argue that "few of the generalizations proposed within the neo-Sufi cliché have much validity."[146] According to O'Fahey and Radtke, those scholars who use the term "neo-Sufi" characterize the neo-Sufi movements as rejecting: (1) the mystical philosophical tradition of Ibn al-ʿArabi; (2) popular ecstatic practices (such as dancing, "noisy" *dhikr*, and saint worship); (3) the *murshid/murid* (teacher/student) relationship; and (4) the idea of the union of the believer with the spirit of Muhammad.[147] O'Fahey and Radtke also assert that scholars who use the term neo-Sufi claim that many of these Sufis embraced political and military measures in defense of Islam.

Although O'Fahey and Radtke assert that Fazlur Rahman was the first scholar to coin the term "neo-Sufism,"[148] they make reference to his works only three times at the beginning of their article, while devoting the rest of the piece to showing the problems in Spencer Trimingham's, B.G. Martin's and John Voll's arguments in favor of the idea of neo-Sufism.[149] They spare Rahman from the bulk of their attack for good reason. Although Rahman may well have coined the term "neo-Sufism," he shows great care regarding the groups to which he applies it. He uses it only three times in *Islam*, once in reference to Ibn Taymiyya and his student Ibn Qayyim al-Jawziyya, whom Rahman says were the first neo-Sufis, and again in reference to Ahmad Sirhindi and the Sanusi brotherhood, respectively.[150] He does not use the term in his other works. In their article, O'Fahey and Radtke do not address Western scholarship on Ibn Taymiyya and Ibn Qayyim al-Jawziyya nor on Ahmad Sirhindi, whom Rahman considers a neo-Sufi, but they do discuss Western scholarship on the political activity of the Sanusi order and this is one area where Rahman's scholarship is vulnerable to their arguments.[151]

Rahman presents the Sanusi order as a Muslim organization which was a vanguard in nineteenth century Muslim resistance to the French advance in Equatorial Africa, to the Italians in Libya, and to the British in Egypt.[152] He writes that this order

> both in its organization and aims, is a representative *par excellence* of neo-Sufism. It is thoroughly activist in its impulse with a purely moral moral-reformist programme, issuing in political action.[153]

O'Fahey and Radtke argue that the Sanusis were far more reluctant to engage in anti-colonial activities than Rahman suggests. They maintain that the Sanusis "were drawn into the war of resistance against the Italians" in Libya in 1911 only after the Turks withdrew from defending the region.[154] According to O'Fahey and Radtke, by the time of the second Italo-Sanusi war (1923–1932), the Sanusi family "were with a few exceptions in exile and the leadership against the Italians had devolved upon . . . the tribal shaykhs."[155] They point to historical evidence that indicates that the Sanusis and other Idrisi-inspired orders largely assigned the leadership and execution of the anti-colonial warfare not to members of their own order, but to local tribal shaykhs.[156] O'Fahey's and Radtke's argument raises doubts about Rahman's claims that the Sanusis are exemplary of a modern Sufi group's enthusiasm in engaging in anti-colonial political activity. Their arguments are sure to spur academic discussion about post-seventeenth century movements for some time to come.[157]

Overall, Mawdudi has a more positive attitude toward Sufism than Rahman, who often uses harsh language to condemn aspects of it with which he disagrees. Like Rahman, Mawdudi criticizes aspects of Sufism that contradict what he perceives to be "true Islam," and supports other aspects of it which reinforce piety among Muslims. However, in his condemnations of certain dimensions of Sufism, Mawdudi is careful not to be overly polemical in his approach, since he traces his Muslim ancestry to members of the Chisti Sufi order who claim to be descendants of the Prophet (sg. sayyid, pl. *asyad*) through his daughter, Fatima. In terms of Mawdudi's criticisms of Sufism, he condemns the "un-Quranic" teachings of various Sufi masters which often elevated the masters and their instructions over that of the Sunna.[158] Mawdudi holds Sufism accountable for the decline of Islam throughout history, referring to it as "lady opium."[159] He believes that Sufism had misled Mughal rulers like Emperor Akbar and his son Dara Shukuh into engaging in syncretic experiments. Their accommodation of Hinduism, as is evident in Akbar's *din-i ilahi* (divine religion) and Dara Shukuh's book *Majma'u'l-bahrain* (*Conglomeration of the Two Seas*), which relied on an esoteric marriage between Islam and Hinduism, was not just religiously suspect; it caused the Mughals to miss a unique opportunity to convert the whole of India to Islam.[160]

Yet, probably because of what Mawdudi believed to be his Sufi ancestry together with the fact that he did not want to alienate the Sufi masses of India from his movement, he curbed the sharpness of his anti-Sufi critique.[161] Since Mawdudi was unwilling to spurn Sufism altogether, he attempted to redefine it.[162] He ascribed to Sufism values and goals which would convert it into an aspect of din, making Sufism another component of his broader message.

Mawdudi maintained that while fiqh "deals with apparent and observable conduct," Sufism "concerns itself with the *spirit* [and intention] of conduct."[163] Mawdudi wrote:

> For example, when we say our prayers, *fiqh* will judge us only by fulfillment of the outward requirements such as ablution, facing toward the Kaba . . . while *tasawwuf* [Sufism] will judge our prayers by our concentration . . . the effect of our prayers on our morals and our manners.[164]

For Mawdudi and the members of the Jama'at, this redefinition constituted a reform of Sufism and the restoration of its true spirit and intent.[165] Mawdudi's redefinition, however, imbued the concept of Sufism with a new and different meaning. According to Mawdudi's understanding, Sufism was not an esoteric movement within Islam, but it was a gauge to measure concentration, morals, and a person's real intentions in following the *fiqh*. Khurshid Ahmad, one of Mawdudi's friends and a member of the Jama'at's leadership council wrote, "Sufism is a sister — parallel — movement to ours. In earlier history it had sought to protect Muslim youth from corruption caused by monarchies."[166] In today's world, the goal of a reformed Sufism was to properly direct the inner life of pious Muslims.

There are some limited parallels in Rahman's and Mawdudi's criticisms of Sufism. They both condemn the excessive influence of Sufi masters, Sufi practices of tomb and ancestor veneration, rituals of dancing and *dhikr* (continual recitation of a single word or phrase) and many Sufis' disregard for various aspects of Sharia. Yet, both affirm that Sufism, when properly reformed, can reinforce the importance of inner piety and sincere belief among Muslims. Rahman's rejection of much of Sufism and Mawdudi's qualified acceptance of it are a bit exceptional insofar as modernists such as Fatima Mernissi,[167] Leila Ahmed,[168] Mohammed Arkoun,[169] and Seyyed Hossein Nasr[170] exhibit a relatively positive attitude towards it, while most Islamic revivalist groups have a tendency to reject most dimensions of Sufism outright.[171]

Rahman's rejection of several forms of Sufism (which encouraged dancing, the meditation on a single word or phrase (*dhikr*) and saint veneration) was probably motivated by at least three factors: (1) his general belief that Sufism genuinely had and was continuing to have a deleterious effect on the life of individual Muslims and the Muslim community as a whole; (2) the danger he thought Sufism posed to rational and exoteric thought; and (3) the influence of other Muslim and Western scholars (including Ibn Taymiyya, Sayyid Ahmed Khan, Jamal al-Din al-Afghani, Muhammad Abduh and H.A.R. Gibb).[172] In terms of the first two factors, Rahman maintained that Sufism's tendency to emphasize internal and emotional states often contradicted Sunni Islam's traditional focus on explicating law and philosophy on the basis of reason and rationality.[173] For Rahman, *ma'rifa* (or the secret knowledge which a mystic was to attain) "was cut off fairly early from 'formulative' reason, and both mystical and dogmatic forms of Muslim thinking suffered as a consequence."[174] Thus, one of the negative outcomes of Sufism was that it had encouraged Muslims to shy away from the path of Islam which encouraged obedience to the law and the clear and rational explication of law and philosophy.

Rahman's attacks against Sufism may also be attributable to the influence of such Muslim scholars as thirteenth century Muslim legist Ibn Taymiyya, and nineteenth century modernists Sayyid Ahmad Khan, Jamal al-Din al-Afghani, and Muhammad 'Abduh. As will be discussed later, Rahman respected the way in which Ibn Taymiyya accepted Sufism's emphasis on inner devotion, and rejected Sufi saint and shaykh veneration as well as Sufi ritual dance.[175] While Rahman does not directly address the works of his modernist forerunners, (such as Sayyid Ahmad Khan, Afghani, and 'Abduh) on the issue of Sufism, Albert Hourani's characterization of late nineteenth and early twentieth century modernist attitudes towards Sufism provides an apt description of Rahman's and his predecessors' views on the issue:

> [The modernists] took from mysticism its emphasis on inner devotion, on sincerity of intention as well as correctness of act, while looking with suspicion on the monistic theology which blurred the distinction between God and his creatures, and repudiating any suggestion that to know God by direct experience was more important than to obey his laws.[176]

Rahman's views on Sufism carry the influence of his teacher H.A.R. Gibb as well. Gibb considered Sufism to be pantheistic, influenced by Buddhism and Hinduism, and contradictory to Islam's orthodox path as embodied in the Sunni tradition.[177] Gibb criticizes Sufism in accordance with his understanding of Christianity much like eighteenth- and nineteenth-century Orientalists evaluated Sufism based on their understanding of Christianity.[178] That is, in his criticism of Sufism, Gibb draws an analogy between the "unorthodox, pantheistic and super-stitious" beliefs of the thirteenth-century Christian mystic Meister Eckhart and those of Sufis who manifest "extremist tendencies" in their own pantheism.[179] Although Rahman does not make parallels between Muslim and Christian mysticism and does not believe that Sufi philosophy was influenced by Buddhism or Hinduism, he condemns Sufi practices such as *dhikr* and Sufi saint veneration, with much the same harshness as Gibb.[180]

Visions for Islam in the Modern World

While Rahman's critiques of various aspects of Islamic history, including his criticisms of Sufism, are intriguing in their own right, they serve as one of the underpinnings of his vision for Islam in the twentieth century and of his ideas for the reform of Islam during the modern period. In the following sections, Rahman's views on three issues which comprise significant features of his vision for Islam in the modern world will be discussed: the structure and method of Islamic education, the proper organization, responsibility, and obligations of the Islamic state, and the role of women in Islam.

Rahman maintains that educational and political leaders in the Muslim world have taken at least two basic approaches to education since the beginning of the colonial period, both of which he criticizes. Those who take the first approach believe that the acquisition of modern knowledge should be limited to the "practical" technological sphere. They maintain that since Islam provides "satisfactory answers to ultimate questions of world view" there is no need to integrate "Western intellectual products into the Islamic educational system."[181] Thus, for members of this group, educational institutions in Muslim countries should focus on integrating Western technical and scientific know-how into their curricula while ignoring other forms of knowledge (such as the humanities and social sciences) which emerge from the

West, since Islam provides the answers to the most important questions regarding human existence.[182]

Those who maintain the second contrasting perspective believe that educational institutions in the Islamic world should convey Western technical and scientific knowledge as well as forms of knowledge in the humanities and social sciences which emerge from the West.[183] Rahman recognizes that these two approaches constitute "ideal types," and that there are "various nuances of these views and also 'middle-term' positions."[184]

He believes that both approaches suffer from serious weaknesses which have resulted in the establishment and perpetuation of some relatively ineffectual educational institutions throughout much of the Islamic world. One of the shortcomings of the first viewpoint is that while accepting Western technology, it does not create an educational environment which is conducive to subjecting the texts and history of Islam to the kind of critical examination which can renew the tradition and make it wholly relevant and potent in the Muslim world. The second perspective does not subject Western forms of knowledge to adequate critical examination and de-emphasizes the role of Islam altogether. Both perspectives suffer from a "blindness to the fact that technology cannot succeed at improving human society unless the mind of man changes — unless he is imbued with a new motivation."[185] Rahman believes that a reinvigorated and substantially reformed Islam can help produce this necessary motivation and dynamic sustenance. Specifically, a revamped and Islamized system of education and knowledge-production could provide the solutions to the hardships of unemployment, poverty, congestion, lack of morality and other challenges which Rahman believes affect many Muslim countries.

Rahman begins his presentation of his idea of the "Islamization" of knowledge and of education by stating that "social sciences and humanities are obviously relevant to values and values are relevant to them."[186] He believes that virtually any form of scholarship or education, including those which are produced in the West, are tied to certain specific metaphysical and ethical presuppositions. That is, while Western education and scholarship are not subjective, the ways in which these forms of inquiry take place presuppose certain specific ideas about human beings, their possible ethical obligations/non-obligations, and their possible purpose/purposelessness in the world.[187] These metaphysical issues can be articulated in terms of questions such as,

"Does our place in the universe or what we study mean anything?" and "Does the content of our study point to a higher will and purpose?"[188]

The Islamization of knowledge for Rahman involves tying all fields of academic endeavor to Islamic ethics and an Islamic metaphysics, both of which would be devoted to answering the above-mentioned questions and relating these metaphysical and ethical standpoints to scholarly enquiry. The task of the Islamization of knowledge is wholly appropriate for the reinvigoration of educational systems in Islamic countries since the Quran contains a full and complete revelation to humanity which has relevance to virtually every area of human endeavor.[189]

The Islamization of knowledge cannot take place immediately. Before knowledge can be Islamized, Muslims must develop a systematic Quranically-based metaphysical, ethical, and theological structure which would be founded upon understanding the Quran as a unity and would also create a method for the proper Islamization of knowledge.[190] Since nobody has yet developed such a system, Rahman does not give specific ideas regarding what an Islamized system of education may look like; he is, however, attempting to demonstrate the need for the Islamization of education, while providing some indication of the steps which Muslims must take in initiating and implementing this process.[191]

For Mawdudi, one of the goals of the Jama'at-i Islami was to educate a cadre of young men who were fully versed in the teachings of the Quran and Hadith so that they could participate in the Islamic revolution and take leadership roles in the Islamic state once it came into being.[192] Unlike Rahman, who believed that one of the purposes of Islamic education was to promote skills in critical thinking and to raise new questions, Mawdudi maintained that the Quran and Hadith contained all the answers people needed and it was his mission as well as that of the Jama'at to create the institutions which would convey these answers to the masses so that they could engage in the process of Islamic revolution.[193]

While Rahman's idea of a Quranically-based and Islamized educational system plays an important role in his vision of Islam in the modern world, his proposals for the implementation of an Islamic state are significant as well. In his writings on the establishment of an Islamic state, Rahman directs his thoughts primarily to the specifics of the Pakistani context; at the same time, he believes that his ideas on this issue carry broad enough guidelines to be relevant to a wide variety of nation-states where Muslims may be in the majority.[194]

The principle underpinning of an Islamic state is the concept of shura. In Rahman's view, the Quran and Hadith indicate that the Prophet utilized a process of mutual consultation when he made important decisions (this consultation usually took the form of the Prophet speaking with his most trusted companions) and Muslims should implement an adapted form of shura within the political organization of a modern Islamic state.[195] In this state, shura would take the form of the elected leader being "aided by a Legislative Assembly which should represent the will of the people."[196] Philosophically and practically, Rahman believes that the "[s]tate organization in Islam receives its mandate from the people, i.e., the Muslim Community, and is, therefore, necessarily democratic."[197] He maintains that the Quranic idea of shura virtually demands that an Islamic state be a democracy.[198] Rahman's stance regarding the democratic nature of the Islamic state also relates to his idea of the Quran's emphasis on justice and egalitarianism.

Mawdudi's vision of an Islamic state contrasts substantially with Rahman's in several ways. One of the most significant differences between these two intellectuals is that while Rahman seems to equate shura with democracy, thus affirming the importance of democratically elected leaders within an Islamic state, Mawdudi intentionally de-emphasizes the role of free elections. Mawdudi maintains that God has absolute sovereignty within a Muslim state and that the emir (as the chief executive would be called) should be given the primary responsibility of acting as God's vice-regent on earth and enforcing Sharia law in this capacity.[199] He downplays the role of shura in favor of his concept of the absolute authority of the emir and of the Islamic state.[200]

Mawdudi also conceives of the Islamic state as having a legislature and judiciary, but their functions would be limited to advising the emir who would be vested with an enormous amount of power so as to apply God's sovereign law in the earthly realm.[201] Mawdudi states that the emir should be selected by public acclamation but, at the same time, he discourages the idea of free election.[202] For Mawdudi, one basis for determining the authenticity and authority of the emir is the extent to which his rule and decrees embody the essential teachings of the Sharia. He argues that the selection of the emir "albeit divorced from a free electoral process would provide a democratic state whose continuity would be guaranteed by a sacrosanct code of law which by definition was just and therefore required obedience."[203]

Mawdudi argued that there were many examples throughout history which demonstrated that the will of the people contradicted Sharia and the sovereignty of God. One way to help assure the implementation of Sharia in its most complete form was by vesting the emir with great power and avoiding electioneering in the process of his selection.[204] While Mawdudi outlines the virtuous qualities of such a leader and strongly discourages popular elections as a means of choosing this leader, he does not make clear how the emir should be selected.[205] In addition to criticizing free election of leaders as a viable mechanism for selecting individuals for political office in an Islamic state, Mawdudi emphasizes that the emir and the state's political apparatus must reserve the right to use coercive powers in order to maintain order and suppress the possibility of chaos or *fitna*.[206]

What could account for Rahman's and Mawdudi's differences of opinion with respect to democracy and free elections in an Islamic state? One factor relates to Mawdudi's and Rahman's views of Islam and the ways in which they believe "truth" can be discovered and known. While Rahman maintains that the Quran and Sunna contain certain general principles (such as the importance of justice and egalitarianism) which are essential aspects of Islam's broader message, he also believes that a diversity of opinions should be encouraged within Islamic educational systems and governmental bodies. Rahman contends that the best political decisions can be made when the electorate and politicians have explored a wide variety of possible options, both in terms of policy decisions and in terms of who the leaders should be.[207]

Mawdudi takes a contrasting viewpoint. He believes that the Quran (and the Sharia) contains one set of monolithic injunctions which are relevant for all times and places. These injunctions are clear and self-evident and it is the task of the emir and his Islamic government to understand these injunctions and implement them decisively and comprehensively.[208] Mawdudi was also suspicious of democracy because he believed that during the colonial era the British had used a democratic system of government to favor the Hindus over the Muslims in the Indian subcontinent.[209] Concomitant with this perception, before the Partition of India and Pakistan, Mawdudi believed that if democracy became the system of government in India, it would *ipso facto* benefit the Hindus since there were more Hindus than Muslims in India.[210]

Even after Partition, one of the factors that discouraged Mawdudi from favoring democracy was his fear that a democratic system in Pakistan would give religious minorities (small as they may be) and "wrong-headed Muslims" too much power in terms of directing the affairs of an Islamic state.[211] The power of leading an Islamic state, in Mawdudi's view, should be given to a powerful emir who fully understands the Sharia and knows how to implement it.[212]

In addition to his perspectives on education and the structure of an Islamic state, the third important feature of Rahman's vision of Islam in the modern world relates to his ideas on the role of women in Islam. In elucidating his position on this issue, Rahman begins by critiquing the Muslim standpoints which have not given women an equal status to men in Islamic societies.[213] Rahman asserts that the inferior status to which Muslim women have "traditionally been relegated in Islamic society has changed very little over the centuries."[214] He goes on to write that their status has been "primarily due to the social milieu that developed in Muslim societies, a result of prevailing social conditions rather than of the moral teaching of the Quran."[215] That is, Rahman believes that the Quran proclaims a relatively egalitarian perspective on the position of women, a principle which many Muslims have historically ignored or violated.[216]

He writes, "[T]he teaching of the Quran on the subject of women is a part of its effort to improve the condition of, and strengthen the weaker segments of society in pre-Islamic Arabia — orphans, slaves, the poor, women, etc. — segments which had been abused by the stronger elements in the society."[217] The Quranic emphasis on justice for the weaker segments of society, including women, stood in contrast to many of the prevailing customs in pre-Islamic Arabian society. According to Rahman, the Quran takes a strong stance against the pre-Islamic practice of infanticide (this behavior was primarily directed against infant girls), slavery of women and men, and the abuse of women.[218] The Quran also contains injunctions which can be interpreted as placing constraints on men in divorcing their wives, which are much stricter than pre-Islamic restrictions.[219]

With respect to polygamy, Rahman writes that the Quranic injunction which limits a man to four wives is a vast improvement over pre-Islamic Arabian practices which allowed men to have many more wives.[220] However, Rahman believes that polygamy is not the ideal which Muslim men are to pursue in their married lives. Rather, Islamic societies, in general, and Muslim men in particular should be guided by

Sura 4:129 which states "You shall never be able to do justice among women, no matter how much you desire to do so."[221] He believes that the Quranic injunctions permitting a man to marry up to four women were purely provisional and that monogamy in marriage constitutes "the moral ideal towards which society was expected to move."[222] Rahman believes that Islamic societies must embrace the moral ideal of monogamy within their laws and customs.[223]

In terms of veiling and the segregation of the sexes, Rahman maintains that the Quran advocates neither; rather he states that the Quran insists on "sexual modesty" in dress and behavior.[224] He also asserts that it is

> certain on historical grounds that there was no veil in the Prophet's time, nor was there segregation of the sexes in the sense Muslim societies later developed it. In fact, the Quranic statements on modesty imply that neither veil nor segregation of the sexes existed. If there had been segregation of the sexes, there would have been no point in asking the sexes to behave with modesty.[225]

In Rahman's interpretation of Sura 24:31, which some traditionalists have interpreted as enjoining Muslim women to wear the veil, he writes that "there is nothing in these verses that calls for the veil as such."[226] Finally, the Quranic ideal of socio-moral justice demands that women "be allowed to work outside the home and to become effective economic entities."[227]

Mawdudi's perspectives on the relationship between men and women contrasts substantially from that of Rahman. Mawdudi maintains on the basis of various passages in the Quran and Hadith that men have a "natural superiority" over women and that men are a "degree above women."[228] This presupposition serves to shape much of Mawdudi's viewpoint on the role of women in Islam. He advocates men working to earn a living and women staying at home and taking care of the various aspects of the domestic sphere, which includes the task of raising children.[229] According to Mawdudi, women are not only obligated to stay at home, but they must ask their husband's permission to leave the domestic sphere, and a husband should only grant his wife this permission under special circumstances, such as when she wants to go to mosque, on the hajj, and attend funerals or visit graves.[230]

Much like other Islamic revivalists in other contexts, Mawdudi takes a very traditional stance regarding the veiling of women. He interprets Suras 24:30–31, 33:32–33, and 33:59 to mean that women must veil themselves when they leave the house, but may leave their faces and hands uncovered if they wish.[231] According to Mawdudi, the extent to which men and women must cover themselves relates to the specific prescriptions regarding male and female forbidden parts or *satar*.[232] The parts of a man which are considered forbidden and must be covered extend from the navel to the knee and for a woman this forbidden area involves the entire body, except for her face and hands.[233] Thus, both men and women must cover certain parts of their body, but he maintains that there is simply some variation regarding the *degree* to which men's and women's bodies should be covered.[234]

In her article "Women's Issues in Modern Islamic Thought," Barbara Freyer Stowasser explains and contextualizes the positions of modernists, such as Rahman, and what she calls "fundamentalists," such as Mawdudi, regarding women's issues.[235] Stowasser observes that modernists perceive Islam as a "'dynamic' religion, and they emphasize its 'openness' and 'permissiveness' as legislated in . . . the Quran and Hadith which allow them to consider the factors of time and societal change in their interpretation."[236] For the modernists, "contemporary social concerns are eminently compatible with the flexible blueprint of original Islam as realized in the way of life of the early Muslim community."[237]

Stowasser states that the "fundamentalists" insist on the static and immutable nature of Islam as stated in the Quran and Hadith.[238] For these Muslims,

> [E]veryday reality is judged as being either 'right' or 'wrong,' 'righteous' or 'sinful.' The objective and absolute criteria by which this distinction is made are the eternally valid norms and laws laid down in the Quran and interpreted in the Prophet's Sunna. According to the fundamentalists, then, social reality and social development have no influence *on* religion, while religion unilaterally shapes and guides them from above. There is one holistic Islam which, revealed to and lived by the Seal of the Prophets, Muhammad, is the final and all-inclusive religion of mankind.[239]

Stowasser's characterizations illuminate the broader streams of Islamic thought into which Rahman's and Mawdudi's thought fit. Rahman's general approach towards constructing his vision of Islam in the modern world and his approach towards women's issues more particularly are shaped by his beliefs regarding the dynamic character of Islamic history and his perception of the flexibility of the blueprint of Islam. While these ideas play an important role in the formation of his thought, he also maintains that on certain historical matters, such as the prevalence of veiling among Muslim women in seventh- and early eighth-century Arabia, the Islamic revivalists are wrong.[240] The differing approaches of modernists and Islamic revivalists have also led to certain basic differences regarding their views on the content of certain aspects of Islamic history. For Mawdudi, regarding women's issues and many other matters, there is one absolute way of understanding Muslims' obligations, which involves enforcing a rather strict segregation of men and women and a rigid division of labor between them in the public and private realms.

Yet while there are some general conceptual similarities among various modernists, on the one hand, and among Islamic revivalists, on the other, there are often differences of opinion between individual thinkers and movements within each of these strands of Islam. For instance, Mawdudi's criticism of democracy and his support of authoritarian forms of government within an Islamic state are points of view which are not shared by other Islamic revivalists. Members of various Islamic revivalist groups in Algeria, Egypt, Syria, Jordan, and in the West Bank and Gaza have come out strongly in favor of free elections as a way of selecting leaders in the Islamic states which they envision.[241]

With respect to the modernists, Rahman's viewpoint regarding Sharia and Sufism contrast distinctly from those of Mernissi and Ahmed. Many of the differences between Rahman, on one hand, and Mernissi and Ahmed, on the other, may be attributable to the fact that Rahman is older than these two intellectuals. He represents a different generation of modernists, especially with respect to feminism. The differences between these scholars are, nonetheless, worth discussing.

Mernissi and Ahmed understand Sharia as containing the legal stipulations which contributed to the oppression and marginalization of women.[242] However, neither in his discussions of women's issues nor in his discussions of Sharia does Rahman address the possible relationship of Sharia with the oppression of women.[243] Mernissi and Ahmed in many of their writings meticulously trace the role of women in Islamic history and the intricacies of historic Quranic and Hadith interpretations as they pertain to women, while gender issues form a relatively small subset of Rahman's thought. He places greater emphasis on the proper structure of educational and governmental systems in the Muslim world, discussing these topics with little regard to the role of women or gender in these institutions. Needless to say, in the works of Mernissi and Ahmed the historical marginalization of women from these institutions and the potential impact they can have upon them in the modern world are of central concern.

Similarly, in his condemnation of Sufism, Rahman gives little attention to the positive influence which various strands of Sufism have had and potentially could have on the lives of women. In Mernissi's article "Women, Saints, and Sanctuaries," she describes the way in which many Moroccan women find refuge from a male-dominated world at the grave sites of legendary Moroccan Sufi masters.[244] Leila Ahmed, for her part, presents her belief of the positive image of women represented in the stories of such Sufi figures as Rabia al-'Adawiyyah and in the speculations of Ibn 'Arabi.[245]

Although Rahman does not give women's issues the kind of prominence they receive in the writings of Mernissi and Ahmed, his contributions in several areas of Islamic thought are significant. One of the most notable features of his perspective, which is emblematic of much of his work, is his desire to create an ethos within Islamic culture that honors diverse points of view while maintaining what he calls a "Quranic" or "Islamic" base for the institutions that influence the lives of Muslims and the future of the umma. While Rahman criticizes Western cultures in many respects, he believes that Western cultures' tendencies to promote diverse and often contradictory viewpoints is one of their strengths.

At the same time, for Rahman the idea of promoting various points of view is not wholly foreign to Islam. Indeed, he believes there have been certain times in Islamic history when encouraging diverse opinions has been endemic to the tradition.[246] Rahman cites the four Sunni madhabs and varying strands of thought within Islamic philosophy as emblematic of diverging movements which are part of the Sunni path.[247]

Thus, Rahman maintains that the most pressing need which Muslims in the modern world face is the development of a proper intellectual method for understanding the past and appropriating it to Muslims' present circumstances. One aspect of this method, at least as far as Quranic interpretation is concerned, involves the "double-movement" of the interpreter from her or his present circumstance to the historical milieu of the text and then back to the present situation. This and other related intellectual methodologies should be open to diverse points of view. One of Rahman's criticisms of Islamic revivalism relates to what he believes to be its lack of intellectualism and its attendant lack of openness to divergent viewpoints. He maintains that Islamic revival-ists believe they have the "divine mission" of "shutting down Islamic intellectual life" and that their assumption that "Muslims can straighten out the practical world without serious intellectual effort, with the aid only of catchy slogans, is a dangerous mistake."[248] This "intellectual bankruptcy" together with Islamic revivalism's "substitution of cliché mongering for serious intellectual endeavor" has contributed to the continued weakening of the Muslim umma vis-à-vis the West in the modern period. Rahman advocates a path of intellectual renewal which upholds Quranic principles of equality, justice, and broad-mindedness as leading the way to the renewal and reform of the Islamic community.

5

MOHAMMED ARKOUN

Mohammed Arkoun's interpretation of Islam's sacred texts and history is guided by his belief that during the course of Islamic history many religious leaders' fear of chaos and mayhem together with their desire for order and obedience played a vital role in determining the content and trajectory of Islamic thought, jurisprudence, and theology. Arkoun is particularly critical of the ulema and caliphs during the Abbasid Period, the founders of the four Sunni Muslim madhabs, as well as modern-day members of the ulema and Islamic Revivalists.[1] Arkoun's interpretive method involves his belief that Islam must free itself from these oppressive constraints and work in partnership with members of other religious traditions (primarily Christians and Jews whose histories, according to Arkoun, overlap significantly with that of Islam) in creating a world that is rooted in mutual understanding, equality, and harmony.[2] Arkoun continually questions the presuppositions which have shaped Islam's sacred textual, interpretive, and legal corpora since the religion's beginnings in the seventh century. These are the ideas undergirding Arkoun's thought. Much of the previous chapters was devoted to analyzing Mernissi's, Ahmed's, and Rahman's thought in comparison and contrast with neotraditionalist or Islamic revivalist strands. In this chapter, Arkoun's ideas will be compared and contrasted with those of Mernissi, Ahmed, and Rahman.[3]

Arkoun's skeptical approach towards Islamic texts and history may well have come as a result of his training in Islamic and Western Philosophy at the Sorbonne, where his dissertation was a translation of eleventh-century Muslim philosopher Miskawayh's treatise on ethics.[4] Robert D. Lee notes that Western scholars such as Jacques Derrida, Max Weber, and Émile Durkheim, play a significant role in Arkoun's thought.[5] The impact of Western philosophical skepticism (such as that embodied in Derrida's philosophy) is evident in Arkoun's works as he questions the ways in which medieval Muslims (particularly al-Shafi'i and the founders of the three other Sunni madhabs) and twentieth century Islamic revivalists interpret the Quran, Hadith, and Islamic history.[6] Arkoun's perspectives on the role which Islamic cultures (particularly North African and Arabian) have played in shaping understandings of Islamic rituals and symbols are influenced by the approaches of Western sociologists of religion.[7]

Arkoun has also devoted many of his works to dialogue between religions as well as his hope for greater understanding between the various countries and societies surrounding the Mediterranean.[8] He maintains there could potentially be greater peace and reconciliation among the "Mediterranean peoples" (which would, of course, include citizens of both predominantly Muslim and non-Muslim countries) if they were, through their educational systems, for example, to learn about the similarities in their histories and cultural customs.[9] Arkoun's viewpoint on this issue may well have been shaped by the fact that he grew up in the southern portion of the Mediterranean region (Algeria) while pursuing his graduate studies and career in the northern portion this region (France).[10] His desire for greater inter-religious dialogue between Jews, Christians, and Muslims could be rooted in the first-hand encounters which he has had with members of these religions in the Mediterranean and during his travels as well as his interest in the academic writings of members of these religious traditions.

Any reading of Arkoun's works indicates that the vast majority of them are not intended for a popular audience, either in the Muslim world or in the West. While some of his writings have been translated from French into Arabic, the bulk of them are published by French academic publishers and are directed at a Western scholarly audience that, Arkoun assumes, already has some familiarity with academic discourse on Islam.[11] Arkoun seems to expect far more from himself than from the "masses" (as he calls them) or from grass roots political movements. For him, it is the intellectuals who must examine the whole of the Islamic tradition and communicate the result to the "undivided and naïve consciousness of the believers."[12] Thus, scholars must be careful to avoid "excessive intellectualization" and stay attuned to popular beliefs.[13] Interestingly, Arkoun sees poetry as a critical link between intellectuals and the masses:

It is through modern poetry, much more than through political or academic pronouncements, that underprivileged persons and members of low-income groups can best perceive and express their own deaths, births and rebirths.[14]

Arkoun's stance on the issues of scholarly over-intellectualization and poetry contradicts his own approach toward expressing his ideas since his writings are neither easy to understand nor are they written in a poetic form. It is not clear from Arkoun's work how he thinks the "true intellectuals," as he calls them, might be able to disseminate their ideas and establish any sort of cohesive movement, political or otherwise. Robert D. Lee notes that Arkoun's work is "largely inaccessible to anyone outside the community of scholars" and that a "crevasse of Himalayan proportions" separates his ideas from non-academics.[15] It certainly remains to be seen the extent to which Arkoun's thought will influence Muslims and non-Muslims outside the academic world.

The Quran

Arkoun's viewpoints on the Quran provide a solid starting point as one attempts to delve into the immensity and complexity of his thought. While Arkoun may agree with modernists such as Mernissi, Ahmed, and Rahman that the Quran can be interpreted as placing an emphasis on the notions of justice and equality, his understanding of the Quran takes a slightly different angle of vision:

> The Quran presents itself as a linguistic form, as a cultural model of mythic, cosmological, institutional, and historic references accessible to the Arab public of the seventh century in order to encourage human beings to be conscious of their human circumstance which is limited by life, death, speech, human minds, politics, and history.[16]

Arkoun indicates the limits and the possibilities of Quranic discourse. Much like Fazlur Rahman, he asserts that throughout much of Islamic history legists and other interpreters who were considered authoritative interpreted the Quran in terms of their own specific circumstances, giving little attention to what may have been the historical milieu within which the Quran was revealed.

With this idea in mind, Arkoun maintains that the Quran provides some general guidance and direction for human beings in the times subsequent to its revelation:

> There is . . . an essentially dynamic Quranic intention: the Quran does not impose definitive solutions to the practical problems of human existence. It carries the purpose of stirring up in human beings a regard for themselves, the world, and the symbols which would constitute for them a metaphysical horizon.[17]

Arkoun understands the initial revelation of the Quran and its subsequent interpretations as existing along a continuum; the interpretations of the Quran throughout Islamic history are related to peoples' perceptions of the importance of the book and individuals who have held power throughout much of Islamic history have utilized their interpretations of the Quran to their own advantage.

Arkoun understands the processes of revelation and interpretation as being best depicted by the following diagram:

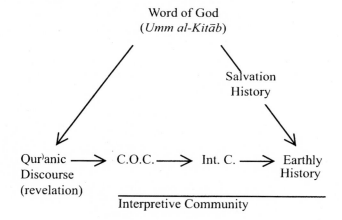

C.O.C. = Closed Official Corpus
Int. C. = Interpretive Corpus

This diagram portrays the movement by which God revealed a part of the Heavenly Book to human beings on the vertical axis, symbolic of the descent of revelation. On the horizontal axis, Arkoun portrays the more earthly activities which were involved in the emergence of the text and its interpretations. The earthly dimension involved Prophetic pronouncements (not all of which, according to Arkoun, were faithfully reported), leading to the Closed Official Corpus and then on to the corpus of interpretation, which is comprised of numerous commentaries written by a diverse set of commentators throughout Islamic history.[18]

In explaining Arkoun's views on the Quran, his ideas on revelation, the Closed Official Corpus, and the corpus of interpretation will be discussed in turn. Arkoun uses the term *wahy* (which he defines as "inspiration, eruption, revelation") to describe the "creative overflow" which Muhammad experienced that caused the Quran to come into existence.[19] Arkoun does not clearly specify the extent to which God may have been involved in this "creative overflow" and the extent to which the Prophet himself may have been involved in it. Arkoun goes so far as to assert that the question as to whether Muhammad knew how to read and write "leads away from the psychological and cultural context of *wahy*"; additionally, he maintains that "to know how to read and write requires . . . an exercise of reason quite apart from the improvisation, inventions, free associations and flashes of thought to be found in prophetic discourse."[20] This statement and other similar ones in Arkoun's works leave open the possibility that *wahy* did not only have a divine source but may have had an earthly or human one as well. The fact that Arkoun shies away from the term *tanzil* (which means descent and is commonly used in tandem with the term *wahy* when discussing Quranic revelation) suggests he may believe that Muhammad was more than a passive recipient in the revelatory process. If this is so, his viewpoint would diverge sharply from traditional lines of discourse among Muslims which explicitly state that Muhammad was illiterate and that the miracle of the Quran is dependent on God actively revealing this book to a Prophet who memorized it and had virtually nothing to do with its creation or composition.

In line with Arkoun's idea of Muhammad's active role in the founding of the Muslim community, he asserts that Muhammad's actions consisted of establishing a new religio-political order by rearticulating the religious symbolism of the covenant (*mithaq*). Muhammad reworked political and religious space at the same time and he did so by moving the qibla (the direction of prayer) from Jerusalem to Mecca, by making Friday the day of "collective celebration in imitative rivalry of Saturday and Sunday" (the days Jews and Christians hold as holy), by building a mosque in Medina and forbidding believers to enter sacred places of other religions, and by returning to Mecca and integrating all the ritual and physical structures of the pagan hajj ("pilgrimage") into a set of significations which came to be understood as distinctly Islamic.[21] By engaging in these and similar tasks, Muhammad was progressively constructing a semiological system which outmoded that of the former Arab society, "outclassed the Jewish, Christian, Sabaean, and Manichean competition, and made possible the edification of a state implementing the new political order."[22]

Arkoun presents a relatively open-ended view of revelation. He does not believe that revelation came to a complete halt with the writing of the Quran but that it is an on-going process which continues even into modern times. He maintains that one could consider revelation to happen "each time that a new vocabulary comes to radically change man's view of his condition, his participation in the production of meaning."[23] He continues by saying that revelation is the acceptance "to the interior space of the human being — to the heart, the *qalb,* says the Quran — of some novel meaning that opens up unlimited opportunities or back currents of meaning for human existence."[24] Revelation occurs in many historical circumstances in many different places when human beings come to new realizations about the meaning or meanings of human existence, of their personal and communal identity or identities, and of the adjustments they must make in their worldviews in light of changed conditions. These revelatory experiences occurred to people during the emergence of the Quran, the Hebrew Bible, the New Testament, and at other times in history. Revelation "feeds a living tradition that permits the community to resupply itself periodically with the radical novelty of the original message."[25]

After the initial revelation comes to and/or emerges within a given individual or community, those enunciations which were at first usually made known orally, are written down, and then form part of a Closed Official Corpus (the Quran, the Torah, the Hebrew Bible, the New Testament, etc.) which comes to be considered as authoritative within the given religious tradition.[26] These books were elevated to the status of Closed Official Corpus according to procedures developed and supervised by scholars.[27] Arkoun uses the term "official" because the formation of the corpora resulted from a set of decisions made by authorities recognized by the community. He uses the term "closed" because "nobody was permitted any longer to add or subtract a word, [or] to modify a reading" in a body of literature "now declared authentic."[28] It is called a corpus in that the Jewish, Christian, and Muslim religious communities more or less view their respective sacred texts as a unified whole.[29] In a "decisive, irreversible, historic event shared by the three interrelated religious tendencies, revelation came to be accessible to the faithful only on the basis of the Closed Official Corpus, more commonly called Holy Scripture or the Word of God."[30]

Arkoun traces the way he believes the Quran came into existence as a Closed Official Corpus within Islam by stating that the assembling of the Quran began at the death of the Prophet in 632. He goes on to assert that "even while [the Prophet] was alive it seems that certain verses were put into writing."[31] He writes that "partial compilations" were made with "rather unsatisfactory materials" since paper was very rarely used among the Arabs and would not be widely used among them until the end of the eighth century. Some years after the death of the Prophet, and the subsequent death of the Companions of the Prophet (primarily those who had journeyed with him from Mecca to Medina in 622) and a "sharpening of debate among surviving Muslims pushed the third caliph, ʿUthman, to gather the totality of the revelation into a single compilation called *mushaf*."[32] After this final, irrevocable, and irreversible decision, "the collection was declared complete, finished, and closed; the text was established without variation and the partial compilations were destroyed to avoid feeding dissent about the authenticity of the revelations selected."[33] These views are generally in line with majoritarian Sunni attitudes on these subjects.

In contrast to much majoritarian Sunni thought, Arkoun's description of the compilation of the Quran in Islamic history relates to his ideas regarding the compilation of the Closed Official Corpus in Judaism and Christianity. He believes that these corpora came into existence through circumstances which were not endemically tied to the original revelation and came as a result of the religious or political objectives of certain individuals who held authority at the time the corpora were deemed closed.

Closely related and subsequent to the final closure of a sacred textual tradition within these three religions is the creation of interpretive corpora which have the task of explaining the universal truths that the writers of these interpretive commentaries believe the sacred texts proclaim. The compilation and completion of a Closed Official Corpus put the "peoples of the Book in a hermeneutic position"; they had to interpret their sacred texts in order to "derive law, prescriptions, and systems of belief and non-belief of the sort that dominated the moral, legal, and political order until the triumph of secularization."[34]

In terms of the other modernists' perspectives on the emergence of the Quran, Mernissi's view of its revelation comes closer to traditional majoritarian lines of interpretation than any of the four thinkers. She asserts that the Quran was revealed to Muhammad over the course of many years through the angel Gabriel, although she does avoid addressing the question of how the Quran came into existence in written form.[35] Ahmed believes that the text of the Quran itself (and that of the Hadith as well) came into existence through "acts of interpretation" and selectivity (influenced by the androcentric perspectives of the compilers). In her view, this interpretive process is one aspect of Islamic history that orthodoxy "is most concerned to conceal and erase from the consciousness of Muslims."[36]

While Rahman states that God revealed the Quran to Muhammad, he rejects the notion that the Quran was revealed through the angel Gabriel and affirms his idea that the Quran came from an external source directly to Muhammad's heart.[37] He contends that there is no adequate Quranic basis for the assertion that the revelation came to Muhammad through the angel Gabriel. According to Rahman, this idea was created sometime in the eighth or ninth century and since it has no foundation in the Quran should be rejected in favor of his position which does have support in the Quran.[38] After Rahman made this viewpoint known in Pakistan in the mid-1960s, many of Pakistan's Islamic Revivalists vociferously attacked him, making Rahman's ideas on the Quran one of the factors which compelled him to leave Pakistan in 1968.[39] For his part, Arkoun does not mention the role of Gabriel in the process of revelation but suggests that, symbolically, this angelic figure (which is present in the Jewish, Muslim and Christian traditions) can form one basis for dialogue between members of these religions.[40]

Unlike the other three modernists in this study, Arkoun places the phenomenon of Quranic revelation in cross-cultural perspective. He analyzes the concept of Quranic revelation in terms of the traditions of Judaism and Christianity and discusses the similarities and differences between the ways these religions have approached the idea of revelation. Arkoun is engaged in a task of analyzing the concept of revelation within the framework of the cross-cultural study of religion while attempting to come to some conclusions about this process philosophically. The three other writers limit their consideration of the idea of revelation to the Islamic context.

The Emergence of a Sunni Orthodoxy and Classic Islamic Reason

For Arkoun, the initial *élan* of the creative Prophetic and Divine semiotic eruptions and reconfigurations which marked the life of the Prophet and the early Muslim communities ended definitively with the "rise of the imperial Umayyad state."[41] Starting with the Umayyad period, a process began where Islam's symbolic capital (the set of signs and significations emerging from Islam's sacred texts as well as the rites and behaviors set in motion by the Prophet) was utilized for the construction and imposition of what Arkoun calls an "official orthodox Islam."[42] This Islam was official because it resulted from political choices of the state which "physically eliminated" opponents who stood for any other interpretations and uses of the symbolic capital; the Shiites and Kharijites are two examples of groups that embodied viewpoints that diverged from what became orthodoxy.[43]

The majoritarian Islamic perspectives can rightly be called orthodox because "the experts accredited by the political authorities gave credence to the idea that it is possible to read the Word of God correctly, to know the prophetic tradition exhaustively in order to deduce . . . from the fundamental sources (*usul*) all the legal provisions that constitute the Divine Law (Sharia)."[44] In this way, during the first two centuries of the rise of Islam (from approximately 632 to 850) what came to be called *fiqh* and *usul al-fiqh* (methodology for Islamic legal interpretation) were developed.[45] During these first two centuries, the legal schools which came into being began to contribute to the development of what Arkoun calls classic Islamic reason. Islamic reason is the historic tendency among Muslim intellectuals and legists to transcendentalize, universalize, and sacralize certain concepts or passages in the Quran, Hadith and/or certain events in Islamic history. One of the major negative consequences of this method of transcendentalizing discourse is that it creates significant misunderstandings and misappropriations of historical events and sacred texts, while marginalizing diverging points of view.[46]

In order to describe and critique this classic Islamic reason, Arkoun has chosen the *Risala* of Shafi'i (767–820) insofar as it is "a limited corpus" and for Arkoun a "test-case" which represents "classic Islamic Reason" in its "form, its contents, and practical results."[47] He does not consult Shafi'i's *Risala* primarily as a manual of methodology, rather as a fundamental source which has hierarchized and defined the sources of authority. Arkoun perceives the *Risala* as "the supreme instance of the legitimization of human power" in Islam and he considers Shafiʻi to be the person who has made the most substantial contribution to formulating Islamic reason into a methodology which was to function as a strategy for quashing other, possibly more accurate, understandings of Islamic history and formulations of law.[48]

Arkoun considers Shafiʻi's use of Quranic verses and Hadith to function as a strategy to reinforce and popularize the most rigid legal methods and to utilize them in a manipulative task which "consists of postulating a structural continuity and a semantic homogeneity between the initial spatial-temporal context within which the Quranic and Hadith texts came into existence and the very different spatial-temporal context when the same texts were re-read and reinterpreted."[49] Arkoun continues:

> Shafiʻi and other Muslim legists drew their conclusions and created their legal treatises without adequately considering the concrete circumstances of the initial irreducible flashes of experience of the Prophet or the accompanying collective action of the Companions. Legists such as Shafiʻi and those of his ilk have a tendency to project their own experiences and actions upon the origins, configuration, and motivations of the earlier Muslim communities within which the Quran and Hadith took shape.[50]

According to Mohamed El Ayadi, this operation of projecting and universalizing which was facilitated by the written or memorized form of the texts reveals how an elaborate system of law

> was disguised and sacralized with respect to the sociological, political, and cultural context of the Hijaz by the first judges and legists who lived in Iraq and Syria in the first and second centuries after the hijra.[51]

Yet, the inaccurate methodologies inhering in classical Islamic reason (from Arkoun's point of view) are not limited to the early and medieval Islamic periods. For him, modern-day Islamic revivalists also engage in endeavors of inappropriately universalizing and transcendentalizing certain passages of the Quran which have led, in Arkoun's view, to the marginalization of women, antiquated marriage laws, distorted portrayals of Jews, Christians, and certain Muslims, as well as a host of other difficulties.[52] According to Arkoun's historical and sociological presentation, Islamic law was in fact legitimized after the creation of a basic theory of law (*usul al-fiqh*) which attached the practical solutions of the judges from the eighth and ninth centuries to the normative religious sources (the Quran and Hadith).[53] Those beliefs which are usually thought of as comprising Islamic orthodoxy are "exposed" by Arkoun as an ideology of a group imposing its supremacy (particularly with the ascendance of the Umayyad state) and the utilization of symbolic capital conveyed by the Quran in order to construct and impose an official monolith of right beliefs and practices on Islam.[54]

There are some general similarities between Mernissi, Ahmed, Rahman, and Arkoun regarding what they believe to be the negative impact of the Umayyad and Abbasid periods on the most important ethical teachings of the Quran and the early Muslim community. While they cite different historical examples of the patriarchally-centered interpretive manipulations during the Umayyad and Abassid periods, Mernissi and Ahmed agree that the forms of majoritarian Islam, which came into existence during these periods, contradicted the essential teachings of the Quran and the early Muslim communities, which taught justice, egalitarianism, the even-handed distribution of power, responsibility, and equal opportunity for men and women.

Rahman criticizes different aspects of the Umayyad and Abbasid periods than Arkoun does. While Arkoun questions virtually all the legal developments which came into existence through the four Sunni Muslim madhabs or legal schools, Rahman believes that these contributions are among the most glorious achievements in Islamic history. However, Rahman condemns the closing of the door of *ijtihad*; this closing being an event which served to block the creative freedom necessary to adapt Islamic law properly to changing historical circumstances.[55]

Arkoun, for his part, condemns *ijtihad* (before and after the closing of the doors) — as well as *qiyas* (analogy), *ra'y* (personal opinion), and *ijma'* — as part and parcel of the emergence of classic Islamic reason. Rahman, in contrast, believes in the continuing value of many of these methods and maintains that they should be reinvigorated together with the practice of *ijtihad* in order to create legal systems in Islam which are true to the message of the Quran and Hadith and are well-adapted to changing historical circumstances.[56] The force of Rahman's critique with respect to the Umayyad and Abbasid periods relates to the narrowness of the Islamic educational system (which, among other weaknesses, discouraged critical thinking) and to the formation of Islamic societies which often blocked free expression and creative intellectual responses to changing historical circumstances.[57] Rahman does not blame the totality of the legal methodologies which were developed during the first two centuries of Islam for these problems.

Rather, he criticizes Islamic educational systems and Islamic cultures which constrained the development of innovative intellectual responses. Arkoun believes the methodologies of Islamic jurisprudence lie at the heart of the problems associated with the formation of what he calls classic Islamic reason and the development of an Islamic orthodoxy.

Applied Islamology

In response to the pervasiveness of the transcendentalizing methods of classic Islamic reason, Arkoun suggests the creation of a discipline he terms "applied Islamology" which would have the goal of demytholo-gizing classic Islamic reason which has contributed to the creation of inaccuracies and stark distortions of Islam's history and sacred texts.[58] Applied Islamologists, who Arkoun believes could be scholars trained in any of a variety of disciplines in the humanities and social sciences, would have at least two tasks. One of these tasks would involve the "purely linguistic and semiotic analysis" of the Quranic text which would permit

> the disengaging of a central mythic structure utilizing symbol and meta-phor in order to confer to all Quranic enunciations the continual poten-tialities of meaning which are actualized in various recurrent existential situations over time.[59]

The second task of applied Islamology would involve "explicating and describing the levels of interaction, the causes of the break between religious forces and the weight of these historic forms, arbitrarily sacralized and transcendentalized" as is the case, among others, in the institutions of the caliphate, of the Sharia, and of the umma in Islam.[60] While the first task of applied Islamology involves analyzing the Quranic text closely, the second tasks involves examining the relation-ship between Islam's sacred texts and the Islamic institutions which were put into place subsequent to the establishment of the sacred texts.

It is necessary to describe these two tasks in greater depth. The first, which engages the scholar in a purely semiotic and linguistic venture of understanding the mythic structure of the Quran, is tied to Arkoun's very specific understanding of myth. He does not translate the term myth as *ustura*, which to many Muslims would connote a legendary tale devoid of truth. Rather, Arkoun translates myth as *qasas,* which is a story that points to some ultimate and fundamental truths about human existence.[61] He accepts the definition of myth as presented by twentieth century structuralist and philosopher Claude Lévi-Strauss:

> The truth of myth does not relate to its privileged content. It consists of logical relationships drained of content, or more exactly, of invariant properties drained of their operative value, since comparable relationships can be established by the elements of a great number of different types of content.[62]

Arkoun considers this type of myth, rehabilitated by social and cultural anthropology after being discredited for a long time by various rationalist thinkers, to be a fruitful notion insofar as it permits one to comprehend the richness of Quranic enunciations and their irreplaceable function in the constitution of the religious imagination.[63]

The second task follows from the first and the intention of this task is for intellectuals to come to terms with the various institutions (such as the caliphate, the Sharia, and the umma) which have come into existence in Islamic cultures over the centuries and to re-evaluate their justifiability on the basis of a re-examination of Islamic texts and Islamic history. The primary questions that this line of enquiry would attempt to answer would be: Is the existence of the various sacralized institutions of Islam that have often contributed to the marginalization and oppression of various individuals and groups justifiable? If so, how could various Islamic institutions be reconstituted or reconfigured to embody the new interpretations and appropriations which would come as a result of applied Islamology? Arkoun does not venture to answer these questions because he believes there is much academic work to be done before they can be properly addressed.[64]

Arkoun's task of applied Islamology has some distinct similarities with Rahman's ideas related to reinvigorating Islamic educational and cultural institutions. Both intellectuals affirm, for example, the importance of reinterpreting Islam's past in a way that remains true to what they perceive as Islam's core principles, while they also advocate the creation of a societal milieu within Islamic countries which would encourage free and creative thought. There are two crucial differences, however, between Arkoun's and Rahman's views on the reinvigoration of Islam in the twentieth century. The first difference has to do with the specific language and concepts each uses in articulating his stance and the second has to do with the degree of skepticism each thinker expresses with respect to developments within Islamic history.

Arkoun's critique of Islamic reason is geared toward questioning the very presuppositions and methodologies which contributed to the formation of Islam's interpretive, legal, and societal structures. Arkoun's approach leads him to criticize these structures at the most rudimentary level; he raises some of the most basic philosophical questions about the nature of revelation, holy scripture, interpretation, and Islamic institutions. In questioning these areas he shows a much greater level of skepticism towards them than Rahman, who accepts certain widely held assumptions about revelation, interpretation, and Islamic institutions. Rahman largely accepts and attempts to reappropriate these entities to the modern situation, while Arkoun questions virtually all of them. Robert Diemer Lee indicates that Arkoun's skepticism about various concepts and institutions related to Islam leads him to "the brink of nihilism."[65]

While Mernissi and Ahmed do not use Arkounian language pertaining to the negative impact of the transcendentalizing force of classic Islamic reason, in their analyses of traditional Islamic interpretations and institutions, they pay very close attention to the ways in which patriarchally-centered, male-generated interpretations of Islamic texts and history have marginalized and oppressed women throughout much of Islamic history. They would agree with Arkoun on the relationship between power, on the one hand, and the creation of knowledge and oppressive interpretive structures, on the other. Indeed, at some point in the future Muslim feminists may find it beneficial to appropriate Arkoun's concepts of classic Islamic reason and his ideas regarding authority in Islamic thought into their own writings.

Marginalized Groups in Islamic History

Three of the groups which Arkoun believes have been marginalized through the transcendentalizing, sacralizing, and institutionalizing forces of Islamic reason and its orthodoxy-centered truth-producing logic are Sufis, Shiites, and women. I will examine Arkoun's viewpoints on each of these groups in turn.

Before delving into Arkoun's perspectives on Sufism, it is important to gain an understanding of two types of religious discourse which Arkoun believes religious communities produce. One type of discourse is based on reason, while the other type is based on what Arkoun terms the imagination (*l'imaginaire*). Discourse based on reason attempts to be logical, explicit, rigorous, and exoteric. This mode of communication attempts to set forward its claims in a manner which actively shies away from mystery.[66] Discourse based on imagination, on the other hand, often relies on emotional or spiritual states, leaves the door open to the supernatural, the miraculous, and magical, and often articulates its stance in terms of esoteric language, which often carries mysterious connotations.[67] These two types of discourse exist on a continuum and are not necessarily mutually exclusive, although the language of orthodoxy is primarily based on the discourse of reason while the language of mystics is primarily based on the discourse of the imagination.[68] Through its "arrogant sovereignty," classic Islamic reason in particular has marginalized and at times actively attacked some of the potentially beneficial images and symbols which have arisen from the Sufi tradition.[69]

Since mystical movements such as Sufism do not set forth an explicit and rigid orthodoxy per se and inasmuch as they often emphasize the universality of love and reappropriate symbols freely, these movements hold the potential of opening the door toward unity among human beings.[70] This is not to suggest that Arkoun is naively proclaiming that mysticism in general or Sufism in particular is a universal solution to humanity's problems. Rather, he attempts to re-evaluate Sufism in terms of the categories of imaginary discourse while he examines the possibilities its language and symbols hold for human unity and for a critique of various aspects of Islamic reason.[71]

He points to the works of the thirteenth century Muslim mystic Ibn 'Arabi as indicative of the type of imaginationally-oriented religious discourse which is open to what Arkoun calls "the unicity of being" (a term Arkoun leaves ambiguous but which he believes holds some promise) and reformulates traditional symbols in such a way that they open the religious imagination to new possibilities — possibilities that Arkoun believes are yet to be explored.[72] In this vein, he quotes a passage from one of Ibn 'Arabi's writings:

> I will respond, my dear friend and very close companion, to the question you asked me about the modalities of the journey to the Master of Omnipotence, the arrival in His Presence and the return—from Him and by Him—to His Creatures without there being any separation, however. For in existence there is nothing other than Allah, His attributes and His acts. Everything is Him, through Him, proceeds from Him, returns to Him; and if He were to hide Himself from the universe, even if only for a second, the universe would cease at once to exist, for it only subsists through His protection and His care. Appearing in His light is so blinding that eyes cannot perceive Him (Sura 6:103), so it is best to say that His appearance is an occultation.[73]

Before reaching the highest state of mental contemplation and understanding of this great being, the believer begins the process of spiritual awakening by recognizing and obeying the "good deeds of God" through respecting the ritual obligations incumbent on all believers (the declaration of faith, prayer five times per day, almsgiving, fasting, and the hajj). A person's increased spiritual understanding is related to his or her practice of various Sufi patterns which leads to a greater and deeper understanding of the cosmos and of "the absolute unicity of being."[74] Arkoun praises Sufism for the ways in which it gives free reign to "religious sensitivity" and "to creative imagination."[75]

Active scholarly analysis of mystical movements such as Sufism "leads to the transgression of conceptual boundaries inherited from dualistic thinking based on the well-known dichotomies between faith and reason, revealed truth and rational truth, religious law and human norms, earthly life and eternal life, good and evil, true and false, and so on."[76] While the transcendentalizing force of classic Islamic reason was primarily tied to the groups which attained power and these groups created an orthodoxy which marginalized such movements as Sufism, Arkoun believes we are living in an age when the imagination-based discourse of mystical movements such as Sufism can be re-examined in order to open new insights for Islam and its relationship to non-Muslim religions. Imagination-based discourse (as contrasted with discourse based solely on reason) such as is found in Sufism and other mystical movements can free Muslim and Western academics from the overly rationalistic type of thinking which has been a characteristic of Islamic reason and of Western academic discourse as well.[77] Thus, Arkoun asserts the importance of analyzing Sufism in terms of classical Islamic reason and he believes that the concepts of imaginationally-based discourse hold very positive potential. Yet, he warns that "mystical discourse gets bogged down in categories as much as dogmatic theological discourse" and that scholars must be aware of this tendency and mysticism's inherent propensity for establishing universal dicta on the basis of certain individual experiences.[78]

Mernissi and Ahmed also believe that Sufism holds the potential of positively influencing Islam's present and future, although they appropriate different aspects of Sufism. Mernissi indicates what she believes to be the very beneficial role Sufi saint sanctuaries play in the lives of many Moroccan women. She contends that sanctuaries function as therapy and as anti-establishment areas; in addition, Sufi sainthood functions as an alternative to male-defined femininity. These sanctuaries are places where many women can go to find rest, relaxation, and refuge from an often male-dominated world.[79]

For her part, Ahmed finds several of the historical manifestations of Sufism to be solid expressions of what she believes to be Islam's ethical monotheism and its original emphasis on justice and equality. She maintains that women played a vital role in Sufism's history and that within various Sufi movements they were understood as having spiritual powers which were equal to or surpassing those of men; these symbols can function as positive models for modern Muslim women and for the Islamic community as a whole. Ahmed, like Arkoun, invokes Ibn 'Arabi in a positive way.[80] Ahmed also indicates that one of the historic merits of Sufism has been its lack of a rigid and authoritarian orthodoxy.[81]

Rahman's viewpoints on Sufism are far more critical. He believes that Sufism is "solely responsible for inculcating, spreading, and perpetuating the most fantastic and grotesque beliefs" and that it "has enchained the minds and spirits of the credulous masses."[82] It seems that Rahman's criticisms of Sufism are related to his positive disposition towards Sharia. Specifically, Rahman believes that the reinvigoration and proper configuration of Sharia is one of the key elements for the revitalization of Islam in the twentieth century and that Sharia, properly formulated and understood, can provide one important foundation for an Islamic society based on human rights, economic opportunity, and sound ethics. Sufi practices such as the veneration of saints, adoration of Sufi masters, and the movement's emphasis on internal spiritual states are some of the many aspects of Sufism that contradict ideas and rules set forth in Sharia. In contrast to Rahman, Mernissi, Ahmed, and Arkoun have a far more skeptical view of Sharia and believe that its abandonment in favor of other egalitarian models within Islam can create freer Muslim societies with more opportunities in education and public life for people.[83]

In considering Arkoun's viewpoints on Shiism, one must first examine how he believes orthodoxies develop. Arkoun points to the emergence of "three orthodoxies" in Islam: those of the Sunni, Shiite, and Kharijite movements. He asserts that in all these cases one sees the "emergence of a religious consciousness bearing claims to rightfulness derived from Islamic teaching and the prophetic model."[84] At the same time, this consciousness takes material form "through political institutions and seeks fulfillment in them to direct the political community postulated by the Quran and the Prophet."[85] These tendencies are confirmed in declarations written by medieval historiographers (often long after the events they purport to report) who are "themselves actors inside the three ideological streams each sublimating [their own tradition's] historical meanderings in a spiritual epic."[86]

Indeed, none of the three groups that considered themselves orthodox could base their orthodoxy solely on the "the only authority unanimously recognized by Muslims, the Quran."[87] That is, each group's interpretation of sacred texts was shaped by the group's own historical situation and presuppositions. Arkoun states that throughout Islamic history there have been divergences in exegesis and that it is difficult to read the Quran in an unequivocal way that would be "binding on all believers and decisive on all debatable points."[88] The great difficulty in formulating orthodoxy in Islam can be explained in terms of the ideological function of any religion. Arkoun maintains that "a religion serves social actors who establish rival groups to assure their own control over symbolic goods with which political power cannot be assumed or exercised."[89] Scholarly enquiry reveals that what various religious groups believe to be orthodoxy is at root the "ideology of each group seeking to assert its supremacy."[90]

Thus, for its part and in accordance with its own particular historic circumstance, Shiism utilized its own form of classic Islamic reason to transcendentalize and sacralize its own interpretations of the Quran, the formation and understanding of its Hadith collections, the establishment of the Shiite Imamate, unique forms of Shiite philosophy and theology, as well as distinctive Shiite rituals. These and many other religious beliefs and practices were transcendentalized within Shiism and played a significant part in the creation and perpetuation of Shiite orthodoxy, an orthodoxy which, like many others, was reconfigured and reappropriated over time.

Arkoun points to the establishment of the Islamic Republic of Iran as one example of the way in which a reformulated Shiism became a revolutionary worldview and subsequently an orthodox religio-political ideology which formed the basis of a Shiite nation-state. Various Iranian Shiite intellectuals transcendentalized certain concepts within Shiism and applied these to the establishment and formation of a new state that manifested a new religio-political orthodoxy never before seen in such a form.[91]

In articulating his viewpoints on the role of women in Islam, Arkoun criticizes both Islamic revivalists and Westerners for the ways they have portrayed the status of Muslim women and Islam's claims about women's status. Arkoun is wary of the Islamic revivalist claims that the Quran improved the status of women, raising them to the same spiritual dignity as men and that Muslim women are not subjected — as are women in the West — to fierce social and economic competition with men.[92] Arkoun objects to the ways which Islamic revivalists have appropriated some of these ideas in their discourse about women. Specifically, Arkoun believes that the Islamic Revivalists have articulated such viewpoints in ways that can lead to misunderstandings and inaccuracies.[93]

For their part, Westerners emphasize the intolerable inferiority of women in Muslim societies, citing polygamy, divorce by repudiation, the wearing of the veil, segregation of the sexes, imprisonment in household tasks, strict dependence on the husband, and lack of legal rights.[94] Arkoun criticizes these Western stereotypes by stating that those who have generated these images "have neglected to begin by considering the givens of the feminine condition common to all societies, givens that persist in our time despite numerous efforts at emancipation, especially in the modern West."[95] Arkoun is suggesting that Western women tend to overlook the difficulties which women may face in Western and other non-Muslim societies when they criticize the situation of Muslim women.

As he does with respect to other sub-fields of Islamic Studies (Sufism, Shiism, Islamic history, etc.), Arkoun suspends final judgments about the position of Muslim women and suggests areas for future research — this research holding the potential for providing a basis to make appraisals regarding the status of women in Islam. The first scholarly task that must be undertaken (which has not been sufficiently addressed in Arkoun's view) is a full-scale historical, sociological, linguistic, and semiotic analysis of the Quranic verses concerning polygamy, divorce by repudiation, inheritance, the "superiority" of men over women, the veil, lineage, and marriage.[96]

While these verses have already been the object of juridical explication throughout Islamic history, it is necessary to subject them to the methods of modern academic analysis in order to attain a deeper understanding of their meaning(s) within their historical context(s). This understanding can provide a basis for interpreting these passages in a sophisticated manner for the modern context. While Arkoun recognizes that Muslims and non-Muslims have used modern scholarly methods to analyze these passages, he finds much of this work inadequate and believes that further investigations should be conducted.[97] Although he asserts the need for further academic study of the Quran, which would facilitate a more sophisticated understanding of the ways in which it addresses gender issues, Arkoun makes the general assertion that at a minimum the Quran recognizes and encourages the dignity of the person.[98]

The second aspect of the task of analyzing and eventually addressing the status of Muslim women involves conducting precise sociological studies of the application of Muslim law in each society which could provide a refinement of the distinction between "the weight, permanence, and preeminence" of cultural and societal structures, on the one hand, and the Quran's call for human dignity on the other.[99] That is, in view of the fact that women have been the object of various exploitative strategies on the part of men throughout history, this second research task would involve analyzing the condition of women in various Muslim societies and developing methods of appropriating the Quran as a normative basis for critiquing and remedying the injustices to which women are being subjected. The specifics of how the status of women is to be concretely addressed awaits a comprehensive academic analysis of the Quran's treatment of gender issues as well as a subsequent study of the Quran's teachings and its relationship to cultural practices relating to women.[100] Nonetheless, Arkoun affirms that the transcendentalizing force of classic Islamic reason has created and legitimized socio-religious structures which have oppressed Muslim women during much of Islamic history.[101]

Mernissi and Ahmed take a much more pro-active and direct stance on women and gender issues than Arkoun. Both unequivocally state their beliefs regarding the need to combat the various religious, societal, institutional, and ideological forces which continue to oppress and marginalize Muslim women. While these two intellectuals share a similar vision about the role of women in Islam, they differ with respect to their methods and points of emphasis regarding how to achieve the goal of the equality of Muslim men and women. Ahmed's primary mode of involvement in women's issues is through her writings and public speeches, while in addition to these tasks Mernissi is actively involved in leading and consulting Muslim women's organizations in North Africa, France, and other parts of the world.[102] In addition, the emphasis in much of Ahmed's scholarly work has been on the role of women and their marginalization during Islamic history while significant portions of Mernissi's work have been devoted to sociological studies of women in modern-day North Africa as well as analyses of materials from the Quran and Hadith.[103]

Visions for Islam in the Modern World

Arkoun sets forth his vision for Islam in the present and future in terms of the concept of the ideal community. Specifically, he suggests that his vision of an ideal community is decidedly *not* related to the concept of Islam as an exclusive cultural system. This means that the sacred texts and history of Islam together with those of Judaism and Christianity can form the beginnings of a basis for an inclusive human community.[104] In presenting the positive potential of these three religions, Arkoun does not exclude the possibility that other religious traditions such as Hinduism, Buddhism, Zoroastrianism, etc. can also contribute to an ideal human community. He begins with these three traditions as a starting point because of what he perceives to be some of their historic and geographic commonalities. He is receptive to the possibility that future academic and religious discourse can incorporate the perspectives of many religions and ideologies within the framework of an ideal community.

In addition to the historical links between these three religions, they can form the beginnings of a framework for an ideal community since each has had an impact on the Mediterranean region. Arkoun believes that the promotion of understanding and peace in this region is an important first step in creating broader reconciliation.[105] Arkoun is not presenting a naive and utopian vision for the future of the Mediterranean and the world through his conception of the ideal community. Rather, he cautiously explores the avenues for dialogue among groups whose relations have often been characterized by misunderstanding and negative stereotypes.

One model of an ideal human community is the *umma muhammadiya* (the community of Muhammad) which was comprised of a group of followers and companions "initially small, weak, and threatened, that grew larger thanks to the direct help of God and the action of the Prophet, who was consistently enlightened by *wahy* [or inspiration]."[106] After the death of the Prophet, the caliphs (according to Sunni belief) and the imams (according to Shiite belief)

> piously and rigorously protected the spiritual heritage, broadened the diffusion of Islam, and consolidated for earthly history the umma's calling as repository, witness, and actor of the final revelation, given to the Seal of the Prophets (*khatam al-anbiya'*).[107]

The fact that Arkoun includes caliphs and imams in his vision of the ideal human community may seem somewhat unusual since in other sections of his works he condemns the caliphate in the Sunni tradition and the imamate in Shiism as the productions of the transcendentalizing forces of classic Islamic reason that have marginalized and oppressed many persons. However, in this discussion, Arkoun does not present these ideas as *historical facts*; rather, he presents them as *mythic representations* of the type of community which Islam *should* represent. He draws from familiar storylines, characters, and symbols within the Islamic tradition to create a self-consciously mythic picture of an ideal Muslim past that Arkoun himself is actively engaged in constructing for the purpose of presenting a paradigmatic model to his audience. Thus, Arkoun is conscious of the fact that he is intentionally drawing on images and concepts familiar to Muslims as he stylizes an Islamic past (part real, part imagined) for the purpose of creating a workable representation of Islamic history, which can function as a model for an ideal human community. Among the four Islamic modernists, Arkoun is not unique in constructing a vision for Islam's future based on its past, but his approach is unique in the sense that it explicitly takes into account the role of symbols in shaping religious identity. One of the enduring components of the Islamic mythological structure that is relevant to the discussion of an ideal human community is the unique relationship that the semiotic system of the Quran proclaims that human beings have with God. Arkoun writes:

> More than angels, jinn, or Satan, human beings are the permanent objects of God's attention. The relationship is lived, experiential, traceable to Quranic discourse, transmissible, and reproducible by this same discourse in each individual experience. Within this relationship the ideal member of the umma takes shape psychologically, spiritually, and corporally (through ritual practices). For that person, the heart is . . . the home of all the energies of the spirit (*ruh*), of the soul (*nafs*), and of the body. The Word of God resounds in the heart, and the spiritual instinct is stimulated there, insofar as other instincts are disciplined enough and trained enough to extract from the verses all the significations, the signs-symbols linking the cosmos, the external world, and profane history with God, bridging the abyss between the act of creation (by fiat, or *kun*) and the objective world so created.[108]

In constructing the foundational ideas for his conception of the ideal community, Arkoun ties the concepts of the early Muslim community with those of the individual believer, his or her relationship with the umma, and the relationship of these two entities with God. In stating his belief that human beings are the permanent objects of God's attention and that the Word of God resounds in the heart, Arkoun is emphasizing the role of the individual believer, his or her own sense of piety, and the relationship of this believer to her or his community and God.

Personal piety or personal understanding of God and his revelation is only a starting point in terms of the formation of an ideal human community. Members of this community have specific rights and obligations with respect to each other and even with respect to God. In line with this idea, Arkoun writes:

> Revelation as collected in the sacred writings contains starting points, strong roots, and carrier concepts for the emergence of the person as a subject equipped with rights and as an agent responsible for the observance of obligations toward God and peers in the political community.[109]

This idea of individuals living in community, all of whom have rights and obligations with respect to each other and to God, is one that Arkoun believes is part and parcel of the mythological structure of the Quran and of the early Muslim community.

Arkoun maintains that the contingent conditions which prevailed in seventh century Arabia (poverty, sociopolitical hierarchy based on birth, social disintegration, and a diminishing of what was formerly sacred) are transcended by the introduction of "absolute" criteria which are comprised of "the cause of God, who is one, living, just, vigilant, helping, forgiving, all-powerful, and welcoming to all those who would open their hearts and enter into the covenant."[110] Thus, the mythic images of the Quran and the early Muslim community provide a general picture and absolute basis for guiding human beings' relationships with each other and with God.

Yet this absolute basis is one which, in Arkoun's view, opposes the mutually exclusive cultural and legal systems of Judaism, Christianity, and Islam and encourages an ethos where different types of people are to live in a state of respect with each other, while honoring their obligations to one another and in living in liberty. He writes:

> The discourse of transcendence and of absoluteness opens an infinite space for the promotion of the individual beyond the constraints of fathers and brothers, clans and tribes, riches and tributes; the individual becomes an autonomous and free person, enjoying a liberty guaranteed by obedience and love lived within the alliance.[111]

Arkoun's vision of the ideal human community is not limited to Islam and Muslims, but draws on certain familiar Islamic images in order to generate possible ideas for the way in which an ideal human community could be construed.

There are several parallels between Mernissi's and Arkoun's visions of Islam for the present and future. One of the most distinctive similarities is that in addition to drawing upon the Quran and the early Muslim community as foundations for constructing their visions of Islam in the modern world they both appeal to United Nations' declarations as legitimate bases for calling upon various Muslim countries to respect human rights.[112] Mernissi calls upon governments in predominantly Muslim countries to respect the tenets of the United Nations Charter (approved in 1945) and the United Nations Declaration of Human Rights (approved in 1948), while Arkoun places similar emphasis on the Universal Islamic Declaration of Human Rights which was prepared on the initiative of the Islamic Council and announced at a UNESCO meeting in 1981.[113] Mernissi and Arkoun believe that the dictates pertaining to human rights which these documents contain are consistent with the ideas regarding the sanctity of human beings as found in the teachings of the Quran, Hadith, and early Islamic community. Arkoun is a bit more guarded in his articulation of human rights than Mernissi in that he recognizes the anachronism of imposing the idea of human rights upon the mythic structure of the Quran and historic configurations of the early Islamic community. Yet, he does seem to believe that something resembling human rights seems to emerge from the mythic renderings of the Quran and the Prophet's community. Rahman is also committed to the idea of human rights. However, his vision for Islam's future is, in many ways, tied to his hopes for Pakistan and he draws primarily upon the Quran, Hadith, and Sharia in calling for the establishment of and respect for human rights in Pakistan and other Muslim countries.[114] While Ahmed is certainly interested in human rights, her vision for Islam's future is largely based on her understanding of the model for justice and equality as found in the Quran, Hadith, the early Islamic community and in aspects of the Sufi, Kharijite, and Qarmatian movements.[115]

One pressing question with respect to Arkoun's perspectives is: Does he fall prey to the transcendentalizing forces of classic Islamic reason in his own works? Are Arkoun's ideas regarding the Prophet's role in reconfiguring semiotic systems or his conception of the Quran as carrying a mythological structure themselves products of Arkoun's own cultural ethos? Arkoun attempts to combat the difficulties that these questions raise by suggesting that there is no innocent discourse and that there is no stepping outside of history, even for the academic.[116]

The problems which these questions raise lead Arkoun toward searching for a meaning in history. Specifically, he seeks to "put back together a domain of meaning that has broken up."[117] The goal of stitching meaning together engages him in the task of analyzing the meanings which have been expressed by various Muslim communities, by non-Muslim religious traditions (particularly Judaism and Christianity), and by intellectuals during much of human history. While this multi-cultural and multi-religious endeavor itself carries the danger of Arkoun imposing cultural presuppositions upon his study (since pluralism is after all one characteristic of the current *Zeitgeist*), it is one risk he is willing to take because of his belief in the human potential to understand and create meanings that are appropriate to changing historical circumstances. Even though concepts such as human rights and justice smack of their own kind of transcendentalism, he believes that meaning for the modern age, however it is symbolically construed, should in the end be integrated with his conception of high ethical ideals.

6

CONCLUSION

Throughout much of Islamic history, Muslims have drawn on the Quran, Hadith, and various moments in the religion's history as bases for guiding their actions and constructing their worldviews. The four intellectuals that this study considers have done much the same in their works. However, one of the dimensions that makes the works of Mernissi, Ahmed, Rahman, and Arkoun unique is that they have spent extended periods of time working within two different types of societies: (1) the countries of their birth and upbringing (Morocco, Egypt, Pakistan and Algeria), where Muslims are in the majority and (2) the countries where they received their graduate education or have taught (France, the United States, Great Britain), where Muslims are in the minority. While there have been many Muslim intellectuals in the modern period who have been influenced by Islamic and Western thought (i.e., Afghani, 'Abduh, Rida, Qutb, and many others), Mernissi, Ahmed, Rahman, and Arkoun are distinctive in that they have made the bulk of their works available to Muslims and non-Muslims in Western languages and through Western presses, while also disseminating them in majority Muslim countries as well.[1] They are among the first Muslim intellectuals in modern times to write in and make their works initially available in Western languages.[2] Thus, these authors can be considered to have "dual identities" (which are not necessarily contradictory) and to be operating within a transnational ethos. This chapter analyzes the works of Mernissi, Ahmed, Rahman, and Arkoun with the following considerations in mind: (1) the roles which interpretations of the Quran, Hadith and Islamic history have played in the collective life of Muslims; (2) the relationship between modernist and Islamic revivalist strands of thought; and (3) the majority Muslim and diaspora societies within which these writers have lived and worked.

Quran, Hadith, Islamic History, and the Notion of Reflexivity

William A. Graham, in his article entitled "Traditionalism in Islam: An Essay in Interpretation." explains the crucial role which the Quran, Sunna, and appropriations of Islamic history have played in the collective and intellectual life of Muslims.[3] Graham uses the terms "traditionalism" and "Islamic traditionalism" as general notions to describe the ways in which Muslims have drawn upon and adapted "the primary, dual authority of the revelation of the Quran and the tradition or practice (Sunna) ascribed to the first few generations of Muslims."[4] In his use of these terms he intends to indicate

> the long-standing, overt predilection in diverse strands of Islamic life for recourse to previous authorities, above all the Prophet and Companions, but also later figures . . . who are perceived as having revived (*jaddada*), reformed (*aslaha*), or preserved (*hafiza*) the vision and norms of true, pristine Islam, and thus as being in continuity and connection with the original community, or umma.[5]

Graham's conceptualization of "traditionalism" and "Islamic traditionalism" provide a basis for understanding the ways in which Muslim modernists and Islamic revivalists appropriate the sacred texts and histories of their religious traditions as they construct their visions of Islam in the modern context. As they reinterpret Islam's authoritative texts to address their own concrete historical circumstances, they are engaging in a task which has a long legacy within the Islamic tradition.

Graham's observations provide one set of ideas for understanding the ways in which the interpretive tasks of modernists and Islamic revivalists fit into Islamic intellectual history. The sociologist Anthony Giddens in his work *The Consequences of Modernity* is more concerned with the ways in which human beings relate to their pasts and attempt to appropriate them to their contemporary circumstances *cross-culturally*; certain aspects of his approach are relevant to Islam.[6] In describing the ways that religious and other types of communities appropriate and understand their pasts, Giddens utilizes the term "reflexivity" and states that it is the defining characteristic of "all human action."[7] Reflexivity takes place when individuals or communities utilize their perceptions of their histories as a way of guiding their present and future actions:

> All human beings routinely 'keep in touch' with the grounds of what they do as an integral part of doing it. I [call this] the 'reflexive monitoring of action,' using the phrase to draw attention to the chronic character of the processes involved. Human action does not incorporate chains of aggregate interactions and reasons, but a consistent . . . monitoring of behavior and its contexts.[8]

Giddens notes that the above definition of reflexivity is not exclusively connected to modernity (i.e., it is a characteristic of other periods in history), but reflexivity is a necessary basis of modernity.

Giddens expresses a similar view to Graham with respect to the role of tradition when he asserts that tradition is a "mode of integrating the reflexive monitoring of action with the time-space organization of the community."[9] Tradition is a means of "handling time and space, which inserts any particular activity or experience within the community of past, present, and future, these in turn being structured by recurrent social practices."[10] In light of all this, tradition is an entity which cultures continually reconstruct:

> Tradition is not wholly static, because it has to be reinvented by each new generation as it takes over its cultural inheritance from those preceding it. Tradition does not so much resist change as pertain to a context in which there are few separated temporal and spatial markers in terms of which change can have any meaningful form.[11]

Islamic modernists and revivalists both draw on the same sacred texts and significations that emerge from those texts in articulating their messages, while members of the two groups often differ in terms of the conclusions they draw from these texts and the ways in which these conclusions are to be implemented. They are both engaged in a "reflexive" task in that they are using authoritative texts and a shared history as ways of constructing their visions for Islam and as guiding the present and future of their communities.

Whereas much of this study has focused on defining and explicating the differences between Islamic modernists and revivalists, it was made clear in Chapter One that these categories function as signposts and have provided useful markers within the study. While maintaining the usefulness of the definitions of modernism and revivalism which were presented in the first chapter and have been foundational throughout this study, it would be helpful to give some attention to the ambiguities and difficulties related to these categories.

William Graham's and Anthony Giddens' definitions of tradition-alism and reflexivity point to some of the similarities which modernists and Islamic revivalists share in terms of their general relationship to Islam's sacred texts and history. That is, while modernists and Islamic revivalists may come to different conclusions regarding what can be learned from Islam's sacred texts and history, they do agree that Islamic sacred texts and history must in some way come into play as issues pertaining to Islam are discussed. At the same time, they *reflex-ively* draw on a common religious tradition and perceive this religious tradition as forming a relevant basis for discourse about the role of Islam in the present and future. In describing this sense of connected-ness to a common history, William Graham points to the term *ittisaliya* (which he defines as "connectedness") as a way of conveying the personal connection (*ittisal*) which Muslims often feel "with the time and the personages of Islamic origins."[12] He asserts that this sense of connection is something "that has been a persistent value in Muslim thought and institutions over the centuries."[13] In addition, whereas Muslims

> have elaborated this emphasis in different ways, at different times, and in different sectors of their collective life, they have always done so in ways that are characteristic, identifiable, and central. Indeed, it is possible to discern a basic, recurrent pattern that is used to express their *ittisaliya*, and hence their traditionalism.[14]

A sense of connectedness to an Islamic past and Islamic sacred texts is another characteristic which Islamic modernism and Islamic revivalism share.

Islamic Modernism and Revivalism

While Seyyed Vali Reza Nasr accepts basic distinctions between Islamic modernism, on the one hand, and Islamic revivalism on the other, he goes so far as to argue that there is a causal linkage between modernism and Islamic revivalism. He asserts that these two strands "share much in their grounding in Western thought, syncretic outlook on religion, reliance on the fundamentals of faith, and idealization of the promise of the future based on the image of the past."[15] Indeed, Nasr contends that much of revivalist thinking is predicated on the kind of discourse which nineteenth and early twentieth century modernism originated. He believes that nineteenth and early twentieth century intellectuals such as Jamal al-Din al-Afghani, Muhammad 'Abduh, Rashid Rida, and Seyyed Ahmed Khan articulated some of the founding discourses of Islamic modernism, aspects of which later Islamic revivalists adopted.

Nasr maintains that the main impact of the Islamic modernism of these and other early Islamic modernists on later forms of Islamic revivalism was at least two-fold. First, modernism initiated the criticism of traditional (primarily ulema) Islam and "opened the door to the possibility of interpreting the religion based on a worldview alien to it."[16] Second, modernism set a precedent "for iconoclasm *vis-à-vis* history, downplaying Islam's civilizational content" and elaborating a "compendium of ideas directed at achieving an ideal that revealed a proclivity for social action."[17] Nasr goes on to show the ways in which the thought of several nineteenth century modernists fit into this two-part pattern and how the ideas of subsequent Islamic revivalists reflected this paradigm as well.[18]

While in what follows I am not interested in arguing for a causal linkage between Islamic modernism and Islamic revivalism, I am interested in utilizing Nasr's two-part paradigm for a different purpose. This model is a helpful analytical tool in coming to terms with some of the similarities in the approaches of the modernists and Islamic revivalists in my study. Specifically, Nasr's paradigm provides one means of understanding the ambiguities inherent in the use of the categories "Islamic modernism" and "Islamic revivalism."

In presenting the first similarity between modernism and revivalism, Nasr suggests that intellectuals within both of these categories criticize various aspects of Islam by interpreting the religion utilizing worldviews that are alien to Islam.[19] This observation does not suggest that Islamic revivalists and modernists use exclusively Western methodologies; rather it suggests that members of these two groups adopt both Islamic and Western-style methodologies in constructing their worldviews.

The distinctive ideas which Fatima Mernissi and Leila Ahmed utilize come from various strands of Islamic and Western feminism which they integrate with various Quranic teachings as they formulate their worldviews, which take very seriously the roles of women in Islamic history and the active part which they should play within Islam today and in the future.[20] One of the many aspects of Western intellectual history that Rahman adopts in constructing his vision emerges from what he perceives to be the West's emphasis on free and critical thinking that he believes should become a hallmark of Islamic democracies and Islamic educational systems.[21] Arkoun draws on the conceptual model of reason (his ideas on this issue carrying the echoes of voices such as Sartre and Bourdieu) as he critiques the manner in which the misapplication of Islamic reason had a deleterious effect on the interpretive methods of pre-modern Islamic legal scholars.[22]

Various individuals involved in Islamic revivalism draw upon certain Western concepts in constructing their visions of Islam for the present and future as well. Mawdudi and members of the Muslim Brotherhood in Syria (among many other revivalists) adapt Western ideas of democracy, human rights, and political revolution as they articulate their religio-political worldviews.[23]

The second observation which Nasr makes is that Islamic modernism and revivalism share an iconoclasm vis-à-vis history; they have a tendency to downplay what Nasr calls "Islam's civilizational content" and they articulate visions of Islam in terms of "a compendium of ideas directed at achieving an ideal that revealed a proclivity for social action."[24] While the four intellectuals in this study articulate their viewpoints in different ways, they all have a deeply critical attitude toward the events in Islamic history that they believe led to the hierarchization of Islamic societies and led away from what they believe to be Islam's initial call to justice and equality. Mernissi and Ahmed believe that various social, legal, and political trends which were put into motion during the Umayyad and Abbasid periods established circumstances that contributed to the oppression and marginalization of women throughout much of Islamic history.[25] Rahman believes that various social, political, and ideological structures which began to be established during the Umayyad period engendered a situation where free thinking within Islamic educational systems was discouraged and where Islam's initial impulse towards democracy was stifled.[26] Arkoun maintains that the founding of Shafiʿi's legal school of thought, together with that of other *madhabs* beginning in the late seventh and eighth centuries, contributed to a series of intellectual and political trends which absolutized rigid and authoritarian religious and political ideologies at the expense of justice and egalitarianism.[27]

In terms of what Nasr terms the modernists' and revivalists' proclivity for social action, Ahmed and Mernissi both take a strong stance on various issues that pertain to the removal of various oppressive constraints that Muslim societies continue to impose on women.[28] In terms of his orientation for social action, Rahman emphasizes the establishment of Islamic educational institutions based on freedom of thought and the introduction of "Islamically-based" democratic reforms in governments throughout much of the Islamic world.[29] In a similar fashion, Arkoun advocates the encouragement of free intellectual enquiry in Islamic societies and hopes for a future where human rights will be respected in the Muslim world and elsewhere.[30] He also tries to lay the groundwork for increased cooperation between Muslims, Jews, and Christians as well as calling for a renewal of ties between various nations and cultures which are in proximity to the Mediterranean.[31]

Members of Islamic revivalist groups criticize developments since the Umayyad period on many counts; they condemn, for instance, the emergence of circumstances which led to individuals becoming illiterate in the teachings of the Quran and Hadith and to people ignoring the social and religious obligations which these texts proclaimed. Mawdudi, for example, believed that the various periods in Islamic history after the first four caliphs can in large part be described as epochs of *jahiliyya* (ignorance), when "three quarters of the religion" was filled with defects as well as wrong beliefs and practices.[32] For Mawdudi, "most Muslims" during these times in Islamic history (led by the obscurantist and godless practices of the caliphs and members of the ulema) had abdicated their responsibilities of *'ibadat* (ritual observance) and *mu'amalat* (proper execution of social and legal transactions).[33]

Nasr's arguments regarding the similarities which modernism and Islamic revivalism share (i.e., differing means of adapting Western discourse and their downplaying of Islam's civilizational content) provide helpful counterweights to and further clarify the distinctions between Islamic revivalism and modernism which R. Stephen Humphreys describes.[34] Islamic revivalists seek to reaffirm traditional modes of understanding and behavior in a radically changed environment whereas modernists articulate the underlying moral purpose of their sacred textual tradition (believing that this purpose should be the model for the religious community). At the same time, both share similar tendencies of adapting strands of Western discourse, expressing a proclivity for social action, criticizing many aspects of Islam after the rise of the Umayyads, and utilizing often-idealized understandings of Islamic history to articulate visions for the present and future.

The Diaspora Contexts

While the above characterizations help illuminate strands of thought within Islamic societies which have shaped or stood in contradistinction to the ideas of Mernissi, Ahmed, Rahman, and Arkoun, Mustansir Mir (a diaspora Muslim scholar and Professor of Islamic Studies at Youngstown State University) presents a deft analysis of various dimensions of Islamic intellectual life in the West.[35] Mir indicates that although Muslim organizations in North America and Europe have developed mechanisms "to facilitate the performance of religious obligations like the *salat,* provide religious education to children and youth, arrange social functions, and facilitate interaction among members," they and the Muslim communities they represent have done little to establish "a solid Islamic academic tradition in the West."[36] He continues:

> Many Muslim scholars and experts who live in the West exist as individuals. Even when they come together at conferences or communicate with one another using different media, they can hardly be said to be members of a scholarly group or organization with well-defined goals and a high degree of cohesion; they are like individuals who are interested in playing football, but are not a football team.[37]

With some qualifications, this characterization describes the circumstances of the four Muslim scholars in this study. Specifically, these intellectuals have not developed a high level of cohesion with other Muslim scholars. Although Mernissi, Rahman and Arkoun have been involved in various activities with Muslim communities in different parts of the world, they have not worked with other scholars to create common goals and a common organizational structure in order to implement their ideals.[38] Neotraditionalist groups in diaspora settings (such as the Muslim Students Association) and Islamic revivalist groups within predominantly Islamic societies (such as the Muslim Brotherhood and Jamaʿat-i Islami) seem to have had far more success in influencing the opinions of Muslims within those contexts than the modernists. The greater impact of the neotraditionalist and revivalist groups within their respective contexts may well be attributable to the clarity of their messages, their high level of organization, and their unity of purpose.[39]

While Mir does not specifically cite the publications of the Islamic Society of North America nor those of the Muslim Students Association of America in his article, he believes that the literature available for Muslims in the West is "weak" and "antiquated."[40] In order to begin creating a strong Islamic academic tradition in the West that would improve Islamic education and literature, Mir suggests scholarships and funding programs for Muslim students so that they may have the opportunity to study Islam in a rigorous academic fashion. According to Mir, the vast majority of Muslim youth in the West "set their eyes on lucrative careers, generally in the fields of science, medicine, and engineering, with only a small number enrolling in humanities programs, for which, indeed, they receive little support from their parents or communities."[41] Mir states that his proposal for funding Muslim students in the West to conduct undergraduate and graduate studies in Islam could be one element which would contribute to these Muslims producing "literature based on the standard sources of Islamic religion and civilization but reflecting their own experiences and concerns."[42] Mir believes that this type of literature does not yet exist.

Ibrahim Abu Rabi', a diaspora Muslim scholar who teaches at Hartford Seminary, concurs with Mir and asserts that there has been a "whittling down of critical thinking and creative intellectual practice" among diaspora Muslims and Muslims in the Islamic world.[43] Rabi' encourages diaspora Muslim scholars and would-be diaspora Muslim scholars to become critical of their past and of "some of the erroneous notions that might still be creeping from the past."[44] This idea of Muslims being critical toward previous Muslim scholarship, is similar to that of Mernissi, Ahmed, Rahman, and Arkoun insofar as they critique the narrowness of previous scholarship within the tradition. Mernissi and Ahmed attempt to expose the weaknesses in androcentric approaches to the Quran, Hadith, and Islamic history. Arkoun critiques the pitfalls of "classic Islamic reason," while Rahman points to various aspects of decay in the medieval period which have contributed to lack of critical thinking in Islamic academic institutions. While Mir, Abu Rabi', and the four intellectuals in this study may disagree on the specific features of future Islamic academic institutions, they agree on the importance of these institutions emphasizing critical thought.

Interestingly, Mir and Abu Rabi''s critiques of Islamic education in the West appeared in *Islamic Horizons*, a magazine produced by the Islamic Society of North America and the Muslim Students Association, which are the very same organizations that produce the kind of literature for diaspora Muslims which Mir and Abu Rabi' call "disappointing" and "monolithic."[45] It remains to be seen what kind of academic tradition or traditions Muslims will establish in the West and to what degree they will incorporate modernist, neotraditionalist, or revivalists perspectives into this tradition or traditions.

A Sketch of Modern Religious Thought Across Cultures

Clearly, Muslims are not the only religious people in modern times who have attempted, in diverse ways, to adapt their sacred textual and historical traditions to the changes of modernity. Modern Jews, Christians, Hindus, and Buddhists have also appropriated their sacred texts and histories in diverging ways to address the changes which have arisen during modern times. Needless to say, it is impossible to address the complexities of these religious traditions' responses to modernity here, but I will briefly point to some salient differences among worldviews within these traditions.

In modern Judaism, for example, scholars have pointed to differing attitudes among various modern Jewish groups regarding the appropriation of their religious tradition and the tradition's relationship to politics. Samuel C. Heilman points to the "quiescent" Jews whose understanding of Torah involves "affirming the Torah in their own lives" while de-emphasizing political involvement.[46] He contrasts this type of religio-political quietism with the political activism of groups such as the Gush Emunim who have engaged in direct political action to claim "Judea and Samaria" (the West Bank) because they believe that the Torah demands they do so.[47]

In the Christian context, one could point to the diverging perspectives of such figures as liberal minister, Jesse Jackson, and conservative minister, Jerry Falwell, whose ideas represent very different trends within contemporary American Christianity. Jackson's interpretation of the Bible and Christian tradition leads him to support such political aims as universal health insurance, generous welfare programs, affirmative action, and reproductive rights.[48] Falwell interprets the same textual and religious tradition as calling for the rejection of those ideals and the affirmation of such conservative principles as prayer and the teaching of Creationism in public schools, tax breaks for parents whose children are in private schools, "pro-life" legislation, and the "sanctity of heterosexual marriage".[49]

In the Indian context, many Hindus who identify themselves with the Hindu nationalist Bharatiya Janata Party (BJP) interpret the sacred textual and historic traditions of Hinduism as containing the notion of *hindutva* which, for these Hindus, means that "everyone who has ancestral roots in India is a Hindu and that collectively they constitute a nation."[50] In contrast, Hindus who are within or empathetic to India's Congress Party generally take a more inclusive stance, often tending to interpret the Hindu tradition in such a way that more fully recognizes the uniqueness of India's religious minorities such as Muslims, Jains, Buddhists, Parsis, Christians and others.[51]

There are also Buddhists, such as Thich Nhat Hanh (who opposed American military involvement in Vietnam)[52] and the Dalai Lama (who continues to struggle against the Chinese occupation of Tibet),[53] whose understandings of Buddhism have led them to taking political action against repressive political domination. These understandings of Buddhism stand in contrast to those of some Buddhists in such places as the United States who de-emphasize the relevance of Buddhism to politics and are almost exclusively interested in Buddhist meditation, chanting, and other practices which they find personally fulfilling.[54] Thus, modern Muslims' diverging interpretations of their sacred textual and historic traditions have apparent corollaries in the responses of other religious traditions to modernity.

This study has attempted to analyze the works of four diaspora Muslim modernists and the relationship of their works to those of Muslims whose viewpoints contrast from theirs. It has endeavored to provide an understanding of some of the contours of Islamic thought in Western countries where Muslims are the minority and in societies where they are the majority. The profiles, practices, and beliefs of these Muslim communities will certainly continue to undergo change as the societies within which they are located change.

Notes

Chapter 1

1. Jonathan Z. Smith, *Imagining Religion* (University of Chicago Press, 1982), 35.
2. Clifford Geertz, *Islam Observed* (Chicago: University of Chicago Press, 1968), 4.
3. Nadia Nagie, *Fez-New York und Zurück: Fatima Mernissi, Ihre Welt und Ihre Geschichte* (Würzburg: Ergon Verlag, 1992), 44–48; Fatima Mernissi, "The Effects of Modernization on the Male-Female Dynamics in a Muslim Society: Morocco" (Ph.D. diss, Brandeis University, 1974). The revised version of Mernissi's dissertation was published as *Beyond the Veil: Male-Female Dynamics in a Modern Muslim Society* (Cambridge, Massachusetts: Schenkman Publishing Company, 1975).
4. Nagie, 46–47.
5. Ursula Günther, *Die Frau in der Revolte: Fatima Mernissis feministische Gesellschaftskritik* (Hamburg: Deutsches Orient-Institut, 1993), 22–26; *Oxford Encyclopedia of the Modern Islamic World*, s.v. "Mernissi, Fatima."
6. www.mernissi.net, www.mernissi.net/about_me.html and other links within Mernissi's website describe these projects.
7. Nagie, 89.
8. Ibid.
9. Fatima Mernissi, *Beyond the Veil: Male-Female Dynamics in Modern Muslim Society* (Bloomington: Indiana University Press, 1987); idem, *Women and Islam: An Historical and Theological Enquiry*, trans. Mary Jo Lakeland (Oxford: Basil Blackwell, 1991); idem, *Islam and Democracy: Fear of the Modern World*, trans. Mary Jo Lakeland (New York: Addison-Wesley Publishing, 1992) idem, *The Forgotten Queens of Islam*, trans. Mary Jo Lakeland (Minneapolis: University of Minnesota Press,

1993); *Scheherazade Goes West: Different Cultures, Different Harems* (New York: Washington Square Press, 2001).

10. *Oxford Encyclopedia of the Modern Islamic World*, s.v. "Mernissi, Fatima."

11. Ibid. Mernissi's Arabic writings have been published by presses in North Africa and Lebanon.

12. Mernissi's "Fundamentalist Obsession with Women" (Lahore, Pakistan: Simorgh Women's Resource and Publication Centre, 1987) was published as "Muslim Women and Fundamentalism" which is the Introduction to the revised edition of *Beyond the Veil* (Bloomington, Indiana: Indiana University Press, rev. ed., 1987), vii–xxx. "Sufis, Saints and Sanctuaries" (Lahore, Pakistan: Simorgh Women's Resource and Publication Centre, 1988) was published as an article under the same title in the Western academic journal *Signs* 31 (Autumn 1977): 101–112. "Women in Muslim History: Traditional Perspectives and New Strategies" (Lahore, Pakistan: Simorgh Women's Resource and Publication Centre, 1989) was published under the same title as a chapter in S. Jay Kleinberg's edited volume *Retrieving Women's History: Changing Perceptions of the Role of Women in Politics and Society* (New York: Berg Publishers, 1988).

13. Leila Ahmed, "The Works of Edward William Lane and Ideas of the Near East in England 1800–1850: The Transformation of an Image" (Ph.D. diss., Cambridge University, 1970). The revised version of this dissertation was published under the title *Edward W. Lane: A Study of His Life and Works and of British Ideas of the Middle East in the Nineteenth Century* (New York: Longman, 1978). Gillian Beer has written extensively in the field of seventeenth through nineteenth century British literature. Her works include *Meredith: A Change of Masks, A Study of the Novels* (London: Athlone, 1970); *The Romance* (London: Methuen, 1970); *Darwin's Plots: Evolutionary Narrative in Darwin, George Eliot, and Nineteenth-Century Fiction* (London: Ark Paperbacks, 1985); *Virginia Woolf: The Common Ground, Essays by Gillian Beer* (Edinburgh: Edinburgh University Press, 1996); *Open Fields: Science in Cultural Encounter* (Oxford, Clarendon Press, 1996). Elisabeth Leedham-Green, Deputy Keeper of the Cambridge University Archives, provided valuable information about Leila Ahmed's academic background at Cambridge.

14. "Notes On Contributors" in *Arabian and Islamic Studies: Articles Presented to R.B. Serjeant on the Occasion of His Retirement from the Sir Thomas Adams Chair of Arabic at the University of Cambridge* (London: Longman, 1983), 280–281. I discuss the impact of Beer, Serjeant, and Arberry on Ahmed's work in Chapter Three.

15. "Biographical Note" in Leila Ahmed, "Feminism and Feminist Movements in the Middle East, A Preliminary Exploration: Turkey, Egypt, Algeria, People's Democratic Republic of Yemen," *Women's Studies International Forum* 5, no. 2 (1982): 153–168 and www.hds.harvard.edu/dpa/faculty/wo/ahmed.html.

16. Significant works by Leila Ahmed include *Edward W. Lane: A Study of His Life and Works and Of British Ideas of the Middle East in the Nineteenth Century* (New York: Longman, 1978), *Women and Gender in Islam: Historical Roots of a Modern Debate* (New Haven: Yale University Press, 1992), *A Border Passage: From Cairo to America—A Woman's Journey* (New York: Farrar, Straus and Giroux, 1999). Additional biographical information was found in the *Middle East Studies Association of North America: 1994 Roster of Members*.

17. The biographical information is from the *Oxford Encyclopedia of the Modern Islamic World*, s.v. "Rahman, Fazlur"; Fazlur Rahman, *Islamic Methodology in History* (Karachi: Central Institute of Islamic Research, 1965); idem, *Major Themes of the Quran* (Minneapolis: Biblioteca Islamica, 1980); idem, *Avicenna's Psychology* (Westport, Connecticut: Hyperion Press, 1981); idem, *Islam and Modernity: Transformation of an Intellectual Tradition* (Chicago: University of Chicago Press, 1982); idem, *Revival and Reform in Islam: A Study of Islamic Fundamentalism* (Oxford: Oneworld, 2000).

18. Fazlur Rahman, "*Avicenna's Psychology*" (Ph.D. diss., Oxford University, 1949). This dissertation was subsequently published as *Avicenna's Psychology* (London: Oxford University Press, 1952). In correspondence with the author, Drs. Tamara Sonn and Frederick Denny, former Ph.D. students of Rahman at the University of Chicago, provided very helpful information about Rahman's academic background.

19. Donald Lee Berry, "The Thought of Fazlur Rahman as an Islamic Response to Modernity" (Ph.D. Diss., The Southern Baptist Theological Seminary, 1990), 53. See also Donald Berry's "Fazlur Rahman: A Life in Review" in *The Shaping of An American Islamic Discourse: A Memorial to Fazlur Rahman*, eds. Earle H. Waugh and Frederick M. Denny (Atlanta, Georgia: Scholars Press, 1998).

20. Berry, "The Thought of Fazlur Rahman," 53.

21. Rahman, "Some Islamic Issues in the Ayyub Khan Era," *Essays on Islamic Civilization* (Leiden: E.J. Brill, 1976), 285.

22. Rahman provides a brief first-hand account of his life and work in Philip L. Berman's *The Courage of Conviction* (New York: Dodd, Mead and Company, 1985), 153–159. Berman's book contains short personal autobiographies from thirty-two well-known twentieth century figures from various walks of life including Joan Baez, Mario Cuomo, the Dalai Lama, Hugh Downs, Billy Graham, and Lech Walesa.

23. Frederick Denny, "The Legacy of Fazlur Rahman," in *The Muslims of America*, ed. Yvonne Yazbeck Haddad (New York: Oxford University Press, 1991), 97.

24. Fazlur Rahman's journal *Islamic Studies* was available in Pakistan. His *Islamic Methodology in History* (Karachi: Iqbal Academy, 1965) and *Intikhabat-i maktubat-i Shaykh Ahmad Sirhindi: Selected Letters of Shaykh Ahmad Sirhindi* (Karachi: Iqbal Academy 1968) were published

through Pakistani presses. Several of his other works have been translated into Arabic, Indonesian, Serbo-Croat, and Turkish. See bibliography for more details.

25. The biographical information may be found in the *Oxford Encyclopedia of the Modern Islamic World*, s.v. "Arkoun, Mohammed"; Mohammed Arkoun, *Lectures du Coran* (Paris: Editions G.-P. Maisonneuve et Larose, 1982); idem, *La Pensé Arabe* (Paris: Presses Universitaires de France, 1991); *Ouvertures sur l'Islam* (Paris: J. Granchet, 1992) and *The Unthought in Contemporary Islamic Thought* (London: Saqi Publishers, 2002). *Ouvertures sur l'Islam* is published in English under the title *Rethinking Islam: Common Questions Uncommon Answers*, trans. Robert D. Lee (Boulder, Colorado: Westview Press, 1994).

26. www.iis.ac.uk/research/academic_publications/arkoun.htm.

27. Robert D. Lee, foreword to *Rethinking Islam*, op. cit., viii.

28. Ibid.

29. Mohammed Arkoun, *Traité d'ethique*. Translation of Ahmad ibn Muhammad ibn Miskawayh's *Tahdhib al-akhlaq*. (Ph.D. diss., Sorbonne University, 1969). This dissertation was published as *Traité d'ethique: traduction française avec introduction et notes du Tahdhib al-akhlaq de Miskawayh*. (Damascus: Institut Française, 1969; 2nd ed., 1988).

30. Arkoun's writings which have been translated into Arabic include: *Al-fikr al-islami: qira'a 'ilmiyya*, a translation of various essays first published in French, (Beirut: Markaz al-Inma al-Qawmi, 1986); *Tarikhiyyat al-fikr al-'arabiyy al-islamiyy*, a translation of various essays first published in French, Beirut: Markaz al-Inma al-Qawmi, 1986; *Al-fikr al-'arabi*, Arabic translation of *La pensée arabe*, (Beirut, Dar al-Saqi, 1990); *Min faysal al-tafriqa ila fasl al-maqal: 'ayna huwa al-fikr al-islamiyya al-mu'asir*, a translation by Hachem Salah of essays originally published in French, (Beirut: Dar al-Saqi, 1992). Information about publication in the other languages was made available through correspondence between the author and Mohammed Arkoun in November 1995.

31. Robert D. Lee, *Overcoming Tradition and Modernity: The Search for Islamic Authenticity* (Boulder, Colorado: Westview Press, 1997), 163–164. See also "Quelques tâches de l'intellectuel musulman aujord'hui," in *Cahiers de la Méditerranée*, 125 (1988), 25.

32. Robert Bellah, et al., *Habits of the Heart: Individualism and Commitment in American Life*. (Berkeley: University of California Press, 1985), 153–154, 213, 249, 251–252.

33. Martin Luther King, Jr., "I Have A Dream," in *I Have A Dream: Writing and Speeches that Changed the World*, James M. Washington, ed. (San Francisco: Harper San Francisco, 1992), 101–106.

34. Mernissi, *The Veil and the Male Elite*, 26.

35. Ibid., 42.

36. Ahmed, *Women and Gender in Islam*, 64–65.

37. Ibid., 65.

38. For Ahmed's relatively empathetic stance regarding veiling, see *Women and Gender in Islam*, 244ff. Ahmed discusses "the coercive patriarchal environment" which necessitates veiling in "Arab Women: 1995" in *The Next Arab Decade* Hisham Sharabi, ed. (Boulder, Colorado: Westview Press, 1988).

39. Rahman, *Islam*, 12.

40. Rahman resisted Hans-Georg Gadamer's notion that knowledge is shaped by our epistemological prejudices. Rahman was convinced that his "double movement theory" of Quranic interpretation was a more stable and valid method. For a detailed discussion of this topic, see Rahman's *Islam and Modernity*, 8–11 and Ebrahim Moosa's introduction to Rahman's *Revival and Reform in Islam*, 20ff.

41. Ibid., 239–240.

42. Ibid., 237.

43. Ibid., 240ff.

44. Robert D. Lee, "Foreword" in *Rethinking Islam*, vii–xiii.

45. One seminal piece with respect to categories of modern Islamic thought is R. Stephen Humphreys' "Islam and Political Values in Saudi Arabia, Egypt and Syria," *Middle East Journal* 33 (Winter 1979): 1–19. There has been substantial debate in academic circles about the value of the terms "Islamic revivalism," "Islamism" or "Islamic fundamentalism" in referring to this current within Islam. I have chosen "Islamic fundamentalism" because it may prove least confusing to a general readership. For perspectives on this topic see: John L. Esposito, *The Islamic Threat: Myth or Reality?* (New York: Oxford University Press, 1999), 5–8; R. Scott Appleby "But All Crabs Are Crabby: Valid and Less Valid Criticisms of The Fundamentalism Project," *Contention* 4, 3 (Spring 1995): 198; Juan Eduardo Campo, "The Ends of Islamic 'Fundamentalism': Hegemonic Discourse and the Islamic Question in Egypt," *Contention* 4, 3 (Spring 1995): 167–195; Mark Juergensmeyer, *The New Cold War? Religious Nationalism Confronts the Secular State* (Berkeley: University of California Press, 1993), 4–5; Martin Marty and Scott Appleby, *Fundamentalisms Observed* (Chicago: University of Chicago Press, 1991), ix–x, 835; William Shepard, "'Fundamentalism': Christian and Islamic," *Religion* 17 (October 1987): 355–378; Bruce Lawrence and Azim Nanji, "Response to the Critiques of 'Fundamentalism: Christian and Islamic,'" *Religion* 19 (July 1989): 285–292.

46. See Humphreys, "Islam and Political Values," 1–19. Some works of Islamic revivalists which address issues pertaining to the Quran are: Sayyid Qutb's *In The Shade of the Quran* (Alexandria, Virginia: Al-Saadawi Publications, 1997) and Sayyid Abu'l-A'la Mawdudi's *Introduction to the Study of the Quran* (Delhi: Maktaba Jama'at-i Islami Hind, 1971). Abdur Rahman I. Doi, a popular neotraditionalist intellectual who taught at the University of Nova Scotia and whose books are available through such places as the Islamic Book Service and Islamic Books and Tapes

International, wrote *Introduction to the Quran* (London: Arewa Books, 1981), which cites the works of Qutb and takes a similar approach to the Quran as he and other Islamic Revivalists.

47. Sayyid Abu'l-A'la Mawdudi in his *Islam: An Historical Perspective*, trans. Ashraf Abu Turab (Leicester: Islamic Foundation, 1974) and Hassan Hathout, a popular Egyptian-born Muslim diaspora writer who is a physician and practices medicine in the United States, in his *Reading the Muslim Mind* (Plainfield, Indiana: American Trust Publications, 1995) both ascribe perfection to the Prophet and the first four caliphs.

48. Mawdudi in his *Purdah and the Status of Women In Islam* (Lahore: Islamic Publications, 1972) is adamant in his support of Muslim women wearing the veil. Huda L. Khattab—a British Muslim writer, author of Muslim children's books, and editor of the Muslim monthly newsletter *Usra*—and Abdur Rahman I. Doi in his *Women In Shariah* (London: Ta-Ha Publishers, 1996) are two of many neotraditionalist writers who favor the wearing of the veil by Muslim women.

49. Mawdudi criticizes many aspects of Western scholarship in *The Religion of Truth* (Delhi: Markazi Maktaba Jama'at-i Islami Hind, 1972) as does neotraditionalist writer Abdul Qader Audah, a leader in the International Islamic Federation of Student Organizations, in his *Islam: Between Ignorant Followers and Incapable Scholars* (Plainfield, Indiana: American Trust Publishers, 1994).

50. Works by Jamal Badawi include *Muhammed in the Bible* (Halifax, Nova Scotia: Islamic Information Foundation, 1982), *The Muslim Woman's Dress: According to the Quran and Sunnah* (London: Ta-Ha Publishers, 1982), and *Gender Equity in Islam: Basic Principles* (Plainfield, Indiana: American Trust Publications, 1995). Works by Abdur Rahman I. Doi include *Hadith: Traditions of Prophet Muhammad: An Introduction* (Chicago: Kazi Publications, 1980), *The Cardinal Principles of Islam According to the Maliki System* (Zaria, Nigeria: Hudahuda Publishing Company, 1981) and *Woman in Shariah* (London: Ta-Ha Publishers, 1987); Suzanne Haneef's works include *Islam: the Path of God* (Chicago, Kazi Publications: 1996) and *What Everyone Should Know About Islam and Muslims* (Chicago, Kazi Publications: 1996). Hassan Hathout's works include *Hajj Pilgrimage: Form and Essence* (Kuwait: Scientific Research House, 1972), *Topics in Islamic Medicine* (Kuwait: International Organisation of Islamic Medicine, 1984), and *Reading the Muslim Mind*, (Plainfield, Indiana: American Trust Publications, 1995); Huda L. Khattab's works include: *The Muslim Woman's Handbook* (London: Ta-Ha Publishers, 1993), *Feminism and Muslim Women* (London: Ta-Ha Publishers, 1996), *Stories from the Muslim World* (London: Ta-Ha Publishers, 1996), *Bent Rib: A Journey Through Women's Issues in Islam* (London: Ta-Ha Publishers, 1997); Sulaiman Mufassir, *Biblical Studies from a Muslim Perspective* (Washington, D.C.: Islamic Center, 1973), *Jesus in the Quran* (India-

napolis, Indiana: American Trust Publications, 1993); *Jesus, A Prophet of Islam* (Indianapolis, Indiana: American Trust Publications, 1993).

51. For example, Amana Publications in Beltsville, Maryland (www.amana-publications.com), Kazi Publications in Chicago, Illinois (www.kazi.com), and Ta-Ha Publishers in London, England (www.taha.co.uk) carry works by Muslim neotraditionalist and Islamic revivalist writers.

52. Adur Rahman I. Doi in his *Woman in Shariah* cites Mawdudi's and Khurshid Ahmad's works several times in support of his arguments. (Ahmad was another important leader in Mawdudi's Jamaʾat-i Islami). See *Woman in Shariah*, 191 n. 4, 193 n. 16, 197 n. 13. Huda Khattab in *The Muslim Woman's Handbook* also cites Mawdudi; see p. 65 of her book.

53. One scholar who has written on the transnational character of certain movements within contemporary Judaism, Christianity, and Islam is Gilles Kepel in *The Revenge of God: The Resurgence of Islam, Christianity, and Judaism in the Modern World* (University Park, Pennsylvania: Pennsylvania State University Press, 1994). There are several articles on the transnational character of Hindu nationalist movements in the special issue of *Ethnic and Racial Studies* entitled *Hindutva Movements in the West: Resurgent Hinduism and the Politics of Diaspora*, Parita Mukta and Chetan Bhatt, Guest Co-editors, 23, no. 3 (May 2000).

Chapter 2

1. Fatima Mernissi, *Beyond the Veil* (Bloomington: Indiana University Press, 1987), xii.

2. Mernisssi refers to the works of Western feminists in *Beyond the Veil* and in her dissertation. Although she shies away from direct reference to these scholars in the text of her dissertation, Mernissi cites the following writings, which have a variety of feminist leanings, in her bibliography: Betty Friedan, *The Feminine Mystique* (New York: Dell Publishing Company, 1964); Robin Fox, *Kinship and Marriage* (New York: Pelican Books, 1967); Ashley Montagu, *The Natural Superiority of Women* (New York: Collier Books, 1970); Kate Millet, *Sexual Politics* (New York: Avon Books, 1971); idem, *The Prostitution Papers* (New York, Avon Books, 1973). For these references, see Mernissi, "The Effects of Modernization on the Male-Female Dynamics in a Muslim Society: Morocco," 271–285. In *Beyond the Veil*, Mernissi also makes passing reference to Una Stannard "Adam's Rib or the Woman Within," *Transaction* 8 (November–December 1970): 24–36 and Gertrude Stern, *Marriage in Early Islam* (London: The Royal Asiatic Society, 1939). For these references, see *Beyond the Veil*, 182 n. 28, 185 n. 37.

3. Mernissi, "The Effects of Modernization on the Male-Female Dynamics in a Muslim Society: Morocco," 7. Mernissi critiques certain

aspects of Qasim's thought and affirms others while addressing the ideas of Salama Musa in *Beyond the Veil*, 13–14, 180–181, 187.

4. Mernissi, "The Effects of Modernization," 7. Mernissi cites Salama Musa's *Woman Is Not the Plaything of Man* (Cairo: n.p., 1955) and Qasim Amin's *The Liberation of Women* (Cairo: n.p., 1928).

5. Mernissi, "The Effects of Modernization," 7–9.

6. Mernissi, *Women in Muslim History: Traditional Perspectives and New Strategies.* (Lahore: Women's Resource and Publication Center, 1986), 8, n. 5.

7. Mernissi as quoted in Nadia Nagie, *Fez-New York und zurück: Fatima Mernissi, ihre Welt und ihre Geschichte* (Würzburg: Ergon Verlag, 1992), 53–54.

8. Ibid.

9. Ibid., 53. Leila Ahmed makes very similar observations about Western feminists' "dress codes" in *A Border Passage*, 295.

10. Mernissi, *Beyond the Veil*, 168.

11. Mernissi, *The Forgotten Queens of Islam* (Minneapolis, Minnesota: University of Minnesota Press), 117.

12. Ibid., 1–5.

13. This quotation is taken from Marmaduke Pickthall, *The Meaning of the Glorious Koran* (New York: Mentor Books, n.d.): Sura 33:35. Mernissi quotes this translation in *The Veil and the Male Elite*.

14. Mernissi, *The Veil and the Male Elite*, 118–119.

15. Sherifa Zuhur, *Revealing Reveiling: Islamist Gender Ideology in Contemporary Egypt* (Albany: State University of New York Press, 1992), 59ff.

16. Ibid.

17. Ibid.

18. Ibid.

19. Barbara Freyer Stowasser, *Women in the Quran, Traditions and Interpretation* (New York: Oxford University Press, 1994), 93.

20. Jennifer Scarce, *Women's Costume of the Near and Middle East* (London: Unwin Hyman, 1987).

21. Ibid., 85ff.

22. Mernissi maintains that one way which the Prophet expressed his original egalitarian vision for the community was through the structure of the first mosque he built in Medina in 622. This mosque allowed his wives and others in the community relatively unencumbered access and was emblematic of the egalitarianism he originally intended for his community (Mernissi, *The Veil and the Male Elite*, 106–109).

23. Ibid., 86–87. Mernissi cites al-Tabari, *Tafsir* (Dar al-Maʿrifa, vol. 22), 26.

24. Mernissi, *The Veil and the Male Elite*, 86–87.

25. Sura 33:54, 59–60 from *The Koran*. N.J. Dawood, trans. (New York: Penguin Books, 1993).

26. Sura 24:31 states "Enjoin believing women to turn their eyes away from temptation and to preserve their chastity; to cover their adornments

(except such as are normally displayed); to draw their veils over their bosoms and not to reveal their finery except to their husbands, their fathers, their husbands' fathers, their sons, their step-sons, their brothers, their brothers' sons, their sisters' sons, their women servants, and their slave-girls; male attendants lacking in natural vigour, and children who have no carnal knowledge of women." (*The Koran.* N.J. Dawood, trans.)

27. *The Veil and the Male Elite,* 85–101.
28. Ibid., 85–89.
29. Ibid., 92.
30. Ibid.
31. Ibid., 89.
32. Ibid., 89–92.
33. Ibid., 92
34. Ibid.
35. Ibid., 91–92.
36. Ibid., 92.
37. Ibid., 180.
38. Ibid., 187.
39. Ibid., 101.
40. Barbara Freyer Stowasser, *Women in the Quran, Traditions, and Interpretation* (New York: Oxford University Press, 1994), 134.
41. Humphreys, *Islam and Political Values,* 4–5; Mernissi, *The Veil and the Male Elite,* 92.
42. Gutbi Mahdi Ahmed, "Muslim Organizations in the United States," in *The Muslims of America,* Yvonne Haddad, ed. (New York: Oxford University Press, 1991): 16–18.
43. Nazhat Afza and Khurshid Ahmed, *The Position of Woman in Islam* (Safat, Kuwait and Singapore: Karamatullah Shaykh Islamic Book Publishers, 1993). The ideas which the authors of these works express about the veil are similar to those of Islamic revivalists in North Africa. In *The Islamic Movement in North Africa,* François Burgat and William Dowell record the "pro-veiling" positions of some North African men and women; see François Burgat and William Dowell, *The Islamic Movement in North Africa* (Austin, Texas: Center for Middle Eastern Studies at The University of Texas at Austin), 100–108. I have chosen to discuss the ideas from the above-mentioned diaspora writers because they provide very detailed and extensive rationale for their stance on the veil.
44. Khattab, *The Muslim Woman's Handbook,* backcover and 15–22.
45. See, for example, Jamal A. Badawi, *The Muslim Woman's Dress* (Plainfield, Indiana: Islamic Book Service, n.d.) and B. 'A'isha Lemu and Fatima Heeren, *Woman in Islam* (Leicester, U.K.: The Islamic Foundation, 1992), 25–26, 49–51.
46. Khattab, 15ff.
47. Khattab cites Badawi's *The Muslim Woman's Dress* and another publication by Abu Bilal Mustafa al-Kanadi *The Islamic Ruling Regarding Wom-*

en's Dress According to the Quran and Sunnah (Jeddah, Saudi Arabia: Abul-Qasim Publishing House: 1991/1411 A.H.) both of which are available through the the Islamic Society of North America's retail arm, the Islamic Book Service.

48. Khattab, *The Muslim Woman's Handbook*, 15–17.
49. Ibid., p. 17.
50. Ibid.
51. Stowasser, *Women in the Quran, Traditions and Interpretation,* 92–93; Zuhur, *Revealing Reveiling,* 29, 77.
52. Khattab, *The Muslim Woman's Handbook,* 18.
53. Khattab is not alone in affirming that women veiling themselves *and* pursuing careers is fully consistent with Islamic teaching. Suzanne Haneef, in her book *What Everyone Should Know About Islam and Muslims* p. 170, makes very similar assertions, "People often suppose that it must be very difficult or impossible to move about freely or do work clad in such a dress. This is not the case, as the vast numbers of Muslim women of all levels and walks of life who wear such clothing in virtually every country of the world can testify. Today numerous high school and university students, teachers, doctors and other women who hold important and responsible jobs in all areas are voluntarily adopting Islamic dress as being a vital expression of their Islamic identity. They lead very active and busy lives, *hijab* constituting no impediment."
54. Doi, *Woman in Shariah,* 14, 21–22.
55. Ibid., "About the Author" section on backcover of *Woman in Shariah.*
56. ʿAʾisha Lemu and Fatima Heeren, *Woman in Islam,* 14–16 and 25–26; Jamal A. Badawi, *The Muslim Woman's Dress,* 3–18; Mohammad Mazheruddin Siddiqui, *Women In Islam* (Delhi, India: Islamic Book Trust, 1981): 102–106; Suzanne Haneef, *What Everyone Should Know About Islam and Muslims* (Chicago: Kazi Publications, 1995): 168–170.
57. See for example Haneef, *What Everyone Should Know About Islam and Muslims,* 168.
58. Ibn Saʿd, *al-Tabaqat,* vol. 8, 166 as quoted in Mernissi, *The Veil and the Male Elite,* 107.
59. Mernissi, *The Veil and the Male Elite,* 107–108. As evidence for her stance Mernissi cites Ibn Saʿd's *Al-Tabaqat al-kubra,* Vol. 8 (Beirut: Dar Sadir, n.d.), 166. Another significant early source provides a similar account; see al-Tabari, *The Foundation of the Community: Muhammad at al-Madina,* vol. 7 of The *History of al-Tabari,* trans. W. Montgomery Watt (Albany: State University of New York Press, 1987), 4–5.
60. This seems to be Mernissi's particular interpretation; cf. W. Montgomery Watt, Translator's Foreward to *The Foundation of the Community: Muhammad at al-Madina,* xvi–xvii and al-Tabari, *The Foundation of the Community,* 4–5.
61. Mernissi, *The Veil and the Male Elite,* 113–114.
62. Mernissi, *Beyond the Veil,* 19.

63. Ibid.
64. Ibid., 32–33. Mernissi cites al-Ghazali, *The Revivification of Religious Sciences*, vol. 2, chapter on Marriage.
65. Mernissi, *Beyond the Veil*, 32 and 33.
66. Qasim Amin, *The Liberation of Women*, (Cairo: n.p., 1928), 18 as cited in Mernissi, *Beyond the Veil*, 31.
67. Mernissi, *Beyond the Veil*, 143–144. Ahmed makes very similar observations about the appropriations of space in Abu Dhabi in *A Border Passage*, 284–285.
68. Ibid., 97.
69. Ibid., 138.
70. For more elaboration on this point see Ursula Günther, *Die Frau in der Revolte: Fatima Mernissis feministische Gesellschaftskritik* (Hamburg: Deutsches Orient Institut, 1993), 64ff.
71. The verses of Sura 33:53–62 which have been interpreted as pertaining directly to the veiling of Muslim women read: "O ye who believe! Enter not the dwellings of the Prophet for a meal without waiting for the proper time, unless permission be granted you. But if ye are invited, enter, and when, when your meal is ended, then disperse. Linger not for conversation. Lo! That would cause annoyance to the Prophet, and he would be shy of (asking) you (to go); but Allah is not shy of the truth. And when ye ask the wives of the Prophet anything, ask it of them from behind a curtain. That is purer for your hearts and for their hearts. And it is not for you to cause annoyance to the messenger of Allah, not that ye should ever marry his wives after him. Lo! that in Allah's sight would be an enormity. . . . It is no sin for thy wives to converse with their fathers, or their sons, or their brothers, or their brothers' sons, or the sons of their sisters or of their own women, or their slaves. O women! Keep your duty to Allah. Lo! Allah is witness over all things. salute him with with a worthy salutation. . . . O Prophet! Tell thy wives and thy daughters and the women of the believers to draw their cloaks close round them when they go abroad. That will be better, that so they may be recognized and not annoyed. Allah is ever forgiving, merciful. . . . " (Quotation from Mohammed Marmaduke Pickthall's *The Meaning of the Glorious Koran*. New York: New American Library, 1953. This is the translation which Mernissi utilizes in her works).
72. Mernissi, *Islam and Democracy: Fear of the Modern World* (Reading, Massachusetts: Addison-Wesley, 1992), 64–65.
73. Ibid., 62–65.
74. Mernissi, *Forgotten Queens of Islam*, 75.
75. Ibid., 76.
76. Ibid., 79.
77. Mernissi, *Islam and Democracy*, 62–63.
78. Ibid.
79. Ibid., 66.

80. John Esposito, *The Islamic Threat: Myth or Reality?*, 186.
81. "Proclamation of Syria's Muslim Brotherhood" in Umar F. Abdallah, *The Islamic Struggle in Syria* (Berkeley: Mizan Press, 1983), 214–218.
82. Ibid., 214.
83. Ibid., 214–218.
84. Ibid., 215.
85. Ibid.
86. Ibid., 216.
87. Ibid., 247.
88. Ibid.
89. Mernissi, *The Fundamentalist Obsession with Women: A Current Articulation of Class Conflict in Modern Muslim Societies.* (Lahore, Pakistan: Simorgh Women's Resource and Publication Centre, 1987), 5–6.
90. Ann Elizabeth Mayer, *Islam and Human Rights: Tradition and Politics* (Boulder, Colorado: Westview Press, 1995), 79–92.
91. Ibid., 79.
92. Ibid.
93. Ibid., 80.
94. Ibid.
95. Ibid.
96. "Proclamation of Syria's Muslim Brotherhood," 247.
97. Mayer, *Islam and Human Rights*, 80.
98. Mernissi, *Islam and Democracy*, 62–63, 68–73.
99. Mernissi, as quoted in Günther, *Die Frau in der Revolte*, 117.
100. Ibid.
101. Ibid., 113. Italics added for emphasis.

Chapter 3

1. Ahmed, *Women and Gender in Islam: Historical Roots of a Modern Debate* (New Haven: Yale University Press, 1992), 64. Ahmed puts her egalitarian vision for Islam in the context of her life in *A Border Passage*, 123–131.
2. Ibid., 65.
3. Ibid., 65ff.
4. Ibid., 65–66.
5. Ibid., 66.
6. Ibid.
7. Ibid.
8. Ibid.
9. Ibid., 67.
10. Ahmed, "Feminism and Feminist Movements in the Middle East, A Preliminary Exploration: Turkey, Egypt, Algeria, People's Democratic

Republic of Yemen," *Women's Studies International Forum* 5, no. 2 (1982): 162.

11. Ibid.

12. Ibid., 162–163.

13. Ibid., 163.

14. Ibid., 162.

15. Ahmed cites Joan W. Scott's "Gender: A Useful Category of Historical Analysis," *American Historical Review* 91, no. 5 (1986): 1053–75; see Ahmed, *Women and Gender in Islam*, 2.

16. Ahmed cites Nancy F. Cott, *The Grounding of Modern Feminism* (New Haven: Yale University Press, 1987) and Judith Butler, *Gender Trouble: Feminism and the Subversion of Identity*, (New York: Routledge, 1990); see Ahmed, *Women and Gender in Islam*, 7.

17. Works which provide some background regarding Ahmed's approach to Middle Eastern strands of feminism are "Feminism and Feminist Movements in the Middle East, A Preliminary Exploration: Turkey, Egypt, Algeria, People's Democratic Republic of Yemen," *Women's Studies International Forum* 5, no. 2 (1982): 153–168 and "Between Two Worlds: The Formation of a Turn-of-the-Century Egyptian Feminist," in *Life/Lines: Theorizing Women's Autobiography*, eds. Bella Brodzki and Celeste Schenk (Ithaca: Cornell University Press, 1998) which examines the life and thought of Huda Sha'rawi. Ahmed also discusses the influences of Sha'rawi, al-Ghazali, and Shafik on her life in *A Border Passage*, 95ff, 122ff, and 154ff. She elaborates on her relationship with Western feminism in *A Border Passage*, 291–296.

18. Ahmed, *Women and Gender in Islam*, 176.

19. Ibid.

20. Ibid.

21. Ibid., 180–181.

22. Ibid., 197.

23. Ibid.

24. Zeynab al-Ghazali, *Ayam min hayati* (Cairo: Dar al-Shuruq, n.d.), 26. Ahmed cites this passage in *Women and Gender in Islam*, 198.

25. Zeynab al-Ghazali, *Ayam min hayati*, 235–236. Ahmed cites this passage in *Women and Gender in Islam*, 198.

26. Ahmed, *Women and Gender in Islam*, 203.

27. Ibid.

28. This quote is from Shafik as contained in Cynthia Nelson's "The Voice of Doria Shafik: Feminist Consciousness in Egypt, 1940–1960," *Feminist Issues* 6, no. 2 (1986): 16. See Ahmed, *Women and Gender in Islam*, 205.

29. Ahmed, *Women and Gender in Islam*, 206.

30. Ahmed expresses her belief regarding Sha'rawi's and Shafik's prejudices in this regard in *Women and Gender in Islam*, 176–179 and 202–203.

31. Ahmed, "Western Ethnocentrism and Perceptions of the Harem" 8, no. 3 (Fall 1982): 526. Ahmed describes the experiences she was having in

America at the time she wrote this piece and further elucidates her position on these issues in *A Border Passage*, 291–297.

32. Ahmed notes the influence of these individuals in *Edward W. Lane: A Study of His Life and Works*, v and in *A Border Passage*, 208. She also discusses the influence of British literature on her intellectual life in *A Border Passage*, 14.

33. Ibid., v. For references to some of Ahmed's works on Islamic history see n. 18, 29, and 32 above.

34. Ahmed, *Edward W. Lane: A Study of His Life and Works*, v.

35. Ahmed, *A Border Passage*, 231.

36. Ahmed, *A Border Passage*, 222, 231–233.

37. Ibid., 231–233.

38. For additional biographical information on Ahmed see her autobiography *A Border Passage: From Cairo to America—A Woman's Journey*, the biographical note in her article "Feminism and Feminist Movements in the Middle East, A Preliminary Exploration: Turkey, Egypt, Algeria, People's Democratic Republic of Yemen," 135 and in the "Notes on Contributors" in *Arabian and Islamic Studies: Articles Presented to R.B. Serjeant on the Occasion of His Retirement from the Sir Thomas Adams Chair of Arabic at the University of Cambridge*, eds., R.L. Bidwell and G.R. Smith (London: Longman, 1981), 280–281.

39. *Women and Gender in Islam*, for example, was published by a Western academic press and Ahmed has written for such journals as *Women's Studies International Forum, Feminist Studies, Feminist Issues*, and *Signs*, all of which are directed to Western academic audiences.

40. Leila Ahmed, *Women and Gender in Islam*, 67.

41. Ibid.

42. Ibid.

43. Ibid.

44. Ibid., 53.

45. Ibid. Ahmed cites *Sahih al-Bukhari* 4:85–86 and Nabia Abbott, "Women and the State on the Eve of Islam," *American Journal of Semitic Languages* 58 (1941): 273.

46. Ahmed, *Women and Gender in Islam*, 70. She bases the claim about Umm Umara on Muhammad Ibn Saʿd's *Biographien/Kitab al-tabaqat al-kabir*, 9 vols., ed. Eduard Sachau (Leiden: E.J. Brill, 1904–1940), 8: 301–304.

47. Muslim histories record such events as the role of Umm Hakim in fighting against the Byzantines at the battle of Marj al-Saffar, of Azdah bint al-Harith in an early Arab Muslim expedition against a Persian seaport, and of Hind bint ʿUtbah and her daughter, Huwairah, encouraging the Muslims at the battle of Yarmuk in 637 (Ahmed, *Women and Gender in Islam*, 70). In this regard, Ahmed cites the following sources: Muhammad Ibn Saʿd, *Biographen/Kitab al-tabaqat al-kabir*, 9 vols., ed. Eduard Sachau (Leiden: E.J. Brill, 1904–40), 8:301–4.; Nabia Abbott, "Women

and the State in Early Islam," *Journal of Near Eastern Studies* (April 1942): 118; William Muir, *The Caliphate: Its Rise, Decline and Fall*, (Edinburgh: John Grant, 1924), 122; Muir, *Annals of the Early Caliphate* (London: Smith and Elder, 1883), 109; and Abbott "Women and the State on the Eve of Islam," *American Journal of Semitic Languages* 58 (1941): 277.

48. Ahmed, *Women and Gender in Islam*, 53.

49. Ibid., 75.

50. Ibid., 75–76.

51. Ibid., 76.

52. Ibid.

53. Ibid.

54. Ibid., 76–78.

55. Sayyid Abuʾl-Aʿla Mawdudi is one of many modern Muslim intellectuals who maintains that Islam improved the condition of women in contrast with *jahiliyya* times. See his *Purdah and The Status of Women in Islam* (Lahore: Islamic Publications, 1972), 2–28.

56. *Women and Gender in Islam*, 43. Ahmed cites W. Robertson Smith, *Kinship and Marriage in Early Arabia* (Cambridge: Cambridge University Press, 1885). She does not provide page numbers.

57. Ahmed, *Women and Gender in Islam*, 43. Ahmed cites W. Montgomery Watt, *Muhammad at Medina* (Oxford: Clarendon Press, 1956), 272–73.

58. Ahmed, *Women and Gender in Islam*, 42.

59. Ibid., 42–43.

60. Ibid., 43.

61. Ibid.

62. Ibid., 45.

63. Denise Spellberg presents some features of these idealized biographies of ʿAʾisha in *Politics, Gender, and The Islamic Past: The Legacy of Aisha bint Abi Bakr* (New York: Columbia University Press, 1994), 17–23. Some of the positive accounts of ʿAʾisha's life to which she refers are: Muhammad Khamis, *Al-sayyida Aisha umm al-muʾminun* (Aleppo: Maktabat Dar al-Daʾwa, 1976); ʿAbd al-Ghani Hamada, *Al-marʾa al-khalida fi tarikh al-Islam*, n.p., n.d.; ʿAbd al-Hamid Tahmaz, *Al-sayyida Aisha* (Damascus: Dar al-Qalam, 1975); ʿAli Ahmad Abu al-ʿIzz, *Umm al-muʾminin: Aisha al-mubarraʾa* (Cairo: al-Maktaba al-Mahmudiya al-Tijariya, n.d.). One book containing an idealized biography of ʿAʾisha, which is widely available in diaspora bookstores and mail-order catalogues, is Ahmad Thomson's *The Wives of the Prophet Muhammad* (London: Ta-Ha Publishers, 1993), 19–42.

64. Muhammad Ibn Saʿd, *Kitab al-tabaqat al-kabir*, op. cit.; Nabia Abbott, *Aisha, The Beloved of Muhammad* (Chicago: University of Chicago Press, 1942). Denise Spellberg notes that Abbott's was the first biography of ʿAʾisha written by a Western scholar; see Spellberg's *Politics, Gender, and the Islamic Past*, 19.

65. Spellberg, *Politics, Gender, and the Islamic Past*, 1–2.
66. Ibid., 20.
67. Ibid., 19.
68. Ibid., 19–20.
69. Ibid., 19.
70. Ahmed, *Women, Gender and Islam*, 43–45.
71. Ibid.
72. Ahmed, *Women and Gender in Islam*, 72.
73. Ibid.
74. Ibid.
75. Ibid.
76. Ibid.
77. Ibid., 72–73.
78. Ibid., 73.
79. Ibid. The "six widely accepted collections" refer to the *Sahih* collections of Muhammad Ibn Isma'il al-Bukhari and Abu-l-Husayn Muslim ibn al-Hajjaj (i.e., Muslim) as well as the other collections of Abu Dawud, al-Tirmidhi, al-Nasa'i and Ibn Maja.
80. Ahmed, *Women and Gender in Islam*, 74.
81. Ibid. See also Cyril Glassé, *The Concise Encyclopedia of Islam* (San Francisco: Harper, 1989): 143.
82. Ahmed, *Women and Gender in Islam*, 79ff.
83. Ibid., 79.
84. Ibid.
85. Ibid.
86. Ibid. One of the sources which Ahmed cites in her description of the role of women in Abbasid society is Nabia Abbott *Two Queens of Baghdad: Mother and Wife of Harun al-Rashid* (Chicago: University of Chicago Press, 1946; Midway Reprint, 1974).
87. Ahmed, *Women and Gender in Islam*, 82.
88. Ibid., 82.
89. Ibid.
90. Ibid., 87.
91. Ibid., 88.
92. Ibid. This viewpoint on the Quran is very similar to that of Fazlur Rahman; see Rahman's *Major Themes of the Quran*, 48ff.
93. Ibid., 88.
94. Joseph Schacht, *An Introduction to Islamic Law* (London: Oxford University Press, 1966), 1.
95. Ahmed indicates this very negative stance towards Islamic law in several sections of her work; see, for example, *Women and Gender in Islam*, 146, 168, 198, 227–228, 230–234.
96. Ismail R. Faruqi, *Humanism and the Law: The Case of the Shariah*. Occasional Paper No. 8. (Lagos, Nigeria: Nigerian Institute of Advanced Legal Studies), 1.

97. Ibid.
98. Ibid.
99. See, for example, the following essays in Yvonne Yazbeck Haddad's *The Muslims of America* (New York: Oxford University Press, 1991): John O. Voll, "Islamic Issues for Muslims in the United States," 205–216 and Sulayman S. Nyang, "Convergence and Divergence in an Emergent Community: A Study of Challenges Facing U.S. Muslims," 236–249.
100. Nyang, "Convergence and Divergence in an Emergent Community," 236–249.
101. John Voll, "Islamic Issues for Muslims in the United States," 209–210; Gilles Kepel, *The Revenge of God,* 34–35.
102. Voll, "Islamic Issues," 209–210. See also Gutbi Mahdi Ahmed, "Muslim Organizations in the United States," in *The Muslims of America* (New York: Oxford University Press, 1991): 11–24.
103. For some Muslim diaspora perspectives on this issue see Abdur Rahman I. Doi, *Shariah: The Islamic Law* (London: Ta-Ha Publishers, 1984), i–ii and 2–40; Doi, *Shariah in the 1500 Century* [*sic*] *of Shariah* (London: Ta-Ha Publishers, 1981): 5–28; Hassan Hathout, *Reading the Muslim Mind* (Plainfield, Indiana: American Trust Publications, 1996): 41–62.
104. John Voll, "Islamic Issues," 209–210; Gilles Kepel, *The Revenge of God,* 34–35.
105. Ismail R. Faruqi, "The Path of Dawah in the West," *The Muslim World League Journal* 14, 7–8 (Rajab-Shaban 1407/March–April 1987), 56 as quoted in Voll, "Islamic Issues for Muslims in the United States," 214.
106. Abdur Rahman I. Doi is an example of one diaspora thinker who employs this distinction as he attempts to guide Muslims in living their lives in accordance with Shariah. See his *Shari'ah: The Islamic Law,* 66, 82, 115, 116, and 207 for his treatment of some specific issues related to *'ibadat.* In addition, the contents of the book itself is divided in two parts, with roughly the first half addressing issues of *'ibadat* and the second half discussing topics related to *mu'amalat.* Barbara Freyer Stowasser analyzes the ways in which concepts related to *'ibadat* and *mu'amalat* function in modern Islamic thought in "Women's Issues in Modern Islamic Thought" in *Arab Women: Old Boundaries, New Frontiers* (Bloomington: Indiana University Press, 1993): 8ff.
107. John Voll, "Islamic Issues," 209–210; Gilles Kepel, *The Revenge of God,* 34–35.
108. Ibid. See also Gutbi Mahdi Ahmed, "Muslim Organizations in the United States," 11–24 and Sulayman S. Nyang, "Convergence and Divergence in an Emergent Community," 236–249. Both of these entries appear in Yvonne Haddad's *The Muslims of America.*
109. Yvonne Haddad's and Adair T. Lummis's *Islamic Values in the United States Islamic Values in the United States: A Comparative Study* (New York: Oxford University Press), 98–121, 155–156 and Kambiz Ghanea-Bassiri's *Competing Visions of Islam in the United States* (Westport, Con-

necticut: Greenwood Press, 1997), 80–81, 107–111 provide extensive discussions of the varieties of North American diaspora Muslim approaches
to daily prayer, almsgiving, participation in hajj, fasting during Ramadan,
as well as attitudes towards loans, interest, and hijra. Haddad's and
Lummis' work focuses on Islamic institutions, social integration, Islamic
laws, Muslim practice and roles of men in women, among Muslim communities in the Midwest, East Coast, and Upstate New York. Gilles
Kepel discusses the problems which some diaspora Muslims in France
have experienced with respect to their dietary duties in *Les banlieues de
l'Islam* (Paris: Éditions du Seuil), 356–361 and the history of the veiling
controversy in France in *Allah in the West: Islamic Movements in America and Europe* (Stanford, California: Stanford University Press, 1997),
174–203.

110. Muhammad Khalid Masud "The Obligation to Migrate: The Doctrine of
jihad in Islamic Law," in *Muslim Travellers: Pilgrimage, Migration, and
the Religious Imagination*, eds. Dale F. Eickelman and James Piscatori
(Berkeley: University of California Press, 1990), 38.

111. For a discussion of the interpretations of hijra among Islamic Revivalist
groups in Egypt, see Gilles Kepel, *The Prophet and Pharaoh: Muslim
Extremism in Egypt* (London: Al-Saqi Books, 1985), 70–102.

112. Kemal H. Karpat, "The *hijra* from Russia and the Balkans: The Process
of Self-Definition in the late Ottoman State" in *Muslim Travellers*, 131–
152.

113. *Oxford Encyclopedia of the Modern Islamic World*, s.v. "hijrah."

114. Ibid., 29–38.

115. Suzanne Haneef, *What Everyone Should Know About Islam and Muslims*
(Chicago: Kazi Publications, 1995), 24.

116. Abdur Rahman I. Doi, *Shari'ah: The Islamic Law* (London: Ta-Ha Publishers, 1984), 21.

117. Ahmed, "Early Feminist Movements in the Middle East: Turkey and
Egypt," in *Muslim Women*, Freda Hussain, ed. New York: St. Martin's
Press, 1984: 111–123.

118. Ahmed, *Women and Gender in Islam*, 95.

119. Ibid.

120. Ibid.

121. Ibid.

122. Ibid.

123. Ibid., 95–96

124. Ibid.

125. Ibid., 96

126. Ibid.

127. Ibid. In one of these stories, the esteemed Sufi leader Hasan al-Basri
declares, "I passed one whole night and day with Rabia speaking of the
Way and the Truth, and it never even passed through my mind that I
was a man nor did it occur to her that she was a woman, and at the end

when I looked at her I saw myself as bankrupt [i.e., as spiritually worth nothing] and Rabia as truly sincere [rich in spiritual virtue]." In addition to repudiating the dominant notion of the time that sexuality governed male-female interactions, according to Ahmed, "the tale also reverses the dominant society's valuation of male over female by representing not merely any man but one of the most revered Sufi leaders describing himself as 'bankrupt' compared with a woman of truly superior merits." Ahmed recounts these stories as presented in Margaret Smith's *Rabi'a the Mystic and Her Fellow-Saints in Islam* (Cambridge: Cambridge University Press, 1928), 14. The first brackets are in the original and the second ones were added by Ahmed.

128. Ibid., 96–98.
129. Ibid., 98–99.
130. Ibid., 99.
131. Ibid.
132. Ibid., 100.
133. Spencer Trimingham, *The Sufi Orders in Islam* (New York: Oxford University Press, 1998), 102–104. Even though certain aspects of Trimingham's work, particularly his notion of neo-Sufism, have come under attack, scholars such as John Voll affirm the apparent accuracy of Trimingham's three-stage approach to the history of Sufism. One extended critique of Trimingham's approach to neo-Sufism is R.S. O'Fahey's and Bernd Radtke's "Neo-Sufism Reconsidered," *Der Islam* 70, 1 (1993): 52–87. John Voll notes that while new research "provides new information and perspectives" regarding the development of Sufi orders, Trimingham's three-stage schema continues "to be useful for students and scholars"; see John O. Voll foreword to the 1998 edition of Trimingham's *The Sufi Orders in Islam*, v.
134. Trimingham, *The Sufi Orders in Islam*, 103.
135. Ibid., 103.
136. Ibid.
137. Ibid.
138. Carl W. Ernst, *The Shambhala Guide to Sufism* (Boston: Shambhala Publications, 1997), 18.
139. Carl Ernst discusses the difficulties and contradictions which have arisen as a result of Orientalists' and Muslims' use of the term "Sufism." See Carl Ernst, *Shambhala Guide to Sufism*, 1–31.
140. Trimingham, *The Sufi Orders in Islam*, 18. Trimingham (p. 114) also discusses women's leadership in Sufi orders in Morocco during the twentieth century.
141. Ernst indicates the predominance of men and male Sufis saints in the tradition while providing a discussion of the importance of Rabia and Bibi Jamal Khatun (d. 1647), a Sufi saint of western India.
142. Ernst, *The Shambhala Guide to Sufism*, 28–30, 66–67, 138, 143.
143. Mernissi, *Women, Saints, and Sanctuaries*, 101–112.

144. For Ahmed's references to the Qarmatians see *Women and Gender in Islam*, 95 and 98–100. Farhad Daftary provides a very helpful discussion of the Qarmatian state in Bahrayn in *The Ismailis: Their History and Doctrines* (Cambridge: Cambridge University Press, 1990), 119, 131, 160–166.

145. Daftary, *The Ismailis*, 119.

146. Ibid. See also *The Encyclopaedia of Islam*, s.v. "Karmati."

147. *Encyclopaedia of Islam*, s.v. "Karmati."

148. Madelung in his article on the Qarmatians in the *Encyclopaedia of Islam* indicates that at the time of the Muslim traveller Nasir-i Khusraw's visit to the Qarmatian state thirty thousand African slaves were employed by the *'Iqdaniyya*. Daftary indicates that Nasir-i Khusraw's visit to the region took place in 1051. See *Encyclopaedia of Islam*, s.v. "Karmati" and Daftary, *The Ismailis*, 120.

149. Daftary, *The Ismailis*, 161–164.

150. *The Encyclopedia of Religion*, Vol. 12, s.v. "Qaramitah" by Ismail K. Poonawala, 127.

151. Marshall G.S. Hodgson. *The Venture of Islam*, Vol. 1: *The Classical Age of Islam*. (Chicago: University of Chicago Press): 490–491; *The Encyclopedia of Religion*, Vol. 12, s.v. "Qaramitah" by Ismail K. Poonawala; Ira Lapidus, *A History of Islamic Societies* (New York: Cambridge University Press, 1991), 132.

152. For an outline of some of the animosities which some Sunnis have directed against certain Sufi groups, see Ira Lapidus, *A History of Islamic Societies*, 257–259; 512–514; and 853–854; Muhammad Abdul Haq Ansari, *Sufism and Shari'ah: A Study of Shaykh Ahmad Sirhindi's Effort to Reform Sufism* (Leicester: The Islamic Foundation, 1986); *The Encyclopedia of Religion*, s.v. "Sufism" by Peter Awn, 121ff.

153. *The Encyclopedia of Religion*, s.v. "Sufism" by Peter Awn, 121ff.

154. See Muhammad Abdul Haq Ansari, *Sufism and Shari'ah*, chapters two and three.

155. For a discussion of some Sufi masters' knowledge of Sharia and the membership of some ulema in Sufi orders, see Carl Ernst's preface to *Early Islamic Mysticism*, by Michael A. Sells (New York: Paulist Press, 1996), 2–3. My use of the term "sharia-minded" has its roots in Marshall Hodgson's *The Venture of Islam: Conscience and History in a World Civilization* (Chicago: University of Chicago Press, 1974), 318–335 and 345–350.

156. The Islamic Society of North America, the Muslim Students Association of North America, the Islamic Book Service, North American Trust Publications (which are have offices in Plainfield, Indiana and Washington, D.C.). The Islamic Foundation (based in Leicester, England) and Islamic Publications International (based in Berkeley, California) offer virtually no literature which portrays Sufism in a positive light. Most of the literature which they do offer on this subject has a distinctly pro-

Wahhabi/anti-Sufi slant. Such publications include Muhammad Ibn 'Abd al-Wahhab, *Kitab al-Tawhid: Essay on the Unicity of Allah*, trans. Ismail Raji al-Faruqi (al-Ain: United Arab Emirates, n.d.) which devotes several chapters to denouncing various Sufi beliefs and practices; Muhammad Ibn 'Abd al-Wahhab *Three Essays on Tawhid* (Plainfield, Indiana: North American Trust Publications); Muhammad Ibn 'Abd al-Wahhab, *Major Sins in Islam* (New Delhi, India: International Islamic Publishers, 1988). A section of a book on the life and work of Ismail Faruqi by Muhammad Shafiq called *Growth of Islamic Thought in North America: Focus on Isma'il Raji al-Faruqi* (Brentwood, Maryland: Amana Publications, 1994), which is another work that is available through such distributers as the Islamic Book Service presents some of the "anti-Sufi" elements of Faruqi's thought (see, for example, p. 89). In addition, Sufism is not addressed in the magazine *The Minaret* which is published by the Islamic Center of Southern California; see Juan E. Campo, "Islam in California: Views from *The Minaret*," *Muslim World* (July–October 1996): 299.

157. Information on the American Sufi Institute, the Sufi Psychology Association, and the Threshold Society are available on their websites whose respective addresses are: www.geocities.com/athens/acropolis, www.sufipsychology.org, www.webcom.web/threshld/society. For discussions of other contemporary Sufi organizations in diaspora settings see John Voll's foreword to Spencer Trimingham's *The Sufi Orders in Islam* and Carl Ernst's *The Shambhala Guide to Sufism*, 199–228.

158. Bernard Lewis, *History: Remembered, Recovered, Invented* (Princeton: Princeton University Press, 1987), 11–12.

159. Ibid.

160. Ahmed, "Arab Women: 1995," in *The Next Arab Decade*, Hisham Sharabi, ed. (Boulder, Colorado, 1988), 211–212, 214.

161. Ahmed, *Women and Gender in Islam*, 5, 14–15, 26.

162. Ibid., 14.

163. Ibid., 53–56. Regarding the possible events in the early period and the *asbab al-nuzul* for the Quranic verses, Ahmed cites Ibn Sa'd's *al-Tabaqat*, Ibn Hanbal's *Musnad*, and al-Bukhari's *Sahih*. In terms of secondary sources, she cites Gertrude Stern's *Marriage in Early Islam*, Nabia Abbott's *Aishah*, and Montgomery Watt's *Muhammad at Medina*.

164. Ahmed, *Women and Gender in Islam*, 55–56.

165. Ibid.

166. Ibid.

167. Some secondary sources which discuss the contemporary trend toward "reveiling" on the part of Muslim women include: John Alden Williams, "A Return to the Veil in Egypt," *Middle East Review* 11, 3 (Spring 1979): 49–54. Fadwa al-Guindi, "Veiling *Infitah* with Muslim Ethic: Egypt's Contemporary Islamic Movement," *Social Problems* 28, 4 (April 1981): 465–485; Yvonne Y. Haddad, "Islam, Women and Revolution in Twentieth-Century Arab Thought," *Muslim World* 74, 3–4 (July/October 1984):

137–160; Sherifa Zuhur, *Revealing Revealing: Islamist Gender Ideology in Contemporary Egypt* (Albany: State University of New York Press, 1992).
168. Ahmed, *Women and Gender in Islam*, 152.
169. Ibid., 153. Ahmed cites the Earl of Cromer's *Modern Egypt*, Volume 2 (New York: MacMillan, 1908), 538–539. The secondary source pertaining to Cromer's perspectives that she cites is A.B. De Guerville, *New Egypt* (London: William Heinemann, 1906), 154.
170. Ahmed, *Women and Gender in Islam*, 153. The quote from Cromer appears in *Cromer Papers*, cited in Judith E. Tucker, *Women in Nineteenth-Century Egypt* (Cambridge: Cambridge University Press, 1985), 122.
171. Ahmed, *Women and Gender in Islam*, 153.
172. Ibid., 153–154.
173. Ibid., 153.
174. Ibid., 163–164.
175. Ibid., 163.
176. Ibid., 224ff. See also Leila Ahmed, "Arab Women: 1995," 211ff and Sherifa Zuhur, *Revealing Reveiling: Islamist Gender Ideology in Contemporary Egypt.*
177. Leila Ahmed, *Women and Gender in Islam*, 224.
178. Ibid.
179. Ibid., 223.
180. Ahmed, "Arab Women: 1995," 214.
181. Ibid.
182. Ibid.
183. Mernissi, *Beyond the Veil*, vii–xxx, 7–9; *Women and Islam*, 1–11. Nadia Nagie, *Fez-New York und zurück: Fatima Mernissi ihre Welt und ihre Geschichte*, 55–56, 89–90.
184. Mernissi, *Women and Islam*, Chapters 3, 4, 5, 10.
185. Ahmed, "Arab Women: 1995," 214.
186. Ahmed, "Feminism and Feminist Movements in the Middle East, A Preliminary Exploration: Turkey, Egypt, Algeria, People's Democratic Republic of Yemen," 163.

Chapter 4

1. Rahman, *Islam and Modernity: Transformation of an Intellectual Tradition* (Chicago: University of Chicago Press, 1982), 15ff. See also Rahman's *Major Themes of the Quran* (Minneapolis, Minnesota: Bibliotheca Islamica, 1989), 37ff. Ebrahim Moosa expands on Rahman's ideas about justice in his introduction to Rahman's *Revival and Reform in Islam*, 9ff. In a related matter, Tamara Sonn provides very insightful observations on Rahman's perspectives on Quranic interpretation in "Fazlur Rahman and

Islamic Feminism" in Waugh's and Denny's *The Shaping of an American Islamic Discourse*, p. 8: "Indeed, all efforts to understand the meaning of the Quran are efforts at interpretation according to Fazlur Rahman, since, as he paraphrases Gadamer, 'all experience of understanding presupposes a preconditioning of the experiencing subject.' Overall, [Rahman] rejects the idea that interpretations are utterly predetermined. However, it is essential to his reasoning that socioeconomic and historical factors, such as one's education and one's political and economic concerns, affect interpretation. Similarly, he rejects the implication that truth as such is inaccessible to humans. For him, the Quran is truth, unquestionably, the revealed word of God. Yet this does not preclude his recognition that even the Quran is an interpretation. In Fazlur Rahman's words, '[C]ertainly, in the case of the Quran, the objective situation is a *sine qua non* for understanding, particularly since, in view of its absolute normativity for Muslims, it is literally God's response through Muhammad's mind . . . to a historic situation. . . .' Earle Waugh articulates a similar stance on Rahman's approach in his "Beyond Scylla and Kharybdis: Fazlur Rahman and Islamic Identity" in Waugh's and Denny's *The Shaping of an American Islamic Discourse*, 21 as does Ebrahim Moosa in his Introduction to Rahman's *Revival and Reform in Islam*, 23.

2. For a comprehensive study of the Jama'at, see Seyyed Vali Reza Nasr, *The Vanguard of the Islamic Revolution: The Jama'at-i Islami of Pakistan* (Berkeley: University of California Press, 1994). See also *Encyclopaedia of Islam*, s.v. "Mawdudi, Sayyid Abu'l-A'la" and *Oxford Encyclopedia of Modern Islamic World*, s.v. "Mawdudi, Sayyid Abu'l-A'la." See also Donald L. Berry, "Fazlur Rahman: A Life in Review" in *The Shaping of an American Islamic Discourse: A Memorial to Fazlur Rahman*, ed. Earle H. Waugh and Frederick M. Denny (Atlanta: Scholars Press, 1998), 37–45.

3. Autobiographical essay by Rahman in Phillip L. Berman's *The Courage of Conviction*, 153–159.

4. Ibid., 154.

5. Ibid.

6. Ibid.

7. Ibid.

8. Barbara Metcalf, *Islamic Revival in British India: Deoband 1860–1900* (Princeton, New Jersey: Princeton University Press, 1982), 95.

9. Rahman, *Islam and Modernity*, 130–162.

10. Autobiographical essay by Rahman in Berman's *The Courage of Conviction*, 153. For an extended discussion of the impact of the Quran on Rahman's thinking see Donald Lee Berry, "The Thought of Fazlur Rahman as an Islamic Response to Modernity," (Ph.D. diss., Southern Baptist Theological Seminary, 1990), 82–119.

11. Rahman's Autobiographical Essay in Berman's *The Courage of Conviction*, 154–155.

12. See for example Rahman, "Law and Ethics in Islam" in *Ethics in Islam*, ed. Richard Hovannisian, (Malibu, California: Undena Publications, 1985), 14ff. and *Islam and Modernity*, 154–157.

13. Denny, "The Legacy of Fazlur Rahman" in *The Muslims of America*, ed. Yvonne Yazbeck Haddad (New York: Oxford University Press, 1991), 96–97; Rahman's Autobiograpical Essay in Berman's *The Courage of Conviction*, 154–155.

14. See Rahman, *Islam*, 128–166 and Gibb's *Mohammedanism: An Historical Survey* (New York: Oxford University Press, 1975), 86–112. Their views on Sufism will be discussed later in this chapter.

15. Rahman, "Some Islamic Issues in the Ayyub Khan Era," in *Essays On Islamic Civilization: Presented to Niyazi Berkes*, ed. Donald P. Little (Leiden: E.J. Brill, 1976), 285.

16. Ibid.

17. Denny, "The Legacy of Fazlur Rahman," 97.

18. For a comparison of the impact which Rahman and Mawdudi had on policy formation in Pakistan, see Berry's "The Thought of Fazlur Rahman as an Islamic Response to Modernity," 98–116. For Rahman's views on what he believes is the proper structure and method for Islamic education in the modern world see his article entitled "The Quranic Solution of Pakistan's Educational Problems," *Islamic Studies* 6 (1967): 315–326; Rahman's *Islam and Modernity*, 130–162 and *Islam*, 181–192. For his position on biomedical and family planning issues, see his book *Health and Medicine in the Islamic Tradition* (New York: Crossroad Publishing Company, 1989), 106–129 and his article "Controversy Over the Muslim Family Laws Ordinance" in *South Asian Politics and Religion*, ed. Donald Smith (Princeton, New Jersey: Princeton University Press, 1966). For his perspectives on interest and banking, see his article "*Riba* and Interest" *Islamic Studies* 3, 1 (March 1964): 1–43. Rahman discusses his understanding of the mechanical slaughter of animals in "Some Islamic Issues in the Ayyub Khan Era," op. cit., 297–298.

19. Denny, "The Legacy of Fazlur Rahman," 97.

20. Nasr, *Mawdudi and the Making of Islamic Revivalism* (New York: Oxford University Press, 1996), 10–13.

21. Ibid., 9. Mawdudi's views on Sufism will be discussed later in this chapter.

22. Nasr, *Mawdudi and the Making of Islamic Revivalism*, 10. For a description of the madrasa at Aligarh and its history, see Barbara Metcalf, *Islamic Revival in British India: 1860–1900*, 315–334.

23. Nasr, *Mawdudi and the Making of Islamic Revivalism*, 10.

24. Ibid., 19.

25. Ibid., 15–19.

26. *The Oxford Encyclopedia of the Modern Islamic World*, s.v. "Mawdudi, Sayyid Abu'l-A'la."

27. Nasr, *Mawdudi and the Making of Islamic Revivalism*, 139–140 and 206–208.

28. Rahman, *Islam and Modernity*, 5.

29. Ibid.

30. Ibid.

31. Rahman, "Islam and Political Action: Politics in the Service of Religion," in *Cities of Gods: Faith, Politics and Pluralism in Judaism, Christianity and Islam*, ed. Nigel Biggar, Jamie S. Scott, and William Schweiker (Westport, Connecticut: Greenwood Press, 1986), 155.

32. Rahman, *Major Themes of the Quran*, 28–29.

33. Ibid. See also Rahman's "Islam and Political Action," 28–29.

34. Rahman, *Islam and Modernity*, 6 and *Major Themes of the Quran*, 37.

35. Rahman, *Major Themes of the Quran*, 48–49. For more on Rahman's interpretations of Quranic passages pertaining to women see Tamara Sonn, "Fazlur Rahman and Islamic Feminism" in Waugh's and Denny's *The Shaping of an American Islamic Discourse*, 123–145.

36. Ibid.

37. Ibid., 49.

38. Ibid.

39. Ibid., 48.

40. Ibid.

41. Ibid.

42. Mawdudi, *Towards Understanding the Qur'an*, trans. Zafar Ishaq Ansari (Leicester: Islamic Foundation, 1988), 1:4.

43. Ibid.

44. Ibid., xiv–xv.

45. Ibid. See also Mawdudi, *Four Basic Quranic Terms*, trans. Abu Asad (Lahore: Islamic Publications, 1982).

46. Mawdudi, *Towards Understanding the Quran*, xiv–xv.

47. Ibid.

48. Mawdudi, *Introduction to the Study of the Quran* (Delhi: Maktaba Jamaat-e Islami Hind, 1971), 43–48.

49. Mawdudi, *Towards Understanding the Quran*, 1:4ff.

50. Ibid., 1:xiv–xv. See also Mawdudi's *Four Basic Quranic Terms*.

51. Mawdudi, *Towards Understanding the Quran* 1:12 and Mawdudi's *Introduction to the Study of the Quran*, 43–48.

52. Rahman, *Major Themes of the Quran*, 48ff.

53. Ibid.

54. Mawdudi, *Introduction to the Study of the Quran* (Delhi: Markazi Maktaba Jammat-e-Islami Hind, 1971), 1–12.

55. Rahman, *Islam and Modernity*, 5. For more on the priority Rahman placed on understanding history in the process of Quranic interpretation see Earle Waugh, "Beyond Scylla and Kharybdis: Fazlur Rahman and

Islamic Identity" in Waugh's and Denny's *The Shaping of an American Islamic Discourse*, 21–23.

56. Mawdudi, *Towards Understanding the Qur'an*, 1:17–20.

57. Rahman, *Islam and Modernity*, 130–162.

58. Mawdudi, *The Process of Islamic Revolution* (Lahore: Islamic Publications, 1980), 17.

59. Rahman, *Islam and Modernity*, 130–162.

60. Mawdudi, *Towards Understanding the Quran*, 1:17–20.

61. Rahman *Islam*, 2nd ed., (Chicago: University of Chicago Press, 1979), 102–103.

62. Ibid., 102.

63. Ibid.

64. Ibid.

65. Ibid.

66. Ibid.

67. Ibid., 103.

68. Ibid.

69. Ibid.

70. Ibid., 4–6.

71. Ibid. and Rahman, *Islam and Modernity*, 29–31.

72. Ibid., 104ff.

73. Ibid., 113.

74. Rahman, "Law and Ethics in Islam," in *Ethics in Islam*, ed. Richard Hovannisian (Malibu, California: Undena Publications, 1985), 14ff.

75. Ibid., 12.

76. Ibid.

77. Ibid.

78. *Islam*, 116.

79. Ibid., 77.

80. Ibid.

81. Ibid.

82. Ibid., 78.

83. Ibid.

84. Ibid.

85. Hallaq makes this argument in "The Gate of *Ijtihad*: A Study in Islamic Legal History" (Ph.D. diss, University of Washington, 1983). A condensed version of some of the arguments in Hallaq's dissertation appear in: "Was the Gate of *Ijtihad* Closed?" *International Journal of Middle East Studies* 16 (1984): 3–41. He also makes his arguments against the idea of the closure of the door of *ijtihad* in "Was al-Shafi'i the Master Architect of Islamic Jurisprudence?" *International Journal of Middle East Studies* 25 (1993): 587–605 and in *Law and Legal Theory in Classical and Medieval Islam* (Aldershot, U.K.: Variorum, 1994), 3–41, 129–141, 172–202, 587–605.

86. See, for example, N.J. Coulson, *A History of Islamic Law* (Edinburgh: Edinburgh University Press), 56; Ignaz Goldziher, *The Zahiris: Their Doctrine and Their History* (Leiden: E.J. Brill, 1971), 20–21; Joseph Schacht, *The Origins of Muhammadan Jurisprudence* (Oxford: Oxford University Press, 1975).

87. Hallaq, "Al-Shafiʿi, Architect of Islamic Jurisprudence?," 592.

88. Ibid.

89. Hallaq, "The Gate of *Ijtihad*: A Study in Islamic Legal History," 9–10.

90. Ibid., 9–10.

91. Ibid., 37.

92. Ibid., 23.

93. Ibid., 23–24, 59–60.

94. Rahman, *Islam and Modernity*, 37–38. Barbara Metcalf discusses the authority of the shaykh in the Deobandi and other Islamic madrasas in *Islamic Revival in British India: Deoband, 1860–1900* (Princeton: Princeton University Press, 1982), 143ff.

95. Nasr, *Mawdudi and the Making of Islamic Revivalism* (New York: Oxford University Press, 1996), 63. For Mawdudi's distinction regarding what is to his mind Islamic and un-Islamic see his *Towards Understanding Islam*, trans. Khurshid Ahmad (Indianapolis: Islamic Teaching Center, 1977), 4, 11–12, 18–19 and his *Let Us Be Muslims*, trans. Khurram Jah Murad (Leicester: Islamic Foundation, 1985), 53–55.

96. Mawdudi, *A Short History of the Revivalist Movement in Islam*, trans. al-Ashʿari (Lahore: Islamic Publications Limited, 1992), 25–28.

97. Ibid. See also Nasr, *Mawdudi and the Making of Islamic Revivalism*, 136.

98. Mawdudi, *A Short History of the Revivalist Movement in Islam*, 28.

99. Ibid.

100. Ibid., 30–31.

101. Ibid., 44–78.

102. Nasr, *Mawdudi and the Making of Islamic Revivalism*, 130. See also Martin Riesebrodt, *Pious Passion: The Emergence of Modern Fundamentalism in the United States and Iran.* (Berkeley: University of California Press, 1993), 24.

103. Rahman, *Islam*, 68–84.

104. Rahman, *Islam and Modernity*, 130–162.

105. Mawdudi, *Four Basic Quranic Terms*, trans. Abu Asad (Lahore: Islamic Publications, 1979), 1–9, 93–103.

106. Ibid., 93–103.

107. Rahman, *Islam and Modernity*, 130–162.

108. Rahman, *Islam*, 77–80.

109. Rahman, *Islam and Modernity*, 137.

110. Mawdudi, *Economic System of Islam*, ed. Khurshid Ahmad, trans. Riaz Husain (Lahore: Islamic Publications, 1984), 298–299, 304. See also Sayyid Abuʾl-Aʿla Mawdudi and Shah Muhammad Abu Zahra, "The Role

of '*Ijtihad*' and the Scope of Legislation in Islam," *Muslim Digest* 9, no. 6 (January 1959): 15–20.

111. Mawdudi and Shah Muhammad Abu Zahra, "The Role of '*Ijtihad*' and the Scope of Legislation in Islam," 15–20. See also Mawdudi's *Process of Islamic Revolution*, 1–8.

112. Nasr, *Mawdudi and the Making of Islamic Revivalism*, 136.

113. Ibid., 107. See also Mawdudi and Shah Muhammad Abu Zahra, "The Role of '*Ijtihad*' and the Scope of Legislation in Islam," 15–20.

114. Rahman, "The Principle of *Shura* and the Role of Umma in Islam," *American Journal of Islamic Studies* 1, no.1 (1984): 2ff.

115. Rahman, "Islam and Political Action," 156.

116. Rahman, "The Principle of *Shura* and the Role of Umma in Islam," 2ff.

117. Rahman, *Islam*, 239.

118. Ibid., 238.

119. Rahman, "Islam and Political Action," 158.

120. Rahman, *Islam*, 239.

121. Ibid.

122. Rahman, *Islam and Modernity*, 31.

123. Ibid. Rahman's characterization of the growth of Islamic education follows George Madkisi's concept of the three-stage development of Islamic education which he describes as initially taking place in the *masjid* (mosque) and subsequently in the *masjid-khan* complex (a mosque with residence hall, or khan, attached or nearby). Makdisi notes that the first free-standing madrasas came into existence in the eleventh century. See George Makdisi, *The Rise of Colleges: Institutions of Learning in Islam and the West* (Edinburgh: Edinburgh University Press, 1981), 27 and 34. Cf. Rahman, *Islam*, 181–184 and his *Islam and Modernity*, 31.

124. Rahman, "Islam and Modernity," 31. See also Rahman's *Islam*, 181–184.

125. Rahman, *Islam and Modernity*, 33. I have used Rahman's transliterations.

126. Ibid., 36.

127. Ibid.

128. Ibid.

129. Ibid.

130. Ibid., 37.

131. Ibid.

132. Ibid. Interestingly, Fatima Mernissi strongly advocates the resurgence of a form of contemporary *jadal* as one way to foster healthy debate among contemporary Muslims. See Mernissi's *Islam and Democracy: Fear of the Modern World*, 2nd ed. (Cambridge, Massachusetts: Perseus Publishing, 2002), xvi–ix.

133. Ibid., 37.

134. Ibid., 38.

135. Ibid.

136. Rahman, *Islam*, 244–246. Michael Sells addresses Rahman's skepticism about Sufism in "Heart-Secret, Intimacy and Awe in Formative Sufism"

in Waugh's and Denny's *The Shaping of an American Islamic Discourse*, 183, n. 1.

137. Ibid., 244.

138. Ibid., 147–148.

139. Ibid., 244. Rahman seems to suggest that, at times, Sufis confuse the coming of Jesus with that of the Mahdi.

140. Ibid., 245.

141. Ibid.

142. Ibid., 206.

143. *Encyclopedia of Islam*, s.v., "Ibn ʿArabi, Abu Bakr Muhammad Muhyi Din."

144. Rahman, *Islam*, 148.

145. Ibid., 208.

146. R.S. O'Fahey and Bernd Radtke, "Neo-Sufism Reconsidered," *Der Islam* 70, 1 (1993): 56–57.

147. Ibid., 57.

148. O'Fahey and Radtke correctly cite Rahman's brief discussion of neo-Sufism in *Islam*, p. 206. However, they incorrectly note that Rahman refers to neo-Sufism on p. 239 of Islam; Rahman's arguments on this page pertain to Ibn Taymiyya's views on the Islamic state, not Sufism. They also mistakenly suggest that Rahman utilizes the term neo-Sufism in his article "Revival and Reform in Islam" in *The Cambridge History of Islam*, vol. 2, ed. Ann Lambton and Bernard Lewis (Cambridge: Cambridge University Press, 1970), 637. Cf. O'Fahey and Radtke, "Neo-Sufism Reconsidered," 55, n. 5.

149. O'Fahey and Radtke state that the primary focus of their arguments is on the interpretation of neo-Sufi movements as presented in: J. Spencer Trimingham, *The Sufi Orders in Islam* (Oxford: Oxford University Press, 1971), 106–107; B.G. Martin, *Muslim Brotherhoods in Nineteenth Century Africa* (Cambridge: Cambridge University Press, 1976), 71–72 and 108 and John Voll, *Islam: Continuity and Change in the Modern World* (Boulder: Westview Press, 1982), 55–59, 65–67, 76–79, 103–104, 134–136. See O'Fahey and Radtke, "Neo-Sufism Reconsidered," 56, nn. 11 and 12 and pp. 57–87.

150. Rahman, *Islam*, 195, 206.

151. O'Fahey and Radtke, "Neo-Sufism Reconsidered," 53, 81–86.

152. Rahman, *Islam*, 208.

153. Ibid., 207.

154. O'Fahey and Radtke, "Neo-Sufism Reconsidered", 84.

155. Ibid.

156. Ibid.

157. John Voll, for example, has pointed to some of the problems related to O'Fahey and Radtke's interpretation of the secondary literature about modern Sufi movements. See John Voll, foreword to J. Spencer Trim-

ingham's *The Sufi Orders in Islam* (New York: Oxford University Press, 1998), x–xi.

158. Masudul Hasan, *Sayyid Abul A'ala Maududi and His Thought* (Lahore: Islamic Publications, 1984), 1:175.

159. Mawdudi, *A Short History of the Revivalist Movement in Islam*, 134–135. See also Nasr, *Mawdudi and the Making of Islamic Revivalism*, 122.

160. Nasr, *Mawdudi and the Making of Islamic Revivalism*, 122. For more on Akbar's and Dara Shukuh's syncretistic experiments, see Daryush Shayegan, *Hindouisme et Soufisme* (Paris: Editions de la Difference, 1979).

161. Nasr, *Mawdudi and the Making of Islamic Revivalism*, 123.

162. Ibid. See also Katherine Ewing, "The Politics of Sufism: Redefining the Saints of Pakistan," *Journal of Asian Studies* vol. 42, no. 2 (February 1983): 251–268.

163. Mawdudi, *Towards Understanding Islam*, trans. Khurshid Ahmad (Indianapolis: Islamic Teaching Center, 1977), 111.

164. Ibid.

165. Nasr, *Mawdudi and the Making of Islamic Revivalism*, 123.

166. Khurshid Ahmad's talk at the University of South Florida, and World and Islamic Studies Enterprise Conference, Tampa, Florida, May 15, 1993. Quoted in Nasr, *Mawdudi and the Making of Islamic Revivalism*, 123.

167. Mernissi, "Women, Saints, and Sanctuaries," *Signs* 31 (Autumn 1977): 101–112.

168. Ahmed, *Women and Gender in Islam*, 95–99, 115–116.

169. Arkoun, *Rethinking Islam: Common Questions, Uncommon Answers* (Boulder, Colorado: Westview Press, 1994), 81–85.

170. See Seyyed Hossein Nasr's *Sufi Essays* (London: Allen and Unwin, 1975) and his *Islamic Spirituality* (New York: Crossroads, 1987).

171. For a brief anaylsis of certain Islamic revivalists' rejections of Sufism see John Esposito's *The Islamic Threat: Myth or Reality?* 50.

172. Frederick Denny, "Fazlur Rahman: Muslim Intellectual," *The Muslim World* 79, 2 (April 1989): 96–97. See also Rahman, "Post-Formative Developments in Islam (I)" *Islamic Studies* vol. 1, no. 4 (1962): 20–21.

173. Rahman, "Post-Formative Developments in Islam (I)," 20–21.

174. Ibid.

175. Rahman, *Islam*, 147. Frederick Denny also describes the impact of Ibn Taymiyya on Rahman's work; see his "Legacy of Fazlur Rahman," 99–102.

176. Hourani, *Arabic Thought in the Liberal Age*, 9. While this passage is meant to outline the approaches of Muslim Arab modernists to Sufism, Hourani, later in the book, provides a brief description of Sayyid Ahmed Khan's philosophy which is consistent with this characterization (cf. Hourani, 124–125).

177. H.A.R. Gibb, *Modern Trends in Islam* (New York: Octagon Books, 1975), vii, 20–21, 49, 83. See also Gibb's *Mohammedanism: An Historical Survey* (New York: Oxford University Press, 1975), 86–99.
178. Carl Ernst points to British Orientalists Sir William Jones (d. 1794) and Sir John Malcolm (d. 1833) as two examples of scholars whose understandings of Sufism were overly determined by their own Christian beliefs; see Carl Ernst, *The Shambhala Guide to Sufism*, 8–11.
179. Gibb, *Modern Trends in Islam*, 20.
180. One of Rahman's most direct attacks against Sufism is in *Islam*, 244–247. Denny provides a brief discussion of Rahman's point of view on Sufism in "The Legacy of Fazlur Rahman," 100–101.
181. Rahman, *Islam and Modernity*, 46.
182. Ibid.
183. Ibid., 46–47.
184. Ibid.
185. Ibid., 90.
186. Ibid., 131–132.
187. Ibid.
188. Ibid., 131.
189. Ibid., 133.
190. Ibid., 141–143.
191. Ibid., 141ff.
192. Ibid.
193. Ismail Ibrahim Nawwab, "Reflections on the Roles and Educational Desiderata of the Islamist," in *Islamic Perspectives: Studies In Honor of Mawlana Sayyid Abu'l-A'la Mawdudi*, ed. Khurshid Ahmad and Zafar Ishaq Ansari (Leicester: Islamic Foundation, 1979), 45.
194. For Rahman's views on the institution and structure of an Islamic state see: "Some Reflections on the Reconstruction of Muslim Society in Pakistan," *Islamic Studies* 6 (1967): 103–120; "Implementation of the Islamic Concept of State in the Pakistani Milieu," *Islamic Studies* 6 (1967): 205–224; "Islam and the Constitutional Problem of Pakistan" *Studia Islamica* 32 (1970): 275–287; "The Principle of *Shura* and the Role of the Umma in Islam" *American Journal of Islamic Studies* 1, 1 (1984): 1–9.
195. Rahman, "Implementation of the Islamic Concept of State in the Pakistani Milieu," 206.
196. Ibid.
197. Ibid., 205.
198. Ibid., 206.
199. Mawdudi, *System of Government Under the Holy Prophet* (Lahore: Islamic Publications, 1978), 6–7.
200. Nasr, *Mawdudi and the Making of Islamic Revivalism*, 89.
201. Mawdudi, *Islamic Law and Constitution*, ed. Khurshid Ahmad. (Karachi: Jamaat-e Islami Publications, 1955), 124.
202. Ibid.

203. Nasr, *Mawdudi and the Making of Islamic Revivalism*, 91. See also Mawdudi, *Islamic Law and Constitution*, 81–93.
204. Mawdudi, *The Political Theory of Islam*, trans. Khurshid Ahmad (Lahore: Islamic Publications, 1960), 29–38.
205. Mawdudi, *Islamic Law and Constitution*, 81–93. See also Nasr, *Mawdudi and the Making of Islamic Revivalism*, 91.
206. Mawdudi, *Islamic Law and Constitution*, 31.
207. For Rahman's views on education, see his article "The Quranic Solution of Pakistan's Educational Problems," *Islamic Studies* 6 (1967): 315–326. For Rahman's views on democracy see "The Principle of *Shura* and the Role of the Umma in Islam," op. cit. and "Implementation of the Islamic Concept of State in the Pakistani Milieu," op. cit.
208. Mawdudi, *The Political Theory of Islam*, 29–38.
209. Nasr, *Mawdudi and the Making of Islamic Revivalism*, 84–85.
210. Ibid.
211. Ibid.
212. Mawdudi, *The Political Theory of Islam*, 29–38.
213. Rahman, "Status of Women in the Quran," in *Women and Revolution in Iran*, ed. Guity Nashat (Boulder, Colorado: Westview Press, 1983): 37.
214. Ibid.
215. Ibid.
216. Ibid.
217. Ibid.
218. Ibid., 37–39.
219. Rahman, "A Survey of Modernization of Muslim Family Law," *International Journal of Middle East Studies* 11 (1980): 451.
220. Rahman, "Status of Women in the Quran," 47–48.
221. Rahman, "Major Themes of the Qur'an," 47.
222. Ibid., 48.
223. Ibid., 48ff.
224. Rahman, "Status of Women in the Quran," 40.
225. Ibid., 40.
226. Ibid., 41.
227. Ibid., 44.
228. Mawdudi, *Purdah and the Status of Woman in Islam*, trans. al-Ash⟨ari (Lahore: Islamic Publications, 1995), 149.
229. Ibid., 141–158.
230. Ibid., 200–210.
231. Ibid., 179–199.
232. Ibid., 173–174.
233. Ibid.
234. Ibid.
235 Barbara Freyer Stowasser, "Women's Issues in Modern Islamic Thought," in *Arab Women: Old Boundaries, New Frontiers*, ed. Judith E. Tucker (Bloomington, Indiana: Indiana University Press, 1993), 3–28.

236. Ibid., 3.
237. Ibid.
238. Ibid., 4.
239. Ibid.
240. Rahman, "Status of Women in the Quran," 40–44.
241. John Esposito, *The Islamic Threat: Myth or Reality?* 169–170, 184–187.
242. The bulk of Mernissi's *Women and Islam* is devoted to these questions. For Ahmed's views on Sharia, see *Women and Gender in Islam*, 227–234.
243. Rahman, *Islam*, 100–116.
244. Mernissi, "Women, Saints, and Sanctuaries," *Signs* 31 (Autumn 1977): 101–112.
245. Ahmed, *Women and Gender in Islam*, 86, 96–98.
246. Rahman, *Islam and Modernity*, 130–162.
247. Rahman, *Islam*, 82–83, 182.
248. Rahman, "Roots of Islamic Neo-Fundamentalism," in *Change and the Muslim World*, ed. Philip H. Stoddard, David C. Cuthell, Margaret W. Sullivan (Syracuse: Syracuse University Press, 1981), 34.

Chapter 5

1. Arkoun, "The Concept of Authority in Islamic Thought," in *Islam: State and Society*, ed. Klaus Ferdinand and Mehdi Mozaffari (Riverdale, Maryland: Riverdale Company, 1988), 53–73.
2. Arkoun, "De la strategie de domination a creatrice entre l'Europe et le monde Arabe," in *Le Dialogue Euro-Arabe*, ed. Jacques Bourrinet (Paris: Economica, 1979); "Explorations and Responses: New Perspectives for a Jewish-Christian-Muslim Dialogue," *Journal of Ecumenical Studies* 26, 3 (Summer 1989): 523–529; "Reflexions d'un Musulman sur le "Noveau" Catechisme," *Revue des Deux Mondes* (April 1993): 18–30.
3. There are two reasons for this approach. First, the general outlines of various Islamic revivalist and neotraditionalist positions on such issues as the Quran, Islamic history, Sufism, women, and Islamic government have already been discussed. Second, this chapter is devoted in part to comparing and contrasting the specifics of various aspects of the four modernists' thought while the conclusion will focus on more general trends in modernist, neotraditionalist, and revivalist thought in Islamic and western societies.
4. *Oxford Encyclopedia of the Modern Islamic World*, s.v. "Arkoun, Mohammed."
5. Lee, *Overcoming Tradition and Modernity*, 146. These and several other observations which Lee makes about Arkoun and his works are based on personal interviews with him; see Lee's *Overcoming Tradition and Modernity*, vii–viii and Arkoun's *Rethinking Islam*, xv.

6. For Arkoun's criticism of the works of al-Shafi'i and other medieval Muslim jurists see *Pour une Critique de la Raison Islamique* (Paris: Maisonneuve et Larose, 1984), 83ff. For his criticism of contemporary Islamic revivalist discourse see "L'Islam dans l'Histoire," *Maghreb-Machreq* 102 (1983): 6–10.

7. See Arkoun, "L'Islam dans l'Histoire," 17–21 and Lee, *Overcoming Tradition and Modernity*, 146, 165.

8. Loc. cit. endnote 3 above.

9. Arkoun, *Rethinking Islam* (Boulder: Westview Press, 1994), 121–130.

10. *Oxford Encyclopedia of the Modern Islamic World*, s.v. "Arkoun, Mohammed."

11. See the bibliography of Arkoun's publications for the names of the publishers who have made his works available. Two collections in Arabic of essays by Arkoun originally published in French are *Al-fikr al-islami: qira'a 'ilmiyya* (Beirut: Markaz al-Inma al-Qawmi, 1986) and *Min faysal al-tafriqa ila fasl al maqal: 'ayna huwa al-fikr al-islami al-mu'asir* (Beirut: Dar al-Saqi, 1992).

12. Arkoun, *Pour une critique de la raison islamique*, 112.

13. Arkoun, La Pensée Arabe (Paris: Presses Universitaires de France, 1975), 106–107. See also Lee, *Overcoming Tradition and Modernity*, 164–165.

14. Arkoun and Louis Gardet, *L'Islam: Hier, Demain* (Paris: Buchet/Chastel, 1978), 244.

15. Robert D. Lee, *Overcoming Tradition and Modernity*, 165–166.

16. Arkoun, *L'Islam, Hier-Demain* (Paris: Burchet-Chastel, 1972): 141.

17. Ibid.

18. Arkoun, *Rethinking Islam: Common Questions, Uncommon Answers*, translated and edited by Robert D. Lee (Boulder, Colorado: Westview Press, 1994), 38.

19. Arkoun, *Rethinking Islam*, 44. See also Arkoun's *Lectures du Coran* (Paris: Editions G.-P Maisonneuve et Larose, 1982), 1–27.

20. Arkoun, Rethinking Islam, 44.

21. Ibid., 21.

22. Ibid.

23. Ibid., 34.

24. Ibid.

25. Ibid.

26. Ibid., 33.

27. Ibid.

28. Ibid.

29. Ibid.

30. Ibid.

31. Ibid.

32. Ibid., 35.

33. Ibid.

34. Ibid., 33.
35. Mernissi, *Islam and Democracy*, 75–77.
36. Ahmed, *Women and Gender in Islam*, 94.
37. Rahman, "Muhammad and the Quran," in *Commitment and Commemoration: Jews, Christians, and Muslims in Dialogue*, ed. André Lacocque (Chicago: Exploration Press, 1994), 9–11.
38. Ibid.
39. Rahman, "Some Islamic Issues in the Ayyub Khan Era," 285.
40. Arkoun, "Supplique d'un Musulman aux Chrétiens," in *Les Musulmans: Consultation Islamo-Chrétienne*, eds. Kamel Hussein and Daniel Pézeril (Paris: Editions Beauchesne, 1971), 121–126.
41. Arkoun, *Rethinking Islam*, 22, 33. See also Arkoun's *Essais sur la pensée islamique* (Paris: Editions Maisonneuve et Larose, 1984), 13–50, and "The Concept of Authority in Islamic Thought," in *Islam: State and Society*, ed. Klaus Ferdinand and Mehdi Mozaffari (Riverdale, Maryland: Riverdale Company, 1988), 53–73.
42. Arkoun, *Rethinking Islam*, 22.
43. Ibid.
44. Ibid.
45. Ibid.
46. Arkoun, "Le concept de raison islamique" in *Pour une critique de la raison islamique* (Paris: Maisonneuve et Larose, 1984), 65–99.
47. Ibid., 67.
48. Ibid., 65.
49. Ibid., 83.
50. Ibid.
51. Mohamed El Ayadi, "Mohamed Arkoun ou l'ambition d'une modernité intellectuelle," in *Penseurs Maghrebins Contemporains*, ed. Abdou Filali Ansary and Mohamed Tozy (Tunis: Cérès Productions, 1993), 64.
52. Arkoun, *Pour une critiqe de la raison islamique*, 83ff.
53. Ibid.
54. Ibid.
55. Rahman, *Islam*, 77–80.
56. Ibid.
57. Rahman, *Islam and Modernity*, 130.
58. Arkoun, *Ouvertures sur l'Islam* (Paris: J. Granchet, 1992), 78.
59. Ibid., 158.
60. Arkoun, *L'Islam: Hier, demain.* (Paris: Burchet-Chastel, 1982), 146.
61. El Ayadi, "Mohamed Arkoun ou l'ambition d'une modernité intellectuelle," 61–62.
62. Claude Levi-Strauss, *Le Cru et Cuit* (Plon, 1964), 246, as quoted in El Ayadi, "Mohamed Arkoun ou l'ambition d'une modernité intellectuelle," 62.
63. El Ayadi, "Mohamed Arkoun ou l'ambition d'une modernité intellectuelle," 62.

64. Arkoun, *L'Islam. Hier, demain.* (Paris: Burchet-Chastel, 1982), 146. See also Arkoun's "Les tâches de l'intellectuel musulman," in *Intellectuels et Militants dans le monde islamique VIIe–XXe* (Nice, France: Université de Nice, 1988).
65. Robert D. Lee, *Overcoming Tradition and Modernity: The Search for Islamic Authenticity,* 156.
66. Arkoun, *Rethinking Islam,* 128ff. See also Robert D. Lee's treatment of this subject in *Overcoming Tradition and Modernity,* 159.
67. Ibid., 128ff.
68. Ibid.
69. Ibid.
70. Arkoun, "The Unity of Man in Islamic Thought," *Diogenes* (Winter 1987): 50–51.
71. Ibid., 59–60.
72. Ibid., 57.
73. M. Chodkiewicz's translation of Ibn Arabi's works in *Le Sceau des Saints,* (Gallimard, 1986), 184–185 as quoted in Arkoun's "The Unity of Man in Islamic Thought," 57.
74. Arkoun, "The Unity of Man in Islamic Thought," 57.
75. Ibid., 48.
76. Ibid., 59–60.
77. Arkoun, "L'Islam dans l'histoire," *Maghreb Machreq* 102 (1983): 16.
78. Arkoun, "The Unity of Man in Islamic Thought," 60.
79. Mernissi, "Women, Saints, and Sanctuaries" *Signs* 31 (Autumn 1977): 101–112.
80. Ahmed, *Women and Gender in Islam,* 99–100.
81. Ibid., 95–98, 115–116.
82. Rahman, *Islam,* 246.
83. Mernissi, *Women and Islam,* 49–84; Ahmed, Women and Gender in Islam, 227–228, 230–234; Arkoun, *Rethinking Islam,* 49ff.
84 Arkoun, *Rethinking Islam,* 47; Arkoun, *La pensée arabe,* 44.
85. Arkoun, *Rethinking Islam,* 47; *La pensée arabe,* 45.
86. Arkoun, *Rethinking Islam,* 47.
87. Ibid.; *La pensée arabe,* 46.
88. Ibid.
89. Ibid.
90. Ibid.
91. Arkoun, *L'Islam morale et politique,* 135–146.
92. Arkoun, *Rethinking Islam,* 60.
93. Arkoun, *Islam dans l'histoire,* 6–10 and his article "Émergences et problèmes dans le monde musulman contemporain (1960–1985)," *Islamo-christiana* 12 (1986): 136–139.
94. Arkoun, *Rethinking Islam,* 60.
95. Ibid.
96. Ibid., 61.

97. Ibid.
98. Ibid.
99. Ibid.
100. Ibid. Although Arkoun suspends final judgment regarding the specifics of Quranic teachings about several issues related to women, he suggests that one of Ibn Rushd's (1126–1198) observations on the status of women in early and medieval Islam can be instructive for the modern period:

> Our state of social affairs does not give women the possibility of contributing in accordance with their ability. They seem uniquely destined to give birth to children and to take care of them. This state of servitude has destroyed their ability to do great things. This is why many do not see women as endowed with moral virtue. Their lives are passed off as those of plants" (Ibn Rushd as quoted in Arkoun's "Les unions mixtes en milieu musulman" in *Pour une critique de la raison islamique*, 259).

Arkoun writes that Ibn Rushd's position on this issue is that of a non-conformist whose ideas could provide a basis for "a modern protest" against certain aspects of the treatment of Muslim women.

101. Arkoun, *Rethinking Islam*, 62.
102. Personal interview with Leila Ahmed, April 10, 1998. Nadia Nagie discusses Mernissi's leadership in various women's groups in *Fez-New York und Zurück: Fatima Mernissi, Ihre Welt und Ihre Geschichte*, 93ff.
103. One of Mernissi's better-known sociological works is *Doing Daily Battle: Interviews with Moroccan Women* (New Brunswick, New Jersey: Rutgers University Press, 1989). She engages in some exegesis of the Qur'an and Hadith in *The Veil and the Male Elite, op. cit.* Ahmed's most important historical work that pertains to the role of women in Islamic history is *Women and Gender in Islam, op. cit.*
104. Arkoun, "Le dialogue euro-arabe: essai d'évaluation critique," in *Cooperation Euro-Arabe: Diagnostic et Prospective*, ed. Bichara Khader (Louvain, France: Le Centre d'Etude et de Recherche sur le Monde Arabe Contemporain de l'Université Catholique de Louvain, 1982), 129–137.
105. Arkoun, "De la strategie de domination à une coopération créatice entre l'Europe et le Monde Arabe," in *Le dialogue euro-arabe*, ed. Jacques Bourrinet (Paris: Economica, 1979), 45–61.
106. Arkoun, *Rethinking Islam*, 53.
107. Ibid.
108. Ibid.
109. Ibid., 55.
110. Ibid., 57
111. Ibid.
112. Their common appeals to United Nations declarations may be attributable to the fact that both of them have worked with or have written for the United Nations. Mernissi undertook research projects and aid activities among North African women as part of the United Nations Economic

Commission for Africa and Arkoun has written extensively for UNESCO publications.
113. Mernissi, *Islam and Democracy*, 62–63; Arkoun, *Rethinking Islam*, 106–107.
114. See, for example, Rahman's *Islam and the Constitutional Problem of Pakistan*, 275–287 and his *Implementation of the Islamic Concept of State in the Pakistani Milieu*, 223.
115. Ahmed, *Women and Gender in Islam*, 95–100.
116. Lee, *Overcoming Tradition and Modernity*, 156.
117. Arkoun, *Pour une critique de la raison islamique*, 7.

Chapter 6

1. Mernissi's *Beyond the Veil*, for example, has been translated into Arabic as *al-jins ka-handasa ijtima'iya baina an-nass wa'l waqi'* (Dar al-Baida, n.d.) and a collection of her essays under the title *al-hubb fi hadaratina al-islamiya* (Beirut: n.pub., n.d.). The citations for the articles which Rahman wrote in Pakistan on such issues as education, family law and the mechanical slaughter of animals appears in chapter four, n. 18. The citations for some of the translations of Arkoun's works into Arabic appears in chapter five, n. 11.
2. Ismail Faruqi, Seyyed Hosain Nasr, Mahmoud Ayoub, and Azizah al-Hibri are other Muslim intellectuals, the bulk of whose work has also originally been made available in Western languages through Western presses.
3. William A. Graham, "Traditionalism in Islam: An Essay in Interpretation," *Journal of Interdisciplinary History* 23, 3 (Winter 1993): 495–522.
4. Ibid., 500.
5. Ibid.
6. Giddens, *The Consequences of Modernity*, (Stanford: Stanford University Press, 1990), 1–55.
7. Ibid., 36.
8. Ibid.
9. Ibid., 37.
10. Ibid.
11. Ibid.
12. Graham, "Traditionalism in Islam," 501.
13. Ibid.
14. Ibid.
15. Seyyed Vali Reza Nasr, "Religious Modernism in the Arab World, India and Iran: The Perils and Prospects of a Discourse," *The Muslim World* 83, no. 1 (January 1993): 46–47.
16. Ibid., 36.
17. Ibid.

18. Ibid., 34–47.
19. Ibid., 36.
20. Mernissi, *Women and Islam*, 25–189; Ahmed, *Women and Gender in Islam*, 41–52, 61–65.
21. Rahman, *Islam and Modernity*, 130–158.
22. For a discussion of the ways in which Arkoun draws upon aspects of Jean-Paul Sartre, see Mohamed El Ayadi's "Mohamed Arkoun ou l'ambition d'une modernité intellectuelle," 53 and for the relationship between Arkoun's worldview and Bourdieu's philosophy see Mohammed Arkoun's "L'Islam dans l'histoire," 11–12, 23.
23. Mawdudi, *Human Rights in Islam*, 1–23 and *The Process of Islamic Revolution*, 5–32; Umar Abd-Allah, *The Islamic Struggle in Syria*, 214ff.
24. Seyyed Vali Reza Nasr, "Religious Modernism," 36.
25. Fatima Mernissi, *The Forgotten Queens of Islam* (Minneapolis, Minnesota: University of Minnesota Press, 1993) and Ahmed, *Women and Gender in Islam*, 63–67, 100–101, 239–240.
26. Rahman, *Islam*, 56–57, 80–87.
27. Arkoun, *Pour une critique de la raison islamique*, 65–99; El Ayadi, "Mohamed Arkoun ou l'ambition d'une modernité intellectuelle," 63–64.
28. Mernissi, *Islam and Democracy*, 149–174; Ahmed, "Feminism and Feminist Movements in the Middle East," 161–163 and "Western Ethnocentrism and Perceptions of the Harem," 521–534.
29. Rahman, *Islam and Modernity*, 130–162.
30. Arkoun, "Origines islamiques des droits de l'homme," *Revue des Sciences morales et politiques* no. 1 (1989): 25–37.
31. Arkoun "Le dialogue euro-arabe: Essai d'evaluation critique," 129–137.
32. Mawdudi, *A Short History of the Revivalist Movement in Islam*, 25. Mawdudi does not provide any indication as to how he comes to the figure of "three-fourths."
33. Ibid., 25–28, 44–78.
34. R. Stephen Humphreys, "Islam and Political Values," 3–5.
35. Mustansir Mir, "Building an Islamic Academic Tradition in the West," *Islamic Horizons*, March/April 1998, 29.
36. Ibid.
37. Ibid.
38. Among other activities, Mernissi has been involved in the leadership of Muslim women's organizations and other human rights organizations pertaining to gender equality in Morocco. (Nagie, *Fez-New York und Zurück*, 94. Nagie does not provide the names of these organizations.) Rahman attempted (unsuccessfully) to influence policy-making and public opinion during the 1960s in Pakistan as the Chair of the Institute of Islamic Research in Karachi, but seemed to find more freedom to express his ideas at the University of Chicago. According to Frederick Denny, "It was at the University of Chicago, that [Rahman's] position as the leading Muslim modernist scholar of his generation was solidified through publi-

cations, consultations, preaching, and religious leadership in the Muslim community, and especially through his training of younger scholars who came from various countries to study under him." (Denny, "The Legacy of Fazlur Rahman," 97). In addition to his scholarly publications, Arkoun lectures extensively to Muslims and non-Muslims in many parts of the world and has been in a leadership position at the Institute of Ismaili Studies in London.

39. For a description of the impact and organizational structure of such diaspora groups as the Muslim Students Association and the Islamic Society of North America (which I have termed neotraditionalist), see Gutbi Mahdi Ahmed, "Muslim Organizations in the United States," 11–24 in Haddad and Lummis, *Islamic Values in the United States*, 5–6, 124, 156. For a description of the influence and structure of Islamic revivalist groups in the Muslim world, see John Esposito, *The Islamic Threat*, 119–167.

40. Mir, "Building an Islamic Academic Tradition in the West," 29.

41. Ibid., 29.

42. Ibid.

43. Ibrahim Abu Rabi‘, "An Islamic Response to Modernity," *Islamic Horizons*, March/April 1998, 44.

44. Ibid., 46.

45. Mir, "Building an Islamic Academic Tradition in the West," 29. Abu Rabi‘, "An Islamic Response to Modernity," 44.

46. Samuel C. Heilman, "Quiescent and Active Fundamentalisms: The Jewish Cases," in *Accounting for Fundamentalisms: The Dynamic Character of Movements*, eds. Martin E. Marty and R. Scott Appleby (Chicago: University of Chicago Press, 1994), 178.

47. Ibid., 175.

48. Frank Clemente and Frank Watkins, eds., *Keep Hope Alive; Jesse Jackson's 1988 Presidential Campaign: A Collection of Major Speeches, Issue Papers, Photographs, and Campaign Analysis* (Boston: South End Press, 1989). This entire volume contains Jackson's positions on various political issues and his speech "The Promise and Politics of Empowerment" to the Ward African Methodist Episcopal Church in Los Angeles in June 1988 shows most clearly the fusion of Jackson's religious and political ideals; see *Keep Hope Alive*, pp. 209–212.

49. Jerry Falwell, *Falwell: An Autobiography* (Lynchburg, Virginia: Liberty House, 1997). The book contains his ideas on these and a host of other issues.

50. Juergensmeyer, *The New Cold War?*, 84.

51. Ibid. I am not suggesting that the Congress Party has always been tolerant of religious minorities in India. During various times since Partition in 1948, certain policies of the Congress Party have had negative ramifications for Indian religious minorities, such as Muslims and Sikhs. For a

discussion of these issues, see Gerald James Larson, *India's Agony Over Religion* (Albany: State University of New York Press, 1995), 234–255.

52. Sallie B. King, "Thich Nhat Hanh and the Unified Buddhist Church of Vietnam: Nondualism in Action," in *Engaged Buddhism: Buddhist Liberation Movements in Asia*, ed. Christopher S. Queen (Albany: State University of New York Press, 1996), 356–389.

53. José Ignacio Cabezón, "Buddhist Principles in the Tibetan Liberation Movement," in *Engaged Buddhism: Buddhist Liberation Movements in Asia*, ed. Christopher S. Queen (Albany: State University of New York Press, 1996), 325–354.

54. The following article provides a discussion of politically and non-politically minded Buddhists in America: David Van Biema, "Buddhism in America: An Ancient Religion Grows Ever Stronger Roots in a New World," *Time*, October 13, 1997, 72–78. There are non-politically minded Buddhists in other countries as well. James Manor provides a brief discussion of a subset of Buddhists in Sri Lanka and southern India, whom he calls "purists," who shy away from political activity. See James Manor, "Organizational Weakness and the Rise of Sinhalese Buddhist Extremism," in *Accounting For Fundamentalisms*, 771.

Bibliography

Works by Fatima Mernissi

Arabic

Mernissi, Fatima. *Ahlam al-nisaʾ: tufulah fi al-harim*. Damascus, Syria: Dar Atiyah, 1997.

———. *Hal antum muhassanun didda al-harim: nass ikhtibar lil-rijal alladhina yaʿshaquna al-nisaʾ*. al-Dar al-Baydaʾ: Nashr al-Fanak, 2000.

———. "Al-hub fi hadaratina al-islamiyya." Beirut: al-Dar al-Alamiya, 1983.

———. *Al-marʾah wa-al-sulat*. Al-Dar al-Baydaʾ: Nashr al-Fanak, 1990.

———. *Nisaʾ ʿala ajnihat al-hulm*. Al-Dar al-Baydaʾ-al-Maghrib: Nashr al-Fanak, 1998.

———. and Fatimah al-Zahraʾ Azruwil. *Nisaʾ al-gharb: dirasah maydaniyah*. al-Dar al-Baydaʾ: Smer, 1985.

———. *Sultanat mansiyah: nisaʾ hakimat fi bilad al-Islam*. al-Dar al-Baydaʾ: Nashr al-Fanak, 2000.

———. *Al-suluk al-jinsi fi mujtamaʿ islami rasmali tabai*. Beirut: Dar al-Hadatha, 1984.

Mernissi, Fatima and ʿAbbas ʿAbd al-Hadi. *Al-harim al-siyasi: al-nabi wa-al-nisaʾ*. Damascus, Syria: Dar al-Hisad, 1993.

Mernissi, Fatima and ʿAʾisha Eshanna and Shuʿayb Halifi. *Miziriya shahadat*. al-Dar al-Baydaʾ: Nashr al-Fanak, 1997.

Mernissi, Fatima and Lallah Laʿzizah Tazi, et al. *Kayd al-nisaʾ? Kayd al-rijal?: hikayah shaʿbiyah maghribiyah*. Al-Dar al-Baydaʾ: Mu'assasat Bin-Shirrah, 1983.

Mernissi, Fatima and Fatimah al-Zahraʾ Zaryul. *Al-jins ka-handasah ijtima'iyah bayna al-nass wa-al-waqi'*. Al-Dar al-Bayda': Nashr al-Fanak, 1987.

Mernissi, Fatima and Muhammad Dabbiyat. *Al-khawf min al-hadathah: al-islam wa-al-dimuqratiyah*. Damascus, Syria: Dar al-Jundi, 1994.

English

Mernissi, Fatima. "Arab Women's Rights and the Muslim State in the Twenty-First Century: Reflections on Islam as Religion and State." In *Faith and Freedom: Women's Human Rights in the Modern World*, edited by Mahnaz Afkhami. London: Tauris, 1995.

———. *Beyond the Veil: Male-Female Dynamics in a Modern Muslim Society*. Cambridge, Massachusetts: Schenkman Publishing Company, 1975.

———. *Can We Women Head A Muslim State?* Lahore, Pakistan: Simorgh, Women's Resource and Publications Center, 1991.

———. *Country Reports on Women in North Africa, Libya, Morocco, Tunisia*. Addis Ababa: African Training and Research Center for Women, United Nations Economic Commission for Africa, 1978.

———. "The Degrading Effect of Capitalism on Female Labour in a Third World Economy: The Particular Case of Crafts Women In Morocco." *Peuples Méditerranées* No. 6 (January–March 1979): 41–57.

———. "Democracy as Moral Disintegration: The Contradiction Between Religious Belief and Citizenship as a Manifestation of the Ahistoricity of the Arab Identity." In *Women of the Arab World: The Coming Challenge?* London: Zed Books, 1988.

———. *Doing Daily Battle: Interviews with Moroccan Women*. New Brunswick, New Jersey: Rutgers University Press, 1989.

———. *Dreams of Trespass: Tales of a Harem Girlhood*. Reading, Massachusetts: Addison-Wesley Publishing Company, 1994.

———. *The Effects of Modernization on the Male-Female Dynamics in a Muslim Society*. Ph.D. dissertation, Brandeis University, 1973.

———. "Femininity as Subversion: Reflections on the Muslim Concept of Nushuz." In *Speaking of Faith: Cross Cultural Perspectives on Women, Religion, and Social Change*. London: The

Women's Press, 1986.

———. *The Forgotten Queens of Islam*. Minneapolis, Minnesota: University of Minnesota Press, 1993.

———. *The Fundamentalist Obsession with Women: A Current Articulation of Class Conflict in Modern Muslim Societies*. Lahore, Pakistan: Women's Resource and Publication Centre, 1987.

———. *The Harem Within*. New York: Bantam, 1995.

———. *Hidden from History: The Forgotten Queens of Islam*. Lahore, Pakistan: ASR Publications, 1994.

———. *Islam and Democracy: Fear of the Modern World*. Reading, Massachusetts: Addison-Wesley Publishing, 1992.

———. "Muslim Women and Fundamentalism." *Arab Women: Between Defiance and Restraint*, edited by Suha Sabbagh. New York: Olive Branch Press, 1996.

———. "The Moslem World: Women Excluded from Development." In *Women and World Development*, edited by Irene Trinker. New York: World Development Council, 1976.

———. "Obstacles to Family Planning in Urban Morocco." In *Studies in Family Planning*. New York: The Population Council, 1975.

———. "Palace Fundamentalism and Liberal Democracy: Oil, Arms and Irrationality." *Development and Change* 27, 1: 251–265.

———. *Participation of Women in Social and Human Scientific Life in the Arab World*. Paris: Division of Human Rights and Peace, UNESCO, 1984.

———. "The Patriarch in the Moroccan Family: Myth or Reality?" In *Women's Status and Fertility in the Muslim World*, edited by James Alman. New York: Praeger Publishers, 1978.

———. *Scheherazade Goes West*. New York: Washington Square Press, 2001.

———. *The Veil and the Male Elite: A Feminist Interpretation of Women's Rights in Islam*. Reading, Massachusetts, 1991.

———. "Veiled Sisters," *New World Outlook*, New Series 31, No. 8 (April 1977).

———. "Virginity and Patriarchy," *Women's Studies International Forum* 5, 2 (1982): 183–192.

———. "Women and the Impact of Capitalist Development in Morocco, Part I." *Feminist Issues* 2, 2 (1982): 69–104. "Part II." *Feminist Issues* 3, 1 (1983): 61–112.

———. *Women and Islam: An Historical and Theological Enquiry*. Oxford: Basil Blackwell, 1991. (British edition of *The Veil and the Male Elite*).

———. *Women in Moslem Paradise*. New Delhi: Kali for Women, 1986.

———. *Women in Muslim History: Traditional Perspectives and New Strategies*. Lahore: Women's Resource and Publication Center, 1989.

———. "Women, Saints, and Sanctuaries." *Signs* 31 (Autumn 1977): 101–112.

———. *Women's Rebellion and Islamic Memory*. Atlantic Highlands, New Jersey: Zed Books, 1996.

———. "Women's Work: Religious and Scientific Concepts as Political Manipulation in Dependent Islam. *Barakat, Halim (Hg.): Contemporary North Africa, Issues of Development and Integration*. London: Sydney 1985, 214–228.

———. www.mernissi.net Mernissi's own website.

———. "Zhor's World: A Moroccan Domestic Worker Speaks Out." *Feminist Issues* 2, no. 1 (1982): 3–31.

——— et al. "Dismantling the Maghreb: Contemporary Moroccan Writing and Islamic Discursivity." In *The Marabout and the Muse: New Approaches to Islam in African Literature*, edited by K.W. Harrow. London: Currey, 1996.

Mernissi, Fatima and Ruth Ward. *Vanishing Orient: Papa's Harem is Shifting to Mama's Civil Society*. Munich: AB 40, 1997.

French

Aït Sabbah, Fatna (Mernissi's Pseudonym), *La femme dans l'inconscient musulman*. Editions le Sycomore, Paris, 1981.

Mernissi, Fatima. *Les Ait-Débrouille: ONG rurales du Haut-Atlas*. Morocco: Editions le Fennec, 1998.

———. *L'Amour dans les pays musulmans*. Casablanca: Editions Maghrébines, 1985.

———. "Les Bonnes." *Al-Asas, Mensuel pour la Société de Demain*, Casablanca, November 1977, 26–34.

———. *Chahrazad n'est pas Marocaine: Autrement, Elle Serait Salariee*. Casablanca: Editions Le Fennec, 1991.

———. "Des Marocaines ou la revolution dévoilée." *Jeune Afrique Magazine*, No. 15, 1988, 10–18.

———. *Développement capitaliste et perceptions des femmes dans la société arabo-musulmane*. Geneva: Organisation international du travail, 1981.

————. *Êtes-vous vacciné contre le 'harem'?: texte-test pour les messieurs qui adorent les dames.* Casablanca: Fennec, 1998, 1997.

————. *Femme partagées: Famille-Travail.* Casablanca: Editions Le Fennec, 1988.

————. *Femme et pouvoirs.* Casablanca: Editions Le Fennec, 1990.

————. "Un Futur sans femmes?" *Lamalif, Revue mensuelle, culturelle économique et sociale.* Casablanca, No. 115, April 1980: 26–31.

————. *Le harem et les femmes.* Bruxelles: Complexe, 1992.

————. *Le harem et l'occident.* Paris: Albin Michel, 2001.

————. *Le harem politique: Le Prophéte et les femmes.* Paris: Editions Albin Michel, 1987.

————. "Kesso cherche un mari." *Jeune Afrique,* Paris, November 19, 1967.

————. "Malheureusement comme une Américaine." *Jeune Afrique,* Paris, October 1, 1967.

————. *Le Maroc reconté par ses femmes.* Rabat: Sociéte Marocaine des Editeurs Réunis (SMER), 1983.

————. *Le monde n'est pas un harem: paroles de femmes du Maroc.* Paris: Albin Michel, 1991.

————. "Des Marocaines ou la révolution dévoilée." *Jeune Afrique Magazine* No. 51: 10–18.

————. "Pas de futur sans femmes, pas de futur sans dialogue." *Lamalif: Revue mensuelle, culturelle Economique et sociale.* Casablanca No. 119 (October 1988): 40–44.

————. *La peur—modernité: conflit Islam démocratie.* Paris: A. Michel, 1992.

————. *Portraits de femmes.* Casablanca: Collection Approches, Editions Le Fennec, 1987.

————. "Pourquoi nos enfants dans les rues." *Lamalif,* No. 105 (1979): 24–30.

————. "Le Prolétariat féminine au Maroc." *Annuaire de l'Afrique du Nord* No. 19 (1980): 345–356.

————. *Le savoir comme champ de discrimination et d'exclusion: le cas des femmes au Maroc.* UNESCO, 1982.

————. *Sexe, Ideologie, Islam.* Rabat: Editions maghrebines, 1985.

————. *Sultanes Oubliées: Femmes Chefs d'Etat en Islam.* Paris: Editions Albin Michel, 1990.

————. "Virginité et patriarcat." *Lamalif* No. 107 (1979): 24–30.

Mernissi, Fatima, Omar Azziman, and Fettouma Benabdenbi. *Marocaines et sécurité sociale.* Casablanca: Editions le fennec, 1992.

Mernissi, Fatima and Alya Chérif Chamari. *La femme et la loi en Tunisie.* Alger: Bouchene: UNU/Wider, 1991.

Mernissi, Fatima and Dalila Morsly, *D'Algérie et de femmes.* Algiers: Fridrich [*sic*] Ebert Stiftung: Groupe Aïcha, 1994.

Mernissi, Fatima and Claudine Richetin. *Rêves de femmes: une enfance au harem.* Paris: Albin Michel, 1996.

German

Mernissi, Fatima. *Die Angst vor der Moderne, Frauen und Männer zwischen Islam und Demokratie.* Hamburg: Zurich, 1992.

Mernissi, Fatima. *Geschlecht, Ideologie, Islam.* Munich: Frauenbuchverlag, 1987.

————. *Der Harem ist nicht die Welt: Elf Berichte aus dem Leben marokkanischer Frauen.* Translated by Edgar Peinelt and Nina Corsten. Darmstadt: Luchterhand Literaturverlag, 1988.

————. *Die Sultanin: die Macht der Frauen in der Welt des Islam.* Hamburg: Luchterhand Literaturverlag, 1993.

————. "In der Nacht vorn 16. bin ich gestorben: Eine Araberin schildert den Krieg aus ihrer Sicht." *Emma-Sonderband: Krieg — Was Männerwahn anrichtet, und wie die Frauen Widerstand leisten,* Cologne (March 1991): 10–14.

Mernissi, Fatima and Edgar Peinelt. *Die vergessene Macht: Frauen im Wandel der islamischen Welt.* Berlin: Orlanda Frauenverlag, 1993.

Spanish

————. *El Haren politico: el Profeta y las mujeres.* Translated by I. Jiménez Morell. Guadarrama: Ediciones del Oriente y del Mediterraneo, 1999.

————. *Marruecos a través de sus mujeres.* Translated by I. Jiménez Morell. 5a ed. Guadarrama: Ediciones del Oriente y del Mediterraneo, 2000.

————. *Somnis de l'harem.* Translated by Dolors Udina. 3a ed. Barcelona: Columna, 2000.

————. *Les sultanes olvidadas.* Translated by M.A. Galmarini. Barcelona: Muchnik, 1997.

Works by Leila Ahmed

Ahmed, Leila. "Arab Culture and Writing on Women's Bodies" *Feminist Studies* 9 (September 1989): 41–55.

————. "Arab Women: 1995." In *The Next Arab Decade: Alternative Futures*, edited by Hisham Sharabi. Boulder, Colorado: Westview Press, 1988.

————. "Between Two Worlds: The Formation of a Turn of the Century Feminist." In *Life Lines: Theorizing Women's Autobiography*, edited by Bella Brodzki and Celeste Shenk. Ithaca: Cornell University Press, 1988.

————. *A Border Passage: From Cairo to America—A Woman's Journey.* New York: Farrar, Straus, and Giroux, 1999.

————. *Edward W. Lane: A Study of His Life and Works and of British Ideas of the Middle East in the Nineteenth Century.* New York: Longman, 1978.

————. "Encounter With American Feminism: A Muslim Woman's View of Two Conferences." *The Second Annual National Women's Studies Association* 8, no. 3 (Summer 1980): 7–21.

————. "Feminism and Feminist Movements in the Middle East, A Preliminary Exploration: Turkey, Egypt, Algeria, People's Democratic Republic of Yemen." *Women's Studies International Forum* 5 (1982): 155–171; also in *Arabian and Islamic Studies: Articles Presented to R.B. Serjeant*, edited by R.L Bidwell and G.R. Smith, 153–168. Harlow: Longman, 1983.

————. "The Return to the Source." *History Today* 30 (Fall 1980): 23–27.

————. "Western Ethnocentrism and Perceptions of the Harem." *Feminist Studies* (October 1982): 521–534.

————. "Women and the Advent of Islam." *Signs* 11 (Summer 1986): 665–91.

————. *Women and Gender in Islam: Historical Roots of a Modern Debate.* New Haven: Yale University Press, 1992.

Works by Fazlur Rahman

Arabic

Rahman, Fazlur. *Al-islam wa darura-t al-tahdith: nahw ihdath tagyir fi al-taqalid al- thaqafiyya* (Translation of *Islam and Modernity*). Translated by Ibrahim al-ʿAris. Beirut: Dar-al Saqi, 1993.

————. ed. ʿAli, Saʿid. *Al-luhun fi ayyam taha ibn husayn*. Shikaghu: S. ʿAli, 1982.

English

Rahman, Fazlur. "A. K. Md. Akbar's Religion." *Journal of the Asiatic Society of Pakistan*. 10 (1965): 121–134.

————. "Approaches to Islam in Religious Studies: Review Essays." In *Approaches to Islam in Religious Studies*, edited by R.C. Martin, 189–202. Tucson: University of Arizona Press, 1985. Reprinted with the same titles in Oxford, England: Oneworld, 2001, pp 189–202; 233–234.

————. "Avicenna and Orthodox Islam: An Interpretive Note on the Composition of His System." *Harry Austryn Wolfson, Jubilee Volume on the Occasion of His Seventy-fifth Birthday.* Vol II. Jerusalem: American Academy for Jewish Research (1965): 667–76.

————. *Avicenna's De Anima: Being the Psychological Part of Kitab al-Sifa*. London: Oxford University Press, 1970.

————. *Avicenna's Psychology: An English Translation of Kitab al-Najat, Book II, Chapter VI, with Historico-Philosophical Notes and Textual Improvements on the Cairo Edition.* Westport, Connecticut: Hyperion Press, 1981.

————. *The Bengali Muslims and English Education, 1765–1835.* Dacca: Bengali Academy, 1973.

————. "Challenge of Modern Ideas and Social Values to Muslim Society." *International Islamic Colloqium, University of Punjab, University of Punjab, 1957–1958, Papers.* Lahore: Punjab University Press, 1960.

————. "Concepts *Sunnah, Ijtihad,* and *Ijma* in the Early Period." *Islamic Studies* 1 (1962), 5–21.

————. "The Concept of *hadd* in Islamic Law." *Islamic Studies* 4 (1965): 237–251.

————. "The Controversy Over the Muslim Family Laws Ordinance." In *South Asian Politics and Religion*. Ed. Donald E. Smith. Princeton, New Jersey: Princeton University Press (1966): 414–27.

————. *Culture Conflicts in East Pakistan, 1947–1971: A Study in the Attitude of Bengali Muslim Intelligentsia Towards Bengali Literature and Islam*. Dacca: Sejuty Prokashani, 1990.

————. "Currents of Religious Thought in Pakistan." *Islamic Studies* 7 (1968): 1–7.

————. "Divine Revelation and the Prophet." *Hamdard Islamicus* Vol. 1, no. 2 (1978): 66–72.

————. "Dream, Imagination, and *'Alam al-Mithal*." In *The Dream and Human Societies*, edited by G.E. von Grunebaum and R. Caillois, 409–419. University of California Press, 1966. Also in *Islamic Studies* 3 (1964): 176–180.

————. "Economic Principles of Islam." *Islamic Studies* 8 (1969): 1–8.

————. "Elements of Belief in the Quran." In *Literature of Belief: Sacred Scripture and Religious Experience*, edited by Neal Lambert. Salt Lake City, Utah: Religious Studies Center, Brigham Young University, 1981.

————. "Essence and Existence in Avicenna." *Medieval and Renaissance Studies*. 4 (1958): 1–16.

————. "Essence and Existence in Ibn Sina: The Myth and Reality." *Hamdard Islamicus* 4, no. 1 (1981): 3–14.

————. "The Eternity of the World and Heavenly Bodies." In *Essays on Islamic Philosophy and Science*, edited by George Fadlo Hourani, 222–237. Albany, New York: State University of New York Press, 1975.

————. "Evolution of Soviet Policy Toward Muslims in Russia: 1917–1965." *Journal of Muslim Minority Affairs*. 1, no. 2 and 2, no. 1 (1979–80): 28–46.

————. "Fazlur Rahman." In *The Courage of Convictions: Prominent Contemporaries Discuss their Beliefs and How They Put Them Into Action,* edited by Phillip L. Berman. Santa Barbara, California: Dodd, Mead, (1985): 153–9.

————. "Functional Interdependence of Law and Theology." In *Theology and Law in Islam*, edited by Gustave E. von Grunebaum, 89–97. Wiesbaden: O. Harrassowitz, 1971.

————. "Fundamental Ideas in the Philosophy of Value." *Pakistan Philosophical Journal* 8 (1964): 1–13.

————. "The God-World Relationship in Mulla Sadra." In *Essays on Islamic Philosophy and Science*, edited by George Fadlo Hourani, 238–253. Albany, New York: State University of New York Press, 1975.

————. *Health and Medicine in the Islamic Tradition: Change and Identity.* New York: Crossroad, 1987.

————. "Human Rights in Islam." *Democracy and Human Rights in the Islamic Republic of Iran.* Chicago: Committee on Democracy and Human Rights, 1982.

————. "Ibn Sina." *A History of Muslim Philosophy.* Vol. I. Ed. M.M. Sharif. Wiesbaden: Otto Harassowitz (1966): 480–506.

————. "Ibn Sina's Theory of the God-World Relationship." In *God and Creation: An Ecumenical Symposium*, edited by David Burrell and Bernard McGinn, 38–55. Notre Dame, Indiana: University of Notre Dame Press, 1990.

————. "The Ideological Experience of Pakistan." *Islam and the Modern Age.* 2, No. 4 (November 1971): 1–20.

————. "Al-Ikhwan al-Muslimun: A Survey of Ideas and Ideals." *Bulletin of the Institute of Islamic Studies* (Muslim University, Aligarh). Vols. 2–3 (1958–1959): 92–102.

————. "The Impact of Modernity on Islam." *Islamic Studies* 5, no. 2 (June 1966): 113–28.

————. "Implementation of the Islamic Concept of State in the Pakistani Milieu." Islamic Studies 6 (1967): 205–224.

————. "Internal Religious Developments in the Present Century of Islam." *Journal of World History* 2 (1954–55): 862–879.

————. "Interpreting the Quran." *Afkar Inquiry* 3, no. 5 (1986): 45–49.

————. *Industrial Development in Pakistan: As Explained By the Honorable Mr. Fazlur Rahman.* Washington: Embassy of Pakistan, October 1948.

————. "Iqbal's Idea of Progress." *Iqbal Review* 4, no. 1 (1963): 1–4.

————. "Iqbal's Idea of The Muslim." *Islamic Studies* 2 (1963): 439–445.

————. "Iqbal, the Visionary; Jinnah, the Technician; and Pakistan, the Reality." *Iqbal, Jinnah and Pakistan: The Vision and the Reality,* Ed. C.M. Naim. Syracuse, New York: Syracuse University, 1979.

————. *Islam.* Chicago: University of Chicago Press, 1979.

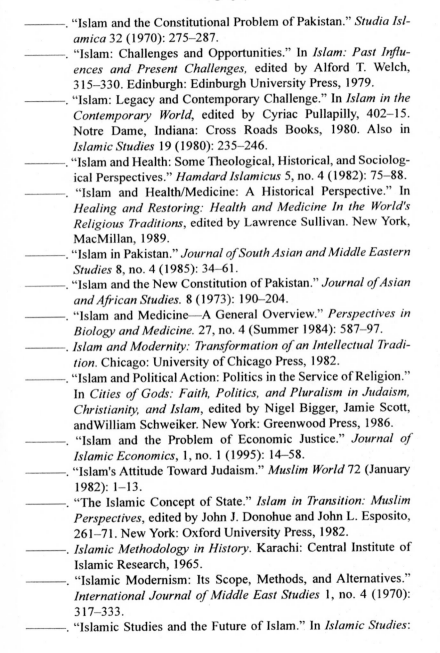

———. "Islam and the Constitutional Problem of Pakistan." *Studia Islamica* 32 (1970): 275–287.

———. "Islam: Challenges and Opportunities." In *Islam: Past Influences and Present Challenges,* edited by Alford T. Welch, 315–330. Edinburgh: Edinburgh University Press, 1979.

———. "Islam: Legacy and Contemporary Challenge." In *Islam in the Contemporary World,* edited by Cyriac Pullapilly, 402–15. Notre Dame, Indiana: Cross Roads Books, 1980. Also in *Islamic Studies* 19 (1980): 235–246.

———. "Islam and Health: Some Theological, Historical, and Sociological Perspectives." *Hamdard Islamicus* 5, no. 4 (1982): 75–88.

———. "Islam and Health/Medicine: A Historical Perspective." In *Healing and Restoring: Health and Medicine In the World's Religious Traditions,* edited by Lawrence Sullivan. New York, MacMillan, 1989.

———. "Islam in Pakistan." *Journal of South Asian and Middle Eastern Studies* 8, no. 4 (1985): 34–61.

———. "Islam and the New Constitution of Pakistan." *Journal of Asian and African Studies.* 8 (1973): 190–204.

———. "Islam and Medicine—A General Overview." *Perspectives in Biology and Medicine.* 27, no. 4 (Summer 1984): 587–97.

———. *Islam and Modernity: Transformation of an Intellectual Tradition.* Chicago: University of Chicago Press, 1982.

———. "Islam and Political Action: Politics in the Service of Religion." In *Cities of Gods: Faith, Politics, and Pluralism in Judaism, Christianity, and Islam,* edited by Nigel Bigger, Jamie Scott, andWilliam Schweiker. New York: Greenwood Press, 1986.

———. "Islam and the Problem of Economic Justice." *Journal of Islamic Economics,* 1, no. 1 (1995): 14–58.

———. "Islam's Attitude Toward Judaism." *Muslim World* 72 (January 1982): 1–13.

———. "The Islamic Concept of State." *Islam in Transition: Muslim Perspectives,* edited by John J. Donohue and John L. Esposito, 261–71. New York: Oxford University Press, 1982.

———. *Islamic Methodology in History.* Karachi: Central Institute of Islamic Research, 1965.

———. "Islamic Modernism: Its Scope, Methods, and Alternatives." *International Journal of Middle East Studies* 1, no. 4 (1970): 317–333.

———. "Islamic Studies and the Future of Islam." In *Islamic Studies:*

A Tradition and Its Problems, edited by Malcolm H. Kerr, 125–133. Malibu, California: Undena Publications, 1980.

———. "Islamic Thought in the Indo-Pakistan Subcontinent and the Middle East." *Journal of Near Eastern Studies* 32 (January–April 1973): 194–200.

———. "Islamization of Knowledge: A Response." *American Journal of Islamic Social Sciences* 5 (September 1988): 3–11.

———. "Law and Ethics in Islam." In *Ethics in Islam* (Ninth Giorgio Levi Della Vida Conference, 1983), edited by R.G. Hovannisian, 3–15. Malibu: Undena, 1985.

———. "Law of Rebellion in Islam." In *Islam in the Modern World, 1983 Paine Lectures in Religion, 8ᵗʰ series*, edited by Jill Raitt. Columbia: University of Missouri-Columbia, 1983.

———. "Ma'sum Khan Kabuli." *Journal of Asiatic Studies* 11, no. 2 (1966): 163–177.

———. *Major Themes of the Quran.* Minneapolis, Minnesota: Bibliotheca Islamica, 1980.

———. "The Message and the Messenger." In *Islam: The Religious and Political Life of a World Community*, edited by Marjorie Kelly. New York: Praeger, 1984.

———. "Mir Damad's Concept of Huduth Dahri: A Contribution to the Study of God-World Relationship Theories in Safavid Iran." *Journal of Near Eastern Studies* 39, no. 2 (1980): 139–151.

———. "Modern Muslim Thought." *Muslim World* 45 (1955): 16–25.

———. "Muhammad and the Quran." *Chicago Theological Seminary Register* 80 (Fall 1990): 5–11.

———. "Muhammad Iqbal and Atatürk's Reforms." *Journal of Near Eastern Studies* 43, no. 2 (April 1984): 157–62.

———. "Mullah Sadra's Theory of Knowledge." *Philosophical Forum.* 4 (1972): 141–52.

———. "Muslim Attitudes Toward Family Planning." Paper presented at Lahore Seminar in March, 1964.

———. "Muslim Modernism in the Indo-Pakistan Subcontinent." *Bulletin of School of Oriental and African Studies* 21 (1958): 82–99.

———. "A Muslim Response: Christian Particularity and the Faith of Islam." In *Christian Faith in a Religiously Plural World*, edited by D.G. Dawe and John Carman, 69–79. Maryknoll, New York: Orbis Books, 1978.

———. "My Belief in Action." *The Courage of Conviction.* Ed. Phillip L. Berman. Santa Barbara California: Dodd, Mead, & Co., 1985.

———. *New Education in the Making in Pakistan: Its Ideology and Basic Problems*. London: Cassell, 1953.

———. "Non-Muslim minorities in an Islamic State." *Journal, Institute of Muslim Minority Affairs*. 7, no. 1 (1986): 13–24.

———. *Pakistan, One and Indivisible*. Karachi: Pakistan Educational Publications, 1960.

———. *Pakistan's Commercial Policy: A Statement Made in Pakistan Parliament on March 19, 1953*. Karachi: Department of Commercial Intelligence, Government of Pakistan, 1953.

———. "The People of the Book and the Diversity of 'Religions'." In *Christianity Through Non-Christian Eyes*, edited by Paul J. Griffiths, 102–110. Maryknoll, New York: Orbis Books, 1990.

———. *The Philosophy of Mulla Sadra*. Albany: State University of New York Press, 1975.

———. "The Post Formative Developments in Islam." *Islamic Studies* 1, no. 4 (1962): 1–23; Vol. 2 (1963): 279–316.

———. "Pre-Foundations of the Muslim Community in Mecca." *Studia Islamica* 43 (1976): 5–24. Reprinted under the same title in *The Arabs and Arabia on the Eve of Islam*. Edited by F.E. Peters. Aldershot: Ashgate, 1999.

———. "The principle of *Shura* and the role of the Umma in Islam." *American Journal of Islamic Studies* 1, no. 1 (1984): 1–9.

———. *Prophecy in Islam: Philosophy and Orthodoxy*. London: Allen and Unwin, 1958.

———. "The Prophet's Society as the Ideal for Contemporary Mulsims." *Journal for Islamic Studies*, 6 (1986): 40–51.

———. "The Quran." In *Religion In India*, edited by T.N. Madan, 26–37. Delhi: Oxford University Press, 1991.

———. "The Quranic Concept of God, the Universe and Man." *Islamic Studies* 6 (1967): 1–19.

———. "The Quranic Solution of Pakistan's Educational Problem." *Islamic Studies* 6 (1967): 315–326.

———. "A Recent Controversy Over the Interpretation of Shura in the Quran." *History of Religions* 20 (May 1981): 291–301.

———. "The Religious Situation of Mecca from the Eve of Islam up to the Hijra." *Islamic Studies* 16, no. 4 (Winter 1977): 289–301.

———. "Revival and Reform in Islam." *Cambridge History of Islam*. Eds. PM Holt et al, Vol. II. Cambridge: Cambridge University

Press (1970): 635–56.

————. "*Riba* and Interest." *Islamic Studies* 3 (1964): 1–43.

————. "The Role of Pakistani Historian." *Journal of the Pakistan Historical Society* 9 (1961): 94–97.

————. "Roots of Islamic Neo-Fundamentalism." In *Change and the Muslim World*, edited by Philip Stoddard and David Cuthell, 23–35. Syracuse, New York: Syracuse University Press, 1981.

————. *Science, Islam and Basic Education.* Dacca: Islamic Academy, 1959.

————. "Sirat al-Nabi of Allamah Shibli." *Journal of the Pakistan Historical Society* 8 (1960), 167–183, 260–270.

————. "Sirat al-Nabi of Allamah Shibli." *Journal of the Pakistan Historical Society* 9 (1961): 1–7, 75–80, 162–169, 235–239; 10 (1962): 66–72; 11 (1963): 139–154, 220–233, 290–303.

————. "Social Change and Early *Sunnah*." *Islamic Studies* 2 (1963): 205–216.

————. "Some Aspects of Iqbal's Political Thought." *Studies in Islam* 5 (1968): 161–166.

————. "Some Islamic Issues in the Ayyub Khan Era." In *Essays on Islamic Civilization*, edited by Donald P. Little, 284–302. Leiden: Brill, 1976.

————. "Some Key Ethical Concepts of the Quran: Iman, Islam, Taqwa." *Journal of Religious Ethics* 11 (Fall 1983): 170–185.

————. "Some Recent Books on the Qur'an by Western Authors: A Bibliographic Essay." *Journal of Religion* 64 (January 1984): 73–95.

————. "Some Reflections on the Reconstruction of Muslim Society in Pakistan." *Islamic Studies* 6 (1967): 103–120.

————. "The Sources and Meaning of Islamic Socialism." In *Religion and Political Modernization*, edited by Donald Eugene Smith, 243–258. New Haven: Yale University Press, 1974.

————. "Sources of Dynamism in Islam." *Al-Ijtihad.* 15, no. 4 (January 1978): 53–64.

————. "The Status of the Individual in Islam." *Islamic Studies* 5 (1966): 319–330.

————. "The Status of the Individual in Islam." *The Status of the Individual in East and West, Report of the Fourth East-West Philosopher's Conference.* Eds. Charles A. Moore and Aldyth V. Morris. Honululu: University of Hawaii Press, 1968.

————. "The Status of Women in Islam: A Modernist Interpretation." In

Separate Worlds: Studies of Purdah in South Asia, edited by H. Papanek and G. Minault, 285–310. Delhi: Chanakya, 1982.

———. "Status of Women in the Quran." In *Women and Revolution in Iran*, edited by Guity Nashat, 37–53. Boulder: Westview Press, 1983.

———. "Sunnah and Hadith." *Islamic Studies* 1, no. 2 (1962): 1–36.

———. "Survey of Modernization of Muslim Family Law." *International Journal of Middle East Studies* 11, no. 4 (1980): 451–465.

———. "The Thinker of Crisis—Shah Wali-Ullah." *Pakistan Quarterly.* 6, no. 2 (1956): 44–8.

———. "Towards a Reformulation of the Theory of Islamic Law.: Sheikh Yamani on Public Interest." *New York University Journal of International Law and Politics.* 12, no. 2 (Fall 1979): 219–24.

———. "Translating the Quran." *Religion and Literature* 20 (Spring 1988): 23–30.

Rahman, Fazlur. et al. *Islam in the Modern World: 1983 Paine Lectures in Religion.* Columbia, Missouri: Columbia University Press, 1983.

French

———. "L'Intellectus Acquistus in Alfarabi." *Giornale critico della filosofia italiana*, Series 3, No. 7 (1953): 351–357.

German

Rahman, Fazlur and al-Faruqi, Ismail R. "Christliches Verständnis des Islam?" *Kairos* 3, no. 3–4 (1961): 225–233.

Encyclopedia Articles

———. "Akl," "Andjuman," "Arad," "Bahmanyar," "Baka wa Fana," "Barahima," "Basit wa Murakkab," "Dhat," and "Dhawk." *Encyclopedia of Islam,* New Edition. Edited by H.A.R. Gibb, et al. Leiden: E.J. Brill, 1979.

———. "Islam," "Iqbal, Muhammad," and "Mullah Sadra." *Encyclopedia of Religion.* Edited by Mircea Eliade. New York: MacMillan

Publishing Company, 1987.

———. "Islamic Philosophy." *Encyclopedia of Philosophy.* Edited by Paul Edwards. New York: MacMillan Publishing Company and the Free Press, 1967.

———. "The Legacy of Muhammad," "Sources of Islamic Doctrine and Social Views," "Doctrines of the Qu'ran," "Fundamental Practices and Institutions of Islam," "Theology and Sectarianism," and "Religion and the Arts." *Encyclopedia Britannica,* 15th Edition. Edited by Philip W Goetz. Chicago: Encyclopedia Britannica, Inc., 1974.

Book Reviews

———. Review of *On Schacht's Origins of Muhammadan Jurisprudence,* by G.M. Azami. *Journal of Near Eastern Studies,* 47 (July 1988): 228–29

Works Translated into Other Languages

Indonesian

———. *Tema Pokok al-Quran [Major Themes of the Quran].* Ed. Ammar Haryono. Trans. Anas Mahyuddin. Bandung: Penerbit Pustaka, 1983.

———. *Membuka Pintu Ijtihad [Islamic Methodology in History].* Ed. Ammar Haryono. Trans. Anas Mahyuddin. Bandung: Penerbit Pustaka, 1984.

———. *Islam dan Modernitas, Tentang Transformasi Intelektual [Islam and Modernity: Transformation of an Intellectual Tradition].* Ed. Ammar Haryono. Trans. Ahsin Mohammad. Bandung: Penerbit Pustaka, 1985.

———. *Islam [Islam].* Ed. Ammar Haryono. Trans. Ahsin Mohammad. Bandung: Penerbit Pustaka, 1985.

Serbo-Croatian

———. *Duh Islama [Islam].* Trans. Andrija Grosberger. Biblioteka Zenit Velike Avanture Coveka Series. Belgrade: Yugoslavia, 1983.

Turkish

————. *Islam [Islam]*. Trans. Mehmet Dag and Mehmet Aydin. Hicri 15, Asir Kulliyat, Series no. 2. Ankara: Selcuk Yayinlari, 1981.

————. *Ana Konulariyla Kur'an [Major Themes of the Quran]*. Trans. Alparslan Acikgenc. Ankara: Fecr Yaninlari, 1987.

————. *Islamiyet ve Iktisadi Adalet Meselesi [Islamic Methodology in History]*. Trans. Yusuf Ziya Kavakci. Islami Ilimler Fakultesi Series, no. 4; Tercüme Serisi, no. 1. Ankara: Islami Ilimler Fakultesi, 1976.

Works by Mohammed Arkoun

Arabic

Arkoun, Mohammed. *Al-almana wa-l-din*. Beirut: Dar al-Saqi, 1997.

————. *Al-fikr al-ʿarabi, ʿuwaydat*. Beirut: Dar al-Saqi, 1979.

————. *Al-fikr al-islami: qiraʾa ʿilmiyya* (translation of various essays first published in French). Beirut: Markaz al-Inma al-Qawmi, 1986.

————. *Al-fikr al-usuli wa-istihalat al-taʾsil*. Beirut: Dar al-Saqi, 1999.

————. *Al-islam: al akhlaq wal-siyasa*. Beirut: Markaz al-Inmaʾ al-Qawmiyy, 1988.

————. *Al-islam, al-ʿuruba wal-gharb*. Beirut: Dar al-Saqi, 1995.

————. *Al-islam: asala wa mumarasa*. Beirut: Dar al-Tawzi li-l-Tibaʿa wal-Nashr, 1988.

————. *Al-islam: naqd wa-jtihad*. Beirut: Dar al-Saqi, 1990.

————. *Al-islam wal-hadatha*. Beirut: Dar al-Saqi, 1990.

————. *Maʿdrik min ajli-l-ansana fi-l-siyaqat al-islamiyya*. Beirut: Dar al-Saqi, 2001.

————. *Min faysal al-tafriqa ila fasl al-maqal: ayna huwa al-fikr al-islamiyya al-muʿasir* (translation by Hachem Salah of essays originally published in French). Beirut: Dar al-Saqi, 1992.

————. *Min al-ijtihad ila naqd al-ʿaql al-islami*. London: Dar al-Saqi, 1991.

————. *Min al-tafsir al-mawruth ila tahil al-khitab al-dini*. Beirut: Dar al-Taliʿa, 2001.

————. *Nazʿat al-ansana fi-l-fikr al-ʿarabi*. Dar al-Saqi, Beirut, 1997.

————. *Qadaya fi naqd al-fikr al-dini.* Beirut: Dar al-Taliᶜa, 1998.

————. *Tarikhiyyat al-fikr al-ᶜarabi al-islami* (translation of various essays first published in French). Beirut: Markaz al-Imma al-Qawmi, 1986.

————. *Al-thaqafah al-ᶜarabiyah fi al-mahjar.* al-Dar al-Baydaᵓ: Dar Tubqal, 1988.

Arkoun, Mohammed and Louis Gardet. *Al-islam al-ams wa-al-ghad.* Beirut, Lebanon: Dar al-Tanwir, 1983.

Arkoun, Mohammed and Siyah Jahayyim. *Nafidah ᶜala al-Islam.* Beirut: Dar 'Atiyah lil-Nashr, 1996.

Arkoun, Mohammed and Maxime Rodinson, et al. *Al-istishraq bayna duᶜatihi wa maᶜaridih.* Beirut: Dar al-Saqi, 1994.

Arkoun, Mohammed and Hashim Salih. *Al-islam, ᶜuruba, al-gharb: rihanat al-maᶜna wa-iradat al-haymanah.* Beirut: Dar al-Saqi, 1995.

————. and Hashim Salih. *Nazᶜat al-ansinah fi al-fikr al-ᶜarabi: fi al-miskawayh wa-al-tawhidi.* Beirut: Dar al-Saqi, 1997.

————. and Hashim Salih. *Al-quran min al-tafsir al-mawruth ila tahlil al-khitab al-dini.* Beirut: Dar al-Taliᶜah, 2001.

English

Arkoun, Mohammed. "The Adequacy of Contemporary Islam to the Political, Social and Economic Development of North Africa." *Africa Studies Quarterly* 4 (1982): 1–2.

————. "The Aga Khan Award as a Process of Thinking." In *Legacies for the Future: Contemporary Architecture in Islamic Societies,* edited by C.C. Davidson. London: Thames and Hudson and the Aga Khan Award for Architecture, 1998.

————. *Architectural Alternatives in Deteriorating Societies.* Geneva: Aga Khan Trust, 1992.

————. "Artistic Creativity in Islamic Contexts." Translated by S. Petit. *The Post-Colonial Crescent: Islam's Impact on Contemporary Literature.* Edited by J.C. Hawley. New York: Lang, 1998.

————. "An Assessment of and Prespectives on the Study of the Quran." *The Quran: Style and Contents,* edited by Andrew Rippin, 297–332. Aldershot: Ashgate, 2001. (Translated from *Lectures du Coran,* pp. 5–33).

————. "The Concept of Authority in Islamic Thought." In *Islam: State and Society,* edited by Klaus Ferdinand and Mehdi Mozaffari.

London: Curzon Press, 1988. Also in *Essays in Honour of Bernard Lewis: The Islamic World From Classical to Modern Times,* edited by C.E. Bosworth, Charles Issawi, Roger Savory, and A.L. Udovitch. Princeton, New Jersey: Darwin Press, 1989.

——. "Chronologie et Préface," to *Le Coran,* translated by Kasimirski. Paris: GF-Flammarion, 2001.

——. "The Concept of Revelation from Ahl al-Kitab to the Societies of the Book." Occasional Papers, Claremont Graduate School, 1988.

——. *The Concept of Revelation: From the People of the Book to the Societies of the Book.* Claremont, Calif.: James A. Blaisdell Programs in World Religions and Cultures, Claremont Graduate School, 1987.

——. "The Death Penalty and Torture in Islamic Thought." In *Death Penalty and Torture,* edited by Franz Bockle and Jacques Marie Pohier, 75–82. New York, Seabury Press, 1979.

——. "Ethics and History According to the *Tajarib al-Umam of Miskawaih.*" Translated by M.S. Khan. *Islamic Culture* 75, no. 2 (2001): 1–40. (Translation into English of "Ethique et histoire d'après les *Tajarib al-Umam*" in Atti del III Congresso di Studi Arabi e Islamici, Naples 1967: 83–112).

——. "Introduction," in *Javidan Khirad* by Ibn Miskawayh. Tehran: Danishgah-Mak Gil, 1976.

——. "Islam, Europe, the West: Meanings-at-Stake and the Will-to-Power." *Islam and Modernity: Muslim Intellectuals Respond.* Edited by John Cooper, R. L. Nettler, and Mohamed Mahmoud. London: Tauris, 1998.

——. "Is Islam Threatened by Christianity?" In *Islam: A Challenge for Christianity,* edited by Hans Küng and Jürgen Moltmann, 48–57. London: SCM Press, 1994.

——. "Islam and the Hegemony of the West." In *God, Truth and Reality: Essays in Honour of John Hick,* edited by Arvind Sharma, 72–86. New York: Saint Martin's Press, 1993.

——. "Islamic Culture, Modernity, Architecture." In *Architecture Education in the Islamic World.* Geneva: The Aga Khan Award for Architecture, 1986.

——. "Islamic Cultures, Developing Societies, Modern Thought." In *Expressions of Islam in Buildings.* Geneva: Aga Khan Trust, 1990.

————. "Manifestations of Arab Thought in Western Islam." *Diogène* 93 (1976).

————. "The Meaning of Cultural Conservation in Muslim Societies." In *Architecture and World Conservation in the Islamic World.* Geneva: Aga Khan Trust for Culture, 1991.

————. "New Perspectives for a Jewish-Christian-Muslim Dialogue." *Journal of Ecumenical Studies* 26:3 (1989).

————. "The Notion of Revelation: from Ahl al-Kitab to the Societies of the Book." In *Die Welt des Islam* (1988).

————. "Present-Day Islam between its Tradition and Globalization." *Intellectual Traditions in Islam.* Edited by Farhad Daftary. London: Tauris (in association with the Institute of Ismaili Studies), 2000.

————. "Religion and Society: The Example of Islam." In *Islam in a World of Diverse Faiths*, edited by Daniel M. Cohn-Sherbok, 134–177. New York: St. Martin's Press, 1991.

————. *Rethinking Islam: Common Questions, Uncommon Answers.* Translated by Robert D. Lee. Boulder, Colorado: Westview Press, 1994.

————. *Rethinking Islam Today.* Occasional Papers Series, Center for Contemporary Arab Studies, Georgetown University, 1987.

————. "Society, State and Religion in Algeria (1962–1985)." In *The Politics of Islamic Revivalism*, edited by Shireen T. Hunter. Bloomington: Indiana University Press, 1988.

————. "The Study of Islam in French Scholarship." In *Mapping Islamic Studies: Genealogy, Continuity and Change.* Berlin: Mouton de Gruyter, 1997.

————. "The Topicality of the Problem of the Person in Islamic Thought." *International Social Science Journal* 117 (August 1988).

————. "The Unity of Man in Islamic Thought." Translated by R. Scott Walker, *Diogène* 140 (1987).

————. *The Unthought in Contemporary Islamic Thought* London: Saqi, 2002.

French

Arkoun, Mohammed. "Actualité d'Ibn Rushd Musulman." In *Multiple Averroës*, edited by Jean Jolivet, 55–56. Paris: Belles Lettres, 1978.

———. "Actualité de la personne dans le pensée islamique." *Welt des Islams* 29 (1989): 1–29.

———. *Actualité d'une culture méditerranéenne*. Tampere, Finlande: TAPRI, (Institut de recherche de la paix à Tampere), 1990.

———. "Actualité du problème de la personne dans la pensée islamique," in *Revue internationale des science sociales*. Paris: UNESCO, 1988.

———. "Algérie 1993: réflexions sur un destin historique." *Revue du monde musulman et de la Meditérranée* 65 (1993).

———. "Les Arabes vus par le Professeur J. Berque." *Esprit* no. 1 (1975).

———. *Aspects de la pensée musulmane classique*. Paris: IPN, 1963.

———. "Avec Mouloud Mammeri à Taourirt-Mimoun." In *Litterature et oralité au Maghrib: Hommage a Mouloud Mammeri*, edited by Charles Bonn. Paris: L'Harmattan, 1993.

———. *Combats pour l'humanisme en contextes islamiques*, Paris (forthcoming).

———. "Comment situer l'Islam dans l'histoire recente?" in *Enciclopedia del Novecento*. Milan: Il Quadrato, 1985.

———. "Le Concept de sociétés du Livre-livre." In *Interpréter: hommage à Claude Geffré*, edited by Jean-Pierre Jossua and Nicholas-Jean Sed, 211–223. Paris: Cerf, 1992.

———. "Construction et signification dans le monde islamique: introduction théorique au Prix Aga Khan d'Architecture" *Mimar* 7 (1983).

———. "De la stratégie de domination à unecoopération créatrice entre l'Europe et le Monde Arabe." In *Le dialogue euro-arabe*, edited by J. Bourrinet. Paris: Economica, 1979.

———. "De l'*Ijtihad* à la critique de la Raison islamique: l'exemple du statut de la femme dans la shariʿa." In *Algérie, passé, présent et avenir*. Paris: Centre Culturel Algerien, 1990.

———. *De Manhattan à Bagdad: Au-delà du bien et du mal*, edited by Maïla, Joseph. Paris: Desclée de Brouwer, 2003.

———. *Deux épîtres de Miskawayh*. Édition Critique, Damascus: BEO, 1961.

———. "Deux médiateurs de la pensee médiévale: Averroës et Maïmonides" Courrier de l'UNESCO (September 1986).

———. "Le dialogue euro-arabe: essai d'evaluation critique." In *Coopération euro-arabe: diagnostic et prospective*, edited by Bichar Khader. Louvain-la-Neuve, 1982.

————. "Discours islamiques, discours orientalistes et pensée scientifique." In *As Others See Us: Mutual Perceptions East and West*, edited by Bernard Lewis. New York: International Society for the Comparative Study of Civilizations, 1985.

————. "Le droit 'dit' musulman en contexte moderne." In *L 'immigration face aux lois de la République*, edited by Edwige Rude Antoine. Paris: Karthala, 1992.

————. "Les droits de l'homme en Islam," *Recherches et documents du Centre Thomas More* 44 (1984).

————. "E possible parlare di un umanesimo islamico?" in *L'Opera al Rosso*. Monferrato: Marietta, 1992.

————. "Emergences et problèmes dans le monde musulman contemporain (1960–1985)." In *Islamochristiana* Volume 12, edited by Maurice Borrmans, 135–61. Italian version in the Enciclopedia italiana, 1989, under "Islamismo."

————. *Essais sur la pensée islamique*. Paris: Maisonneuve et Larose, 1984.

————. *L'ethique musulmane d'après Mawardi*. Paris: Geuthner, 1964.

————. *L'Etrange et le merveilleux dans l'islam médiéval: actes du colloque tenu au Collège de France à Paris, en mars 1974*. Paris: Editions J.A., 1978.

————. "L'Expansion de l'Islam dans la Méditerranée occidentale." *Revue de l'Occident musulman et de la Mediterranée* no. 1 (1976).

————. "Fondments arabo-islamiques de la culture maghrébine," *Französische Heute*, no. 2 (1984).

————. "Les fondements arabo-islamiques de la culture maghrébine." In *Gli interscambi culturali*, Proceedings of the International Congress in Amalfi December 5–8, 1983, Naples, 1986.

————. "Les horizons de la pensée arabe classique" *Courier de l'UNESCO* (1977).

————. *L'humanisme arabe au IVe/Xe siècle: Miskawayh philosophe et historien*. Paris: Vrin, 1982.

————. "Imaginaire social et leaders dans le monde musulman contemporain." *Arabica* 35 (1988).

————. *L'immigration, défis et richesses: LXXIIe session des Semaines sociales de France, tenue à Issy-les-Moulineaux et intitulée Les migrants, défi et richesse pour notre société*. Paris: Bayard Editions/Centurion, 1998.

————. "Introduction à une étude des rapports entre Islam et politique."

In *Religion et Politique* by Mohammed Arkoun et al., 9–27. Lille: Centre National De La Recherche Scientifique, 1979.

———. "Islam et développement dans le Maghreb indépendant." *Arab Studies Quarterly* 4 (1982): 23–53; also in *Arabica* 29, no. 2: 113–42.

———. "Islam dans l'histoire." *Magreb-Machreq* 102 (1983).

———. "Islam, pensée, histoire, l'Orientalisme." *Peuples méditerrranéens* 50 (1990).

———. "L'Islam actuel devant sa tradition." *Aspects de la foi de l'Islam.* Brussels: Facultes universitaires Saint-Louis, 1985.

———. "L'Islam actuel devant sa tradition et la mondialisation." *Islam et Changement Social.* Lausanne: Payot, 1998.

———. *L'Islam: approche critique.* Paris: J. Grancher, 1998.

———. "L'Islam devant la Gritica Moderna l'Hegemonia de l' Occident." *l'Avenç* 46 (1991).

———. "L'Islam face à la modernité." In *Le modèle de l'Occident: 17ᵉ colloque d'intellectuels juifs de langue française du congrès juif mondial.* Paris: Presses universitaires de France, 1977.

———. *L'Islam: Hier, demain* (with L. Gardet). Paris: Burchet-Chastel, 1978; partially translated into Arabic by Hachem Salah as *Al-Islam: asala wa mumarasa*, Beirut: Dar al-tanwir, 1983.

———. "L'Islam et la laïcite." *Bulletin du Centre Thomas More* 24 (1987). Translated into Arabic as *Al-ʿalmaniyya wal-din.* London: Dar al-Saqi, 1990.

———. *L'Islam, morale et politique.* Paris: UNESCO, Desclee de Brouwer, 1986; translated into Arabic by Hachem Salah as *Al-Islam al-akhlaq wal-siyasa*, Beirut: Markaz al-Inma al-Qawmi, 1990.

———. "L'Islam, organisation, règles et pouvoirs" *Awraq* (1990).

———. "L'Islam et les problèmes de développement." In *Communauté musulmane: 18ᵉ congrès juif mondial.* Paris: Presses Universitaires De France, 1978.

———. *L'Islam, religion et société* (with M. Arosio and M. Borrmans). Paris: Editions du Cerf, 1982.

———. "Islam, révélation et révolutions." *Dieux en Sociétés*, Autrement, 127 (1992).

———. "Kémalisme dans une perspective islamique." *Diogène* 127 (1984).

———. "Langues, société et religion dans le Maghreb indépendant." In *Les Cultures Maghreb*, edited by Maria Angels Roque, Paul

Balta, and Mohammed Arkoun. Paris: L'Harmattan, 1996.

―――. "Lecture de la Fatiha: Sura 1." *Melanges d'Islamologie: Volume dedie a la memoire de Armand Abel*, edited by Pierre Salmon, 18–44. Leiden: Brill, 1974.

―――. *Lectures du Coran*. Paris: Maisonneuve et Larose, 1982.

―――. "Lire la ville africaine contemporaine." In *Actes du Colloque de Dakar*. Aga Khan Award for Architecture, 1983.

―――. "La liberté religieuses comme critique de la religion a partir du coran et de la tradition Islamique." In *La liberté religieuse dans la Judaisme, le Christianisme et l'Islam*, edited by Émile Poulet, 109–125. Paris: les Editions du Cerf, 1981.

―――. "La Méditerrranée: une approche multi-rivages." *L'evènement européen* (1988).

―――. "Le Message de Mouloud Mammeri." *Awal* 18 (1998): 9–12.

―――. "Le IXe séminaire de la pensée islamique à Tlemcen." *Revue de l'Occident musulman et de la Mediterranée* 70 (1976).

―――. *Les Musulmans: Consultation islamo-chrétienne entre Muhammed (sic) Arkoun [et al.] et Youakim Moubarac*. Paris: Editions Beauchesne, 1971.

―――. "Origines islamiques des droits de l'homme." *Revue des sciences morales et politiques* no.1 (1989).

―――. *Ouvertures sur l'Islam*. Paris: J. Granchet, 1992.

―――. "La peine de mort et la torture dans la pensée islamique." *Concilium* 140 (1987).

―――. *Pélrinage à la Mecque*. (with Azzedine Guellouz and Abdelaziz Frikha). Tunis: Sud Editions, 1977.

―――. *La pensée arabe*. Paris: Presses universitaires de France, 1991; translated into Arabic as *al-fikr al-ʿarabiyy*, Beirut: Dar al-Saqi, 1990; into English as *Arab Thought*, New Delhi: S. Chand, 1988.

―――. *Penser l'islam aujourd'hui*. Alger: Laphomic, 1993.

―――. "Pensiero Religioso e Pensiero Scientifico Nel Contesto Islamico." In *La Passione del Conoscere*, edited by Lorena Preta. Rome-Bari: Laterza, 1993.

―――. "La perception arabe de l'Europe." *Awraq* 10 (1989).

―――. "La place et les fonctions de l'histoire dans la culture arabe." In *Histoire et diversité des cultures*. Paris: UNESCO, 1984.

―――. "Positivisme et tradition dans une perspective islamique: Le cas du kémalisme." *Diogéne* 127 (July–September 1984).

―――. *Pour une critique de la raison islamique*. Paris: Maisonneuve et Larose, 1984.

———. "Pour une sociologie de l'échec et de la réussite dans la pensée islamique: l'example d'Ibn Rushd." In *Le Choc Averroës: Comment les philosophes ont fait l'Europe*, special edition of Internationale de l'Imaginaire 17–18 (1991).

———. "Preface." In *Le Coran*, translated by S. Kasimirski. Paris: Flammarion, 1970.

———. "Le probléme de l'authenticité divine du Coran." In *Recherches d'Islamologie: Recherches d'Islamologie recueil d'articles offert à Georges C. Anawati et Louis Gardet par leurs collegues et amis*, edited by S.A. Ali, 21–34. Louvain: Editions Peeters, 1977.

———. "Le problème des influences en histoire culturelle d'après l'exemple arabo-islamique." In *Lumieres Arabes Sur l'Occident Medieval*, edited by Henri Loucel and Andre Miquel, 147–54. Paris: Editions Anthropos, 1978.

———. "Propositions pour une autre pensée religieuse." In *Islamochristiana* Volume 4, edited by Maurice Borrmans, 197–206. Rome: Pontificio Istituto di Studi Arabi, 1978.

———. "Quelques réflexions sur les difficiles relations entre les musulmans et les chrétiens." *Revue de l'Institut Catholique de Paris* (1982).

———. "Raison émergente et modernités dans le contexte arabe musulman. Entretien avec Mohamed Arkoun." *Le Monde Arabe dans la Recerche Scientifique* 10–11 (1999): 97–112.

———. *Recherches sur l'Islam: histoire et anthropologie.* Paris: A. Colin, 1980.

———. "Reflexions breves sur le djihad." *Etudes Theologiques et Religieuses* 56, no. 1 (1981): 103–106.

———. "Reflexions d'un musulman sur le 'nouveau' catechisme." *Revue des deux mondes* (April 1993).

———. "Reflexions sur la notion de raison islamique." *Archives de Sciences Sociales des Religions* 32 (January–March 1987): 125–32.

———. *Religion et laïcité: Une approche laique de l'islam.* L'Arbrelle: Centre Thomas Moore, 1989.

———. "Une rencontre islamo-chrétienne en Tunisie." *Maghreb-Machreq* 69 (1975).

———. "Les sciences de l'homme et de la société appliquées à l'etude de l'Islam." In *Les sciences sociales aujourd'hui.* Algiers: University of Oran, 1986.

————. "Les tâches de l'intellectuel musulman." In *Intellectuels et militants dans le monde islamique VIIe - XXe siecle, Cahiers de la Mediterranée*, 1988.

————. *Traité d'ethique: traduction française avec introduction et Tahdhib al-akhlaq de Miskawayh.* Damascus: Institut Francais, 1988.

————. "L'unité de l'homme dans la pensée islamique." *Diogène* 140 (1987).

————. "Les villages socialistes in Algerie." In *Villages socialistes en Afrique*, edited by Alberto Arecchi. Dakar, 1982.

Arkoun, Mohammed and Rémy Leveau. *L'Islam et les musulmans dans le monde.* Beyrouth: Centre culturel Hariri, Recherches et documentation, 1993.

German

————. "Die Frage nach dem Staat am islamischen Beispiel." In *Freiheit der Religion: Christentum und Islam unter dem Anspruch*, edited by Johannes Schwärtlander, 294–315. Mainz: Matthias Grünewald, 1993.

————. "Der Glaube in beständinger Prüfung durch die Zeit." In *Freiheit der Religion: Christentum und Islam unter dem Anspruch*, edited by Johannes Schwärtlander, 376–379. Mainz: Matthias Grünewald, 1993.

————. *Der Islam: Annäherung an eine Religion.* Heidelberg: Palmyra, 1999.

————. "'Westliche' Vernunft Kontra 'islamische' Vernunft? *Versuch einer Kritischen Annäherung.*" In *Der Islam im Aufbruch? Perspektiven der Arabischen Arabischen Welt*, edited by Micheal Luders, 261–274. Munich: Piper, 1992.

————. "Was ist 'Islam' und Wer ist ein 'Muslim'?" *Der Arabische Almanach* 10 (1999–2000): 14–17.

Italian

————. *Cultura araba e societa multietnica: par un'educazione interculturale.* Edited by L. Operti. Turin: Bollati Boringhieri, 1998.

Spanish

―――. "Se puede Hablar De Un Retorno Del 'Moro' en España." In *Preface à Immigracion Magrebi en España*, edited by Bernabe Lopezyotros. Madrid: Mapfre, 1993.

Encyclopedia Entries

―――. "Les expressions de l'Islam," *Encyclopedia Universalis*, Supplement for 1983.

―――. "L'Islam face aux sciences religieuses." In *Le grand atlas des religions*. Paris: Encyclopedia Universalis, 1991.

Works by Islamic Revivalists and Neotraditionalists

Afza, Nazhat and Khurshid Ahmed. *The Position of Woman in Islam.* Safat, Kuwait: Islamic Book Publishers, 1993.

Audah, Abdul Qader. *Islam: Between Ignorant Followers and Incapable Followers.* Riyadh, Saudi Arabia: International Islamic Publishing House, 1994.

Badawi, Jamal. *Gender Equity In Islam: Basic Principles.* Plainfield, Indiana: American Trust Publications, 1995.

Badawi, Jamal. *The Muslim Woman's Dress.* Plainfield, Indiana, Islamic Book Service, n.d.

―――. *Polygamy in Islamic Law.* Plainfield, Indiana: American Trust Publications, n.d.

―――. *The Status of Woman in Islam.* Plainfield, Indiana: The Islamic Society of North America, 1996.

"Charter of the Islamic Resistance Movement (HAMAS) of Palestine." *Journal of Palestine Studies* 22, no. 4 (Summer 1993): 122–134.

Doi, Abdur Rahman I. *Shariah: The Islamic Law.* London: Ta-Ha Publishers, 1984.

―――. *Shariah in the Fifteen Hundredth Century of Hijra: Problems and Prospects.* London: Ta-Ha Publishers, 1981.

————. *Woman in Shariah.* London: Ta-Ha Publishers, 1996.

Haneef, Suzanne. *What Everyone Should Know About Islam and Muslims.* Chicago: Kazi Publications, 1982.

Hathout, Hassan. *Reading the Muslim Mind.* Plainfield, Indiana: American Trust Publications, 1995.

Lemu, B. ʿAʾisha and Fatima Heeren. *Woman in Islam.* Leicester, U.K.: The Islamic Foundation, 1992.

"Proclamation of Syria's Muslim Brotherhood." In *The Islamic Struggle in Syria* by ʿUmar Abdallah. Berkeley, California: Mizan Press, 1983.

Mawdudi, Sayyid Abuʾl-Aʿla. *First Principles of the Islamic State.* Lahore: Islamic Publications, 1983.

————. *Fundamentals of Islam.* Delhi: Markazi Maktabah-i Islami, 1978.

————. *Human Rights in Islam.* Leicester: Islamic Foundation, 1976,

————. *Introduction to the Study of the Quran.* Delhi: Maktaba Jamaat-e-Islami Hind, 1971.

————. *The Process of Islamic Revolution.* Lahore: Islamic Publications, 1980.

————. *Purdah and The Status of Women in Islam.* Lahore: Islamic Publications, 1972.

Thomson, Ahmad. *The Wives of the Prophet Muhammad.* London: Ta-Ha Publishers, 1993.

Khattab, Huda. *The Muslim Woman's Handbook.* London: Ta-Ha Publishers, 1993.

Secondary Sources on the Works of Fatima Mernissi, Leila Ahmed, Mohammed Arkoun, and Fazlur Rahman

Abu Izz al-Din, Amin. "La religion et la laïcité dans les Theses de Mohammed Arkoun." Translated by H. de la Hougue. *Études Arabes: Dossiers* 91–92 (1996–1997) 78–91.

Arnhold, B. Interview with Fatima Mernissi in *Cahier d'Études Maghrebines* 8–9 (1995–1996): 135–139.

Arnhold, B. "Fatima Mernissi par elle meme." *Cahier d'Etudes Maghrebines* 8–9 (1995–1996): 140–148.

Ayadi, Muhammad. "Mohammed Arkoun ou l'ambition d'une modernité intellectuelle." In *Penseurs Maghrebines Contemporains*. Collectif: Tunis, 1993.

Berry, Donald Lee. *The Thought of Fazlur Rahman as an Islamic Response to Modernity*. Ph.D. diss., The Southern Baptist Theological Seminary, 1990.

Cragg, Kenneth. "Fazlur Rahman of Karachi and Chicago." In *The Pen and the Faith: Eight Modern Muslim Writers of the Quran*. London: George Allen and Unwin, 1985.

Denny, Frederick M. "The Legacy of Fazlur Rahman." In *The Muslims of America*, edited by Yvonne Haddad. New York: Oxford University Press, 1991.

Donadey, Anne. "Portrait of a Maghrebian Feminist as a Young Girl: *Fatima Mernissi's Dreams of Trespass*." *Edebiyat* 11, no. 1 (2000): 85–103.

Gibbins, C. "Dismantling the Maghreb: Contemporary Moroccan Writing and Islamic Discursivity." In *The Marabout and the Muse: New Approaches to Islam in African Literature*, edited by K.W. Harrow. London: Currey, 1996.

Günther, Ursula. *Die Frau in der Revolte: Fatima Mernissi's feministische Gesellschaftskritik*. Hamburg: Deutsches Orient-Institut, 1993.

Hussain, Waheed. "A Philosophical Critique of Fazlur Rahman's Islam and Modernity." *Harvard Middle Eastern and Islamic Review*, 6 (2000–2001): 53–81.

Lang, G. "Jihad, *Ijtihad*, and other Dialogical Wars in *La mere du printemps*, *Le harem politique*, and *Loine de Medine*." In the *Marabout and the Muse: New Approaches to Islam in African Literature*, edited by K.W. Harrow. London: Currey, 1996.

La Cocque, André. *Commitment and Commemoration: Jews, Christians, and Muslims in Dialogue*. Chicago: Exploration Press, 1994.

Lee, Robert D. "Arkoun and Authenticity." *Péuples mediterranéens* no. 50 (January–March 1990): 75–106.

Lee, Robert D. *Overcoming Tradition and Modernity: The Search for Islamic Authenticity*. Boulder: Westview Press, 1997.

Marchand, L. "Distorted Histories or the Origins of a Misunderstanding in the Ideological Labyrinth: Interview with Mohammed Arkoun." *Rive: Review of Mediterranean Politics and Culture* 3 (1997): 53–56.

Matthes, M. "Shahrazad's Sisters: Storytelling and Politics in the Memoirs of Mernissi, el Saadawi and Ashrawi." *Alif* 19 (1999): 68–96.

Nagie, Nadia. *Fez-New York und zurück: Fatima Mernissi, ihre Welt und ihre Geschichte.* Würzburg: Ergon Verlag, 1992.

O'Sulliva, P. "The Comparison and Contrast of the Islamic Philosophy, Ideology, and Paradigms of Sayyid Qutb, Mawlana Abu'l A'la Mawdudi and Fazlur Rahman." *Islamic Quarterly* 42, no. 2 (1996): 99–124.

Oxford Encyclopedia of the Modern Islamic World, s.v. "Arkoun, Mohammed." By Fedwa Malti-Douglas.

Oxford Encyclopedia of the Modern Islamic World, s.v. "Mernissi, Fatima." By Amal Rassam.

Oxford Encyclopedia of the Modern Islamic World, s.v. "Rahman, Fazlur." By Tamara Sonn.

Shafiq, Muhammad. "Islamization of Knowledge: Philosophy and Methodology and Analysis of the Views and Ideas of Ismail R. al-Faruqi, Seyyed Hossein Nasr, and Fazlur Rahman." *Hamdard Islamicus* 18, no. 3 (1995): 63–75.

Sonn, Tamara. "Fazlur Rahman's Islamic Methodology." *Muslim World* 81 (July–October 1991): 212–230.

Waugh, Earle H. and Frederick M. Denny, editors. *The Shaping of an American Islamic Discourse: A Memorial to Fazlur Rahman.* Atlanta, Georgia: Scholars Press, 1998.

General Bibliography

Abdallah, 'Umar F. *The Islamic Struggle in Syria.* Berkeley: Mizan Press, 1983.

Abedin, Syed Z. and Ziauddin Sardar. *Muslim Minorities in the West.* London: Grey Seal, 1995.

Bellah, Robert. *Habits of the Heart: Individualism and Commitment in American Life.* Berkeley: University of California Press, 1985.

Binder, Leonard. *Islamic Liberalism: A Critique of Development Ideologies.* Chicago: University of Chicago Press, 1988.

Boullata, Issa J. *Trends and Issues in Contemporary Arab Thought.* Albany: State University of New York Press, 1990.

Campo, Juan Eduardo. "The Ends of Islamic Fundamentalism: Hegemonic Discourse and the Islamic Question in Egypt." *Contention* 4, no. 3 (Spring 1995): 167–195.

———. "Islam in California: Views from the Minaret." *Muslim World*

86, nos. 3–4 (July–October 1996): 294–312.

Ernst, Carl. *The Shambhala Guide to Sufism.* Boston: Shambhala Publications, 1997.

Esposito, John L. *The Islamic Threat: Myth or Reality?* New York: Oxford University Press, 1992.

Faruqi, Ismail. *Humanism and the Law: The Case of the Shariah.* Occasional Paper No. 8. Lagos, Nigeria: Nigerian Institute of Advanced Legal Studies, 1977.

Gadamer, Hans-Georg. *Truth and Method.* Translated by Joel Weinsheimer and Donald G. Marshall. New York: Continuum, 1994.

Geertz, Clifford. *Islam Observed.* Chicago: University of Chicago Press, 1968.

GhanneaBassiri, Kambiz. *Competing Visions of Islam in the United States: A Study of Los Angeles.* Westport, Connecticut: Greenwood Press, 1997.

Giddens, Anthony. *The Consequences of Modernity.* Stanford: Stanford University Press, 1990.

Haddad, Yvonne. *A Century of Islam in America.* Washington, D.C.: American Institute for Islamic Affairs, 1986.

———. *Mission to America: Five Islamic Sectarian Communities in North America.* Gainesville: University Press of Florida, 1993.

———. ed. *The Muslims of America.* New York: Oxford University Press, 1991.

Haddad, Yvonne and Jane Idleman Smith, eds. *Muslim Communities in North America.* Albany, New York: State University of New York Press, 1994.

Haddad, Yvonne and Adair Lummis. *Islamic Values in the United States: A Comparative Study.* New York: Oxford University Press, 1987.

Hallaq, Wael B. *Law and Legal Theory in Classical and Medieval Islam.* Hampshire, U.K.: Variorum, 1994.

Hourani, Albert. *Arabic Thought in the Liberal Age: 1798–1939.* London: Oxford University Press, 1962.

Humphreys, R. Stephen. "Islam and Political Values in Saudi Arabia, Egypt and Syria." *Middle East Journal* 33, no. 1 (Winter 1979): 1–19.

Juergensmeyer, Mark. *The New Cold War? Religious Nationalism Confronts the Secular State.* Berkeley: University of California Press, 1993.

Kepel, Gilles. *Allah in the West: Islamic Movements in America and Europe.* Translated by Susan Milner. Stanford: Stanford University Press, 1997.

———. *Les Banlieues de l'Islam: naissance d'une religion en France.* Paris: Editions du Seuil, 1987.

———. *The Revenge of God: The Resurgence of Islam, Christianity and Judaism in the Modern World.* Translated by Alan Braley. University Park, Pennsylvania: Pennsylvania State University Press, 1994.

Koszegi, Michael and J. Gordon Melton, eds. *Islam in North America: A Sourcebook.* New York: Garland Publishing, 1992.

Kurzman, Charles, ed. *Liberal Islam: A Sourcebook.* New York: Oxford University Press, 1998.

———. *Modernist Islam, 1840–1940: A Sourcebook.* New York: Oxford University Press, 2002.

Lawrence, Bruce. *Defenders of God: The Fundamentalist Revolt Against the Modern Age.* San Francisco: Harper and Row Publishers, 1989.

Lewis, Bernard. *History: Remembered, Recovered, Invented.* Princeton: Princeton University Press, 1975.

Liebman, Charles. "Religion and the Chaos of Modernity: The Case of Contemporary Judaism." In *Take Judaism, For Example: Studies Toward The Comparison of Religions*, edited by Jacob Neusner. Chicago: University of Chicago Press, 1983.

Marty, Martin and R. Scott Appleby. *Fundamentalisms Observed.* Chicago: University of Chicago Press, 1991.

Metcalf, Barbara. *Islamic Revival in British Deoband: 1860–1900.* Princeton: Princeton University Press, 1982.

Nasr, Seyyed Vali Reza. *Mawdudi and the Making of Islamic Revivalism.* New York: Oxford University Press, 1991.

Safi, Omid, ed. *Progressive Muslims: On Justice, Gender, and Pluralism.* Oxford, England: Oneworld Publications, 2003.

Scarce, Jennifer. *Women's Costume of the Near and Middle East.* London: Unwin Hyman, 1987.

Schacht, Josef. *An Introduction to Islamic Law.* London: Oxford University Press, 1966.

Sivan, Immanuel. *Radical Islam: Medieval Theology and Modern Politics.* New Haven: Yale University Press, 1985.

Smith, Jonathan Z. *Imagining Religion.* Chicago: University of Chicago Press, 1982.

Stowasser, Barbara Freyer. *Women in the Quran: Traditions and Inter-pretation.* New York: Oxford University Press, 1994.

Waugh, Earle H. Baha Abu-Laban, and Regula B. Qureshi, eds. *The Muslim Community in North America.* Edmonton: University of Alberta Press, 1983.

Zuhur, Sherifa. *Revealing Reveiling: Islamist Gender Ideology in Contemporary Egypt.* Albany: State University of New York Press, 1992.

Index

Abbasid Caliphate, 42, 49–51,
55–56, 58, 63–64, 67, 69, 87,
91, 93–94, 113, 123, 144
Abbott, Nadia, 52–53
ʿAbduh, Muhammad, 101, 143
Abu Bakr, 54, 93
Adams, Charles, 5
Advisory Council of Islamic
Ideology (Pakistan), 78
Afghani, Jamal al-Din, 101, 139,
143
Africa, 99, 132
African-Americans, 7
Ahmad, Khurshid, 100
Ahmed, Leila: on misogyny and
medieval Islamic History, 53-
56; on the Quran and Sharia,
56-62; sources of thought, 44-
48; on Sufis and Qarmatians,
62-69; the veil and veiling,
69-75; on women in early
Islamic history, 48-53
Ain Shams University, 4, 48
Aleppo, 65
Algeria, 4, 6, 13, 35, 72, 110,
114, 139

Aligarh, 79
Allah, 19, 22, 31, 36, 59, 61, 127
American Revolution, 37
American Sufi Institute, 68
American Trust Publications, 60
Amin, Qasim, 15, 30
Applied Islamology, 124–125
Arab, 6, 11, 16, 18, 34, 38, 45,
48, 51, 67, 95, 107, 114–115,
118–119
Arabia, 23, 49, 51, 67, 80, 82–83,
107, 110, 114, 135
Arabic, 3, 5–6, 13, 16, 25, 27, 38,
52, 57, 114
Arberry, A.J., 4, 47
Arkoun, Mohammed: on Applied
Islamology, 124-126; on Islam
in the modern world, 133-
137; on marginalized groups
in Islamic history, 126-132;
on the Quran, 115-120
Aryana, 31
al-Assad, Hafez, 33
Assyria, 69
Ayadi, Mohamed El, 122

Badawi, Jamal, 12
Badr, Battle of, 21
Baghdad, 65
Bangladesh, 35
Barclay Bank, 46
Basra, 66
al-Basri, Hasan, 63
Beer, Gillian, 4, 47
Berber, 6
Bergh, S. Van Den, 78
Bharatiya Janata Party, 148
Bint al-Nil, 46
Boston, Massachusetts, 17
Brandeis University, 3, 16
Britain (Great Britain), 27, 46,
    139
British Men's League for
    Opposing Women's Suffrage,
    71
Buddhism, 102, 133, 148–149
al-Bukhari, 27, 49, 54
Butler, Judith, 45, 46
Byzantine Empire, 69

Cairo, 4–5, 20, 45–46, 48, 65
Caliphs, 34, 43, 54, 87, 89, 91,
    93, 113, 119, 133, 145
Central Institute of Islamic
    Research, 5, 78
China, 149
Christians (Christianity), 7, 10–
    11, 14, 48, 102, 113–114, 117,
    119–120, 122, 133, 135, 137,

145, 148–149
Closed Official Corpus, 116–119
Conservatism, 11
Cott, Nancy F., 45–46
Creationism, 148
Cromer, Lord Evelyn Baring, 71

Da'wa, 59–60
Dalai Lama, 149
Declaration of Independence, 7,
    37
Delhi, 80
Democracy, 1, 3, 7–8, 10, 13,
    32–36, 39, 105–107, 110, 144
Democratic, 29, 33–36, 39, 65,
    105–107, 145
Deobandi School, 77–78
Derrida, Jacques, 113–114
Dhikr, 64, 98, 100–102
Diaspora, 1–2, 12, 26, 58–61, 68,
    140, 146–147, 149
Din, 83–84, 86, 92, 100
Doi, Abdur Rahman, 61
Doi, Abdur Rahman I., 12, 27, 61
Durkheim, Emile, 113
Dutch, 4, 6

Eckhart, Meister, 102
Egalitarianism, 8–9, 14, 21, 24,
    28, 31–33, 36–37, 41–42, 48–
    49, 57–58, 62, 64–68, 75, 87–
    88, 93, 105–107, 123, 129, 144

Egypt, 4, 13, 20, 25, 35, 45, 46, 48, 50, 60, 71–73, 98–99, 110, 139

Egyptian Feminist Union, 45

Ernst, Carl, 65

Europe, 3, 11, 14, 58, 71, 146

Falwell, Jerry, 148

Faruqi, Ismail, 24, 57–59

Fiqh, 57–58, 86–87, 89, 94, 96, 100, 121, 122

Fitna, 29–30, 106

Fodio, Shehu Usuman dan, 60

France, 3, 6, 114, 132, 139

French, 3, 6, 13–14, 38, 71, 99, 114

Gabriel, 120

Gaza, 110

German, 4, 6

al-Ghazali, Abu Hamid Muhammad, 30, 88

al-Ghazali, Zeynab, 25, 30, 45–47

Gibb, H.A.R., 5, 77–78, 101–102

Giddens, Anthony, 140–142

God, 1, 8, 13, 19, 24, 28, 41, 54, 59, 67–68, 80–89, 91–92, 94, 97–98, 102, 105–106, 116–117, 119–121, 128, 133–135

Graham, William A., 140–142

Günther, Ursula, 38

Gush Emunim, 148

Hadith, 7–9, 12–13, 26–27, 38, 45, 49, 52, 54, 57, 61, 72, 74, 80–81, 84, 93–95, 104–105, 108–110, 114, 120–123, 130, 132, 136, 139–140, 145, 147

Hafsah, 55

Hajj, 84, 108, 117, 128

al-Hallaj, Husayn ibn Mansur, 67

Hallaq, Wael, 89–90

Hanafi, 21

Hanbali, 20, 90

Haneef, Suzanne, 12, 60–61

Hashwis, 90

Hathout, Hassan, 12

Hebrew Bible, 118

Heilman, Samuel C., 148

Hermeneutics, 7–8, 10, 14–15, 17–19, 24, 32, 34–35, 41, 43, 68, 77, 86

Hijab (*higab*), 9, 20, 22–26, 29, 32, 70

Hijaz, 122

Hijra, 58, 60, 122

Hindus (Hinduism), 100, 102, 106, 133, 148–149

Hourani, Albert, 101

Hudud, 30

Humphreys, R. Stephen, 145

Ibn ʿAqil, 90

Ibn ʿArabi, 97, 111, 127, 129

Ibn al-ʿAwwam, Zubair, 50

Ibn al-Jawzi, 68

Ibn Qayyim al-Jawziyya, 98

Ibn Saʿd, 52–53

Ibn Sina, 88

Ibn Taymiyya, 68, 91, 97–98, 101

Ijmaʿ, 35–36, 86, 88, 123

Ila, 83, 92

Imam, 28, 67, 90

India, 35, 60, 77–80, 97, 100, 106, 148–149

Indonesia, 2, 97

Indonesian, 6

Institute for Islamic Studies, 5

Institute of Islamic Research, 79

International Association of Sufism, 68

Iqbal, Muhammad, 24

al-ʿIqdaniyya, 66

Iran, 21, 130

Iraq, 67, 122

Islam, 1–2, 4–16, 18–21, 23–27, 29–30, 32–39, 41–53, 55–72, 74–75, 77–80, 82–117, 119–136, 139–147, 149

Islamic feminism, 43–44, 46, 126, 143

Islamic fundamentalism, 5, 11–12, 25, 38, 111–112, 142–145

Islamic liberalism, 11–12

Islamic majoritarianism, 42, 51,

56–57, 60, 62, 67–68, 74, 119, 121, 123

Islamic modernism, 11–12, 13, 24, 36, 101, 109–110, 115, 119–120, 134, 140–146, 149

Islamic neotraditionalism, 11–14, 25, 27, 60–61, 113, 146, 148

Islamic philosophy, 5

Islamic revivalism, 5, 11–13, 25, 36–38, 72, 79, 108, 110–114, 120, 122, 130–131, 140–145, 148

Islamic traditionalism, 11, 82, 108, 140, 142

Islam, Five Pillars of, 12

Islamic feminism, 1, 3, 5, 8–9, 15–18, 39, 41, 43–48, 65, 68, 71, 74, 110, 126

Islamic Society of North America, 25, 60, 146–147

Islamic Studies, 5, 6, 27, 57, 79, 131, 146

Israel, 46

Italian, 6, 98

Italo-Sanusi War, 99

Ittisal, 142

Ittisaliya, 142

Jackson, Jesse, 148

Jadal, 95

Jahiliyya, 49–52, 91, 145

Jains (Jainism), 149

Jamaʿat al-Tabligh, 60

Jama'at-i Islami, 5
Jerusalem, 117
Jesus, 97
Jews (Judaism), 10, 14, 113–114, 117–120, 122, 133, 135, 137, 145, 148
Jordan, 35, 110
Judea, 148

Kabylia, 6
Kashmir, 35
Khadija, 51–52
Khan, Muhammad Ayyub, 79
Khan, Seyyed Ahmed, 79, 143
Kharijites, 42, 121, 129, 136
Khattab, Huda, 12, 25–27, 70
Khilafat movement, 60
Khomeini, Ayatollah Ruhollah, 25
King, Martin Luther Jr., 7
Kufa, 66
Kuwait, 35

Lane, Edward, 4–5, 47–48
Lapidus, Ira, 44
Le Brun, Eugénie, 71
Lee, Robert D., 10, 113, 115, 126
Lévi-Strauss, Claude, 125
Lewis, Bernard, 68–69
Libya, 98–99

Ma'rifa, 101
Madhabs, 86–87, 111, 113–114, 123, 144
Mahdi, 97
Malik, Anas Ibn, 22
Manazil, 28
Manicheanism, 118
Martin, B.G., 98
Massachusetts, 3–4, 17, 48
Mawdudi, Sayyid Abu'l-A'la, 5, 12, 25, 77, 79–80, 83–86, 90–93, 99–101, 104–110, 144–145
Mayer, Ann E., 36–37
Mecca, 23, 58–59, 66, 70, 117, 119
Medina, 21–23, 27–29, 58–59, 70, 117, 119
Mediterranean Sea, 114, 133, 145
Mernissi, Fatima: on active female sexuality, 29-30; on democracy 35-39; on division of public and domestic space, 30-32; on Quranic interpretation, 19; on seclusion of women, 27-29; on the veil and veiling, 19-27; on visions of Islam in the modern world, 32-35
Metcalf, Barbara, 78
Miami, Florida, 27
Middle East, 5, 21, 37, 44, 47, 71, 73–74, 90
Mir, Mustansir, 146–147
Miskawayh, Ibn, 6, 113

Mithaq, 117

Monasticism, 91

Monotheism, 9, 13, 129

Montreal, 5

Morocco, 2–4, 13, 28, 74, 139

Mosque, 28–29, 33, 66, 108, 117

Mu'amalat, 59, 145

Mufassir, Sulaiman, 12

Mughal Emperor Akbar, 100

Muhaggabat, 20

Muhammad, 3, 9, 13, 21–24,
    26–29, 31–36, 41–42, 49–56,
    58–59, 61–62, 70, 77, 79, 82,
    86–87, 89–90, 93–94, 98–99,
    101, 105, 108–109, 117, 119–
    122, 129, 133, 136, 140, 143

Muhammad V University, 3

Mujaddids, 91

Mujtahidun, 93

Munafiqun, 21, 23–24, 32, 70

Musa, Salama, 15

Mushaf, 119

Muslim Brotherhood, 35–37,
    144, 146

Muslim Students Association of
    America, 25, 60, 146–147

Mysticism, 63, 97, 101–102,
    127–128

Nafs, 134

Nasr, Seyyed Hossein, 101

Nasr, Seyyed Vali Reza, 90–91,
    142–145

Nassef, Malak Hifni, 45–46

National Research Center in
    Rabat, 3

Nawazil, 90

New Testament, 118

Nhat Hanh, Thich,, 149

Nisa'ism, 16–19, 24, 32, 34, 38

Niyazi, Mawlana 'Abd al-Salam,
    80

North Africa, 3, 11, 97, 114, 132

O'Fahey, R.S., 98

Oxford University, 5, 77–78

Pakistan, 4–6, 13–14, 25, 35, 60,
    77–80, 104, 106–107, 120,
    136, 139

Parsis. See Zoroastrianism

Persia, 69

Persian Studies, 5

Qarmatians, 41, 56–57, 62, 64,
    66–69, 75, 136

Qibla, 117

Quran, 5, 7–14, 19, 24, 26–27,
    29–31, 38, 41, 45–46, 54–58,
    60–63, 67–70, 72, 74, 77–89,
    91–96, 99, 104–112, 114–125,
    129–132, 134–136, 139–140,
    143, 145, 147

Qutb, 139

Qutb, Sayyid, 12

Rabb, 83, 92
Rabiʿ, Ibrahim Abu, 147
Radtke, Bernd, 98
Rahman, Fazlur: on the Quran, 80-83; on Sharia, 86-93; on medieval political structures and education, 93-96; on Sufism, 96-102; on Islam in the modern world, 102-112
Ramadan, 59
Reflexivity, 140
Rida, Muhammad Rashid, 139, 143
Risala, 89, 121–122
Ruh, 134
Russia, 60

Salat, 84, 146
Samaria, 148
Sanusi, 97–99
Satan, 134
Satar, 109
Scarce, Jennifer, 21
Scott, Joan W., 44, 46
Shaʿrawi, Huda, 45–47
al-Shafiʿi, Muhammad ibn Idris, 20, 89, 114, 121–122, 144
Shafik, Doria, 45–47
Sharia, 11–12, 27, 37, 56–62, 68–69, 74, 81, 84, 86, 88–89, 91–92, 96–98, 100, 105–107,

110, 121, 124–125, 129, 136
Shiites, 11, 67, 97, 121, 126, 129–131, 134
Shirazi, Sadr al-Din, 88
Shura, 35–36, 87, 93–94, 105
Sinai, 46
Sirhindi, Shaykh Ahmad, 91
Slater, Philip, 3
Smith, Jonathan Z., 1
Smith, W. Robertson, 51
Sorbonne, 3, 6, 113
Spellberg, Denise, 52–53
Stowasser, Barbara, 24, 109
Sudan, 35
Sufi Psychology Association, 68
Sufis (Sufism), 4, 14, 41–42, 56–57, 62–69, 75, 78–79, 96–102, 110–111, 126–129, 131, 136: Chisti Sufi order, 79, 99; murshids (Sufi masters), 64; tariqas (Sufi orders), 64
Sunna, 2, 13, 19, 26, 29, 46, 59, 70, 73, 86, 89, 91, 99, 106, 109, 140
Sunni, 1, 14, 42–43, 49, 56–57, 60, 62, 67–68, 74–75, 87, 91, 94, 101–102, 111, 113–114, 119, 121, 123, 129, 133–134
Syria, 33, 35–37, 110, 122, 144

Tanzil, 117
Taourirt-Mimoun, 6
Taqwa, 81

Theology, 10, 80, 87–88, 90–91, 94–95, 101, 113, 130
Threshold Society, 68
Tibet, 149
Torah, 118, 148
Transnationalism, 13–14, 139
Trimingham, Spencer, 64, 98
Tripartite Aggression, 46
Tunisia, 4, 33, 35
Turkey, 21
Turkish, 38
Turks, 99

Uhud, Battle of, 21, 23, 49
Ulema, 37, 42, 68, 81–82, 86–89, 91, 93–95, 113, 143, 145
ʿUmar ibn al-Khattab, 29
Umayyads, 50–51, 58, 87, 91–94, 121, 123, 144–145
Umm ʿUmara, 49
Umm Khulthum, 50
Umm Salama, 54
Umma, 24, 57–58, 68, 81, 87–88, 94, 111–112, 124–125, 133–134, 140
Umma muhammadiya, 133
UNESCO, 136
United Nations (UN), 33–34, 136
United Nations Charter, 33–34, 136
United Nations Declaration of Human Rights, 136
United States Constitution, 7, 37

United States of America, 3–5, 7, 14, 16–17, 25, 27, 37, 58, 60, 68, 74, 139, 146, 148–149
Universal Declaration of Human Rights, 33–34, 38
University of Ahmadu Bello, 27
University of California, Los Angeles, 5–6, 79
University of Cambridge, 4, 47–48
University of Chicago, 5, 79
University of Durham, 5, 78
University of Harvard Divinity School, 4, 48
University of the United Arab Emirates, 4, 48
ʿUqraba, Battle of, 49
Urdu, 38
Usra, The Muslim Family Magazine, 25
Usul al-fiqh, 89, 121–122

Veil, 8–9, 12, 15, 17, 19–22, 24–27, 29, 31–32, 39, 42, 45, 69–74, 108, 131
Voll, John, 98

Wahhabis, 67
Waliullah, Shah, 91
Watt, Montgomery, 51
Weber, Max, 113
West Africa, 60

West Bank, 110, 148

Women, 3–5, 8–9, 13–39, 41–43,
    45–56, 58, 62–66, 68–75, 82,
    102, 107–111, 122–123, 126,
    128–132, 143–144

Women and Gender in Islam, 5,
    47, 49

World War II, 72

Yathrib, 22, 58

al-Zahiri, Dawud, 90

Zaid, ʿAtika bint, 50

Zaria, Nigeria, 27

Zeinab bint Jahsh, 21–22, 70

Zeitgeist, 137

Zoroastrianism, 133

Zuhur, Sherifa, 19–20

About the Author

Jon Armajani is Assistant Professor of World Religions and Theology in the Theology Department at the College of St. Benedict and St. John's University in Minnesota. His writing and teaching focus on the history of religions, Islam, Christianity, and Muslim-Christian relations.

Related Titles from the
Rowman & Littlefield Publishing Group

R. Scott Appleby, *The Ambivalence of the Sacred:
Religion, Violence, and Reconciliation*

Noam Chomsky, *Middle East Illusions*

Alan Dundes, *Fables of the Ancients? Formulas and Folktales in the Quran*

Amitai Etzioni, *My Brother's Keeper: A Memoir and a Message*

Yvonne Yazbeck Haddad and Jane I. Smith, editors,
Muslim Minorities in the West: Visible and Invisible

Nezar al-Sayyad and Manuel Castells, editors, *Muslim Europe or Euro-Islam:
Politics, Culture, and Citizenship in the Age of Globalization*

Earle H. Waugh and Frederick M. Denny, editors, *The Shaping of an
American Islamic Discourse: A Memorial to Fazlur Rahman*

Related Titles from
University Press of America

Khaled M. Abou El Fadl, *And God Knows the Soldiers:
The Authoritative and Authoritarian in Islamic Discourses*

Khaled M. Abou El Fadl, *Conference of the Books:
The Search for Beauty in Islam*

Mary Boyce, *A Persian Stronghold of Zoroastrianism*

Caesar Farah, *Decision Making and Change in the Ottoman Empire*

M. R. Ghanoonparvar, *Prophets of Doom:
Literature as a Socio-Political Phenomenon in Modern Iran*

Jacob Neusner, *Israel and Iran in Talmudic Times: A Political History*

Haggay Ram, *Myth and Mobilization in Revolutionary Iran:
The Use of the Friday Congregational Sermon*

Abdul Aziz Said and Meena Sharify-Funk, editors, *Cultural Diversity and Islam*

Lamin Sanneh, *The Jakhanke Muslim Clerics:
A Religious and Historical Study of Islam in Senegambia*